W9-CJB-407

THE ARMCHAIR GUIDE TO MURDER AND DETECTION

THE ARMCHAIR GUIDE TO MURDER AND DETECTION

David Peat

DENEAU

Published by
Deneau Publishers
411 Queen Street
Ottawa, Canada K1R 5A6

First printing 1984

Canadian Cataloguing in Publication Data

Peat, F. David, 1938-
Murder and detection

Includes index.
ISBN 0-88879-059-7

1. Criminal investigation. 2. Murder. I. Title

HV6515.P42 363.2-5 C83-090091-8

Contents

Foreword

In 1881, the German police were called in to investigate the death of a mother and her five children. All had been found dead in a room that was bolted from the inside. The window was also locked from the inside. The mother had apparently killed the children, then committed suicide by hanging herself from a hook in the wardrobe. The inspector in charge of the case took an instant dislike to the husband, a man named Fritz Conrad, but had to agree that there was no way he could have been involved in the deaths of his family. Then, glancing idly through a few books on the shelf, the inspector picked out a volume called *Nena Sahib* by John Ratcliffe. It fell open at a certain page, and the inspector found himself reading a description of how a man murdered someone in a room, then made it look like suicide. He drilled a hole in the door, inserted a horsehair which he tied round the end of the bolt, then locked the room from the outside by pulling the horsehair; afterwards, he sealed up the hole in the door with brown wax. The inspector went and slid back the bolt in the death room. Underneath it, he found a tiny hole. On the outside of the door, the hole had been sealed with brown sealing wax...Fritz Conrad was charged with the murder of his wife and family — he was hoping to marry another woman — and executed.

This is the type of criminal drama that fascinates the modern public — the battle of wits between the policeman and the murderer. Yet when Fritz Conrad murdered his family, the public knew little of such matters. The very word "detective" had been invented a mere twenty-five years earlier, by Charles Dickens, who introduces his Inspector Bucket (in *Bleak House*) as a "detective officer." It would be another five years before a young and unsuccessful doctor named Conan Doyle would invent the most famous of all detectives, Sherlock Holmes. Indeed, the story of modern criminology began only two years earlier, in 1879, in the police headquarters in Paris. A thin, undistinguished young man named Alphonse Bertillon began working for the Sûreté in March of that year, copying and filing descriptions of criminals. It was dreary and boring work. But Bertillon came from a family of scientists, and his grandfather had often aired his theory that no two human beings have identical physical measurements — for example, length of forearm, circumference of skull, chest measurements. Bertillon asked permission to take various measurements of convicts who passed through the headquarters. It was granted, and within a matter of weeks, Bertillon had become convinced that his grandfather was correct. A few people might have one, or even two, measurements in common; but never more than that. Unfortunately, Bertillon's superiors thought he was a crank, and it took him three years, until 1882, before he could even persuade them to allow him to try out his new methods on an experimental basis. He was given three months to prove his point. And when the time was almost up, Bertillon had his first small success, identifying a petty crook who had given a false name in an attempt to qualify for treatment as a first offender. He followed up this success by identifying a number of nameless corpses that had been fished out of the Seine. And within a few years, Bertillon's system of identification was being used in police forces all over the world.

Unfortunately for its inventor, an even more efficient method had already been invented by an Indian civil servant named William Herschel — fingerprinting. One of Herschel's jobs was to pay pensions to Indian ex-soldiers, and to the English eye, they all looked very much alike; so some of them succeeded in collecting twice. Herschel made them sign for their pensions by making an inky fingerprint beside their name on the list. And even while Bertillon was becoming famous as the first scientific crimefighter in Paris, Sir Francis Galton was busy devising a simple method by which fingerprints could be classified and filed. His book *Fingerprints* appeared in 1892, the year Bertillon scored one of his most spectacular triumphs. His method of classification trapped an anar-chist bomber named Ravachol, and revealed him to be a wanted murderer called Konigstein. Bertillon, a suspicious and bad-tempered individual, fought grimly for his own system; but in a short time it had been replaced by fingerprinting.

The next great step occurred in 1900, when Paul Uhlenhuth discovered how to test blood to find out if it was human. Blood serum — the watery liquid in which the red cells float — will develop defensive properties against germs (which is how we build up "resistance") and also against organic substances. If a rabbit is injected with human blood, its serum develops a defense against it. If the rabbit's blood is then sucked out with a hypodermic syringe, and left in a test tube, it "clots," and the serum separates out from the brown bloodcells. Now if a drop of human blood, no matter how tiny, is introduced into the serum, the serum turns a milky colour. Uhlenhuth found that it even worked on very old bloodstains; they only had to be dissolved in salty water, and they would still react to the rabbit serum. Just after the turn of the century, a sadistic sex-killer named Tessnov was convicted through Uhlenhuth's test. Children had been found literally hacked to pieces on the island of Rügen; Tessnov, a travelling carpenter, was arrested, and insisted that the stains on his clothing were wood-stains. Uhlenhuth's serum not only revealed that he was lying; it also revealed that other blood-spots were of sheep's blood — and some sheep had also been sadistically mutilated at the same time as the children. Tessnov was executed.

Acknowledgements

Inspector R. Kelly and the Ottawa City Police, the Royal Canadian Mounted Police and their forensic staff, the New York City Police, the London Metropolitan Police, the City of Liverpool Police; pathologists Dr. D. King and Dr. G. Tolnai; coroner Dr. J.A. Thompson; legal council A. Cogan, G. Dzoba and L. Shore and to Rev. E. Jenkins for providing important details in the Laughan and Cameo murder cases.

Introduction

It is a few hours before dawn and, with the exception of the occasional taxicab driving home a late-night drunk, the streets are empty. At this hour even the operations room of the police station is quiet. Sitting back in their chairs, with headsets perched over their ears, the duty officers log each routine report made by a patrol car or an officer on the beat. Callers complain about noise from a next-door apartment or of a suspicious character lurking about. These complaints are logged and relayed to the officer working in the relevant part of town.

Suddenly one of the officers stiffens in his chair; this call is different, the caller almost incoherent. He says he called a half-hour ago to complain about the shouting in the house next door. Now he has heard screams and what sounded like a gunshot. "My God," he cries, "why don't you do something!"

The duty officer logs the time of the message and asks the caller to repeat his exact name, address and telephone number. "Someone will be right over," he says. "Just sit tight and wait."

The duty officer examines the wall map in front of him and sends out an immediate call to the patrol car in that area. The murder hunt has begun.

Hours, days or even years later the killer is arrested. What happens in between? What trail leads from a battered corpse to the identity of its murderer? In the case of the Barlow murder in Bradford, England, a frantic husband woke his next-door neighbour and told him to call the police — his wife had collapsed in the bath. It took considerable forensic deduction before the truth was uncovered: that the man who had first raised the alarm was himself the killer.

The murder of Belle Crippen was brought to the notice of Scotland Yard when friends became worried after her sudden alleged departure for the United States. Despite Dr. Crippen's assurances that he had received letters from his wife, Belle's friends wondered why she would leave without taking her jewellery.

How are the police able to track down a multiple murderer through a crowded city, or determine the way in which a doctor poisoned his nagging wife? When a corpse is found hidden in a patch of dense undergrowth, or a "suicide" is found in suspicious circumstances, or a businessman is found shot beside his open safe, how do the police go about discovering the path that leads to the killer, and how do they present a cast-iron case to the prosecution?

Modern police work ranges from intense research in the most up-to-date scientific laboratories to the routine rounds of an officer on the beat, from the comparative study of thousands of fingerprints to the intuitive probings of an experienced detective.

The forensic scientist and police pathologist may adopt a definite scientific routine but there are no rules of procedure for solving a killing, no sure-fire technique that can be learned at a police-training school. All murders, like all people, are uniquely different and solving each requires its own approach.

Most murders, however, have something in common in that they generally begin with the discovery of a corpse and end with the apprehension of a killer. Yet there are even exceptions to this rule: corpses that are never found, murders without solution, victims without a name. But for now, let's begin with a body.

It is necessary to offer this brief outline of the beginning of scientific criminology, for the changes that have taken place in the past eighty years have been immense, and this book is basically concerned with the world of today. There have been a number of excellent histories of crime detection — notably, Jurgen Thorwald's two-volume classic, comprising *The Century of the Detective* and *Crime and Silence*, and Frank Smyth's *Cause of Death*. What David Peat has written is a volume that would have filled Sherlock Holmes with ecstatic excitement, and that every writer of detective stories will keep on his small shelf of indispensable reference books. As I read it, I found myself wishing that it had been written ten years ago, when I started writing my own "procedural detective story," *The Schoolgirl Murder Case*. This opens with the discovery of a girl's body in a Hampstead garden, in the typical position of a sex murder; she is dressed in school uniform. The following day, the detective in charge of the case learns that the girl is older than she looks; she is a young prostitute who offers her services to clients of peculiar tastes. How would a policeman set out to investigate such a case? I had written more than half the novel when I met a London policeman who is also a writer, Donald Rumbelow, and asked him to read it. His comments made it obvious that I had to scrap the book and start all over again. To begin with, I had not realized that the man who superintends the first examination of the site of the murder is a Scene of Crimes Officer, usually an ordinary constable with specialized training. Until the body has been photographed, examined and removed to the site of the post mortem, he is in charge, and can overrule anyone — even the Commissioner of Police himself — who tries to interfere. If David Peat's book had been on my shelf, I would not have made such an elementary mistake as allowing the Chief Superintendent to examine the body before the photographer has arrived.

But if Peat's book was concerned only with police procedure, it would be of interest only to experts. In fact, its real value lies in the cases that he uses to illustrate his explanations. Some of these will be familiar to students of real-life crimes; for example, the classic Blackburn murder case, in which the police ended by fingerprinting everybody in the town. (It must have been a moment of tremendous drama when the policeman looking through the latest batch of fingerprints suddenly shouted: "I've got it!") Others, like "the corpse in the freezer," the Hepplewhite case, the Dunning case, the "fingerprint forgery," the Arthur Kendall murder and the "clicking alibi" case, were unknown to me, and will be unknown to the majority of readers.

But the cases that excited me most were those in which a psychiatrist had been able to offer some kind of a profile on the criminal based on the crimes themselves — as in the "mad bomber" explosions or the crimes of the Boston Strangler. Here, it seems to me, criminology is moving into a field that is potentially the most fruitful of all. After all, the real problem of modern crime is not how to detect it scientifically, but simply how to understand the terrifying increase in the crime figures from year to year. When I wrote my *Encyclopedia of Murder* in 1960, the American murder rate was about 10,000 a year; now, in 1982, it is more than double that figure. (Yet England, with a population nearly a third the size of America's, has a mere 500 a year.) Checking the violence of the modern world will require a concerted effort of policemen, politicians and criminologists; and of these three, the contribution of the criminologist could well be the most important. Certain practical measures can certainly improve the situation — like the current experiment in New York of giving habitual violent offenders *very* long terms in prison, on the proven assumption that such offenders account for a large percentage of violent crimes. But deeper understanding remains the primary need. The policeman of the future will need to be trained in psychology as well as in more practical disciplines. In a recent case in Daytona Beach, Florida, a suspect named Gerald Stano was pulled in by the police on suspicion of killing a girl. The investigating officer, Detective-Sergeant Paul Crow, had taken the trouble to learn something about "body language," the unconscious gestures that reveal what we are thinking or feeling. Crow noticed that Stano would sit straight upright when telling the truth, and lean back, crossing his legs, when about to lie. By the time Stano himself realized that these gestures were giving him away, Crow had found out enough to convince him that Stano was a man the police wanted for the killing of six prostitutes and many attacks on others. Stano was given three consecutive life sentences.

Two centuries ago, England was suffering from the greatest crime wave in its history — a crime wave that began around 1700 with the introduction of the new cheap drink called gin (twopence a gallon). Two brothers called Henry and John Fielding halted the crime wave by forming their own force, the Bow Street Runners, and taking various other practical and sensible measures. Books like David Peat's make us aware that the solutions to our own problems about crime may be closer than we think.

COLIN WILSON

Chapter 1

AT THE SCENE OF A MURDER

Arriving at the Scene

The person who arrives first at the scene of a murder is generally not a detective or forensic expert but simply an officer on the beat who is nearest to the crime. Responding to the shouts of a passerby or a call from his headquarters, the officer who goes to the scene of a violent crime can find himself face-to-face with anyone from a killer with a gun still smoking, to an hysterical relative. The officer takes charge of the situation according to an established routine.

His immediate priority is to make sure the victim is indeed dead and not in need of emergency medical attention. If his instinct is to attempt to revive an apparently lifeless body, he must take care not to disturb any forensic evidence that later may be crucial in solving the case.

After his examination of the murder victim, the officer seals off the scene of the crime to guarantee that no evidence is touched or removed. He next turns his attention to any witnesses or suspects, making a mental note of their composure, the state of their dress, their position in the room, and anything they say. Finally, he calls his headquarters to report the murder, giving brief details of any witnesses or suspects held.

As soon as possible the officer must write down his observations in the form of brief notes, which are entered in his notebook and dated. Months later, when he gives evidence at the trial, he will be allowed to refer to these on-the-spot notes. They may prove crucial.

At the end of his day on duty the officer returns to the station and fills out a detailed Incident Report which is then dated and signed. This report is an expanded version of his notes at the crime scene and contains additional information on suspects and witnesses.

The Dying Declaration

A dying victim can point a finger at his killer. His last words can hand the police a cast-iron case.

"A dead man can tell no tales," they say. In fact, as far as the law is concerned, a dying man can tell only the truth. What is known as a "dying declaration," when made in the prescribed fashion, can have a crucial impact on a murder trial.

A report of hearsay — what a witness heard a friend say, for example — is not normally admitted as evidence into a court of law. But if a witness is about to die, then his reported words have all the significance of evidence given under solemn oath.

The dying declaration is usually taken down by a police officer at the scene of a murder, or by a doctor in the hospital to which the victim has been taken. For the declaration to be legally valid the victim must understand that he is dying and has no hope of recovery. It must begin with a statement to this effect:

"Being without hope of recovery, I, John Smith, do say..." Then follows a complete description of the crime, the identity of the killer and everything the dying man witnessed. The declaration is written down and, if possible, given to the dying man to sign. But, in an emergency, it is sufficient for those present to remember the words and write them down later.

In court, the defence's only hope of weakening the impact of a dying declaration is to suggest that the dying man was rambling or out of his senses. Witnesses for the prosecution who were present during the declaration would then testify that the victim was rational and able to make clear answers to any questions put to him. In such a case, a dying declaration stands as a damning indictment against the accused.

The Dead May Walk

Gaping wounds and a floor awash in blood do not necessarily mean that a victim is dead, nor does the deep coma of a poisoned victim. In fact, there are cases in which it may be difficult for the medically unsophisticated to diagnose death.

As a strict rule death should not be assumed unless a heart beat is absent for five minutes and a mirror, held before the victim's mouth for the same period, shows no condensation.

In the case of an electrocution, drowning or drug overdose, the victim can remain in a state of suspended animation with no obvious signs of a heart beat or respiration. If the police officer has the slightest doubt that the victim is dead, he should continue attempts at revival until expert medical help arrives.

Keith Simpson, the forensic scientist, tells of the case of a seventy-eight-year-old woman who was discovered with a suicide note and an empty box of sleeping pills beside her bed. The doctor who had examined the body pronounced her dead and she was moved to the mortuary. To everyone's surprise, six hours later, just as the post-mortem was to begin, the pathologist realized that the "corpse" was still breathing.

Sealing the Scene of a Murder

To give the investigating team the best possible chance to gather evidence, the whole area of the crime must be sealed off and no one allowed to enter until the murder squad arrives. Even the act of moving the body can destroy any chance of determining an accurate time of death. Forensic deductions that can be made from hairs, dust and fibres on the body will also be compromised. As a precautionary measure, a patrol man stands guard at the door to a room but in more complicated killings he will seal off the surrounding area with ropes and tape. This area usually includes not only the room where the murder took place, but all connecting rooms, corridors, elevators, entrances, and exits to the building. A murder in a private home, for example, could have been committed by a burglar who left tool marks on a basement window and footprints on the soft earth outside; there may even be tire marks from the getaway car in a laneway. The killer who leaves an apartment may leave his fingerprints on an elevator button or in the lobby.

Witnesses and Suspects

The officer at a crime scene keeps a sharp eye on witnesses and suspects for a quirk of behavior or casual remark that may give rise to an important lead. There are certain obvious features the officer looks for: scratches on the face, torn clothing or upset furniture. These would indicate a struggle, whereas a composed appearance and a tidy room could give the lie to a story of a killing done in self-defence. A husband who claims to have run out into the night to get help for his dying wife naturally arouses suspicion if he first took time to dress himself.

No observation, no matter how insignificant, should escape the officer's notebook. The witnesses' state of composure, their tendency to talk or remain silent, their state of dress, the smell of alcohol are all factors which the officer may have to relate in court many months later.

The Top Ten Poisons of Crippen's Day

Corrosive acids
Lysol (domestic disinfectant)
Oxalic acid (used for cleaning metal)
Opium and Laudanum
Cyanide
Ammonia
Strychnine
Liniments
Phosphorus

The Power of a "Verbal" or "Spontaneous Utterance"

Gossip and hearsay evidence are not admitted as evidence in a trial, but in addition to dying declarations, what is known as a "spontaneous utterance" has a special status. A statement made shortly after a crime is, in law, an extension of the whole drama of the crime itself and can be used in court. For example:

"God, I didn't know it was loaded."

"He just came at me...I didn't know what to do."

"I put my hands around her throat — then everything went blank."

"I only meant to frighten him..."

"God, what have I done? I was so drunk I didn't know what I was doing."

Such spontaneous utterances, made within minutes of a killing, can become a chilling indictment of the accused. Bloodstains, fingerprints and ballistic comparisons are hard facts, but set against time, the drama of the "verbal" can sway a jury. A verbal may not indicate guilt in any rational and arguable sense, yet it can create in a jury's mind the impression of a violent or impulsive person — but a short step from imagining that the accused is capable of murder.

Verbals

Making a statement to the police, or even a spontaneous utterance, is not always in the best interests of the accused.

On November 12, 1935 British journalist Tom Driberg found himself in the Old Bailey on a charge of indecent assault. The following exchange took place:

Crown: *When you were arrested you said "fantastic." When formally charged you said nothing?*
Driberg: *No.*
Crown: *You knew what a serious charge it was?*
Driberg: *Certainly, yes.*
Crown: *Why, when formally charged did you say nothing? Is that the act of an innocent man?*
Judge: *He had already said "fantastic." What more could an innocent man say? Is there any obligation for a man to make a statement?*
Crown: *He made no reply, My Lord.*
Judge: *That is what a wise man does — he keeps his mouth shut — when he is in the presence of the police on a serious charge.*

Ruling Passions, *Tom Driberg. Quartet Books, London, 1978.*

The Murder Hunt Begins

In most countries the responsibility for a murder investigation falls into the hands of the coroner. Dating as far back as the Middle Ages the office of the coroner was created to investigate violent and suspicious deaths as well as those occurring in prisons.

After the police have notified him, the coroner will take formal charge of the case and of the corpse itself. In practice the actual work is done by the police and their forensic assistants. However, the coroner will usually suggest that the body be taken to a pathologist of his choice, who will then perform the autopsy. Following the police investigation the coroner can order an inquest into the death, or pass on the case to the crown or state prosecutor if a suspect has been identified.

Interpol

International cooperation between police forces has been in operation since the turn of the twentieth century. In the chase and arrest of Dr. Crippen, for example, the police forces of Britain, Canada and the United States were involved.

In 1923, at the Criminal Police Congress, a decision was made for formal ties to be established through an organization to be called "Interpol." Its goal was to facilitate the fight against crime except those involving political, religious or military matters. Interpol's first headquarters were established in Vienna and were funded by its member countries.

With the rise of the Nazi party in Austria, Interpol files fell into German hands. At the end of the war, many of the files were lost or destroyed and had to be built up again. The organization was relocated in St. Cluid, Paris, staffed by members of the Sûreté Nationale and the Paris Prefecture.

Today Interpol is not so much concerned with tracking down and arresting a criminal as in acting as a clearing house for information. Its files are identified by a colour code: red for urgent, immediate arrest and extradition; blue for general background details; and green for surveillance.

Each member country of Interpol sets up a national office in radio or telegraph communication with the Paris headquarters. In this way details of criminal records and fingerprints can be transmitted or received, as well as information on legal and forensic matters.

The official languages of the organization are English, French, Spanish, and a unique phonetic system created at the centre. Since many requests are made by telephone and shortwave radio, the problem of different languages and a variety of accents had become severe. A phonetic system — pronounced with a Parisienne accent — was devised for verbal descriptions of fingerprints and the "Portrait Parlé," a checklist of 177 possible characteristics of a criminal, was compiled for easy transmission by telephone or radio.

To avoid their services being misused by terrorist forces and political police, Interpol will provide information only if an actual crime has been committed and hard evidence established against the suspect. The issuing of an arrest weapon or an extradition order also provides access to Interpol files on a suspect.

The files themselves are limited to information on top criminals, descriptions of important stolen items, car registrations, certain passport numbers, information about mysterious deaths, and a list of ships known to have carried drugs.

Contrary to the way they are depicted in fiction, Interpol agents do not chase their suspects across continents or make dramatic arrests of international criminals. Interpol is simply a clearing house for information on international crime and suspects who may have fled across national borders.

The Murder Squad

With the formal authority for the investigation in the hands of the coroner, police headquarters calls out the murder squad who rush to the scene of the crime. The squad consists of two teams: the detectives and the forensic or evidence expert.

The Detectives

Detectives usually work in pairs consisting of a senior, experienced officer and a junior partner. Since their work may involve a great deal of travel, the team is increased by the addition of a police driver.

If the case is likely to involve a large number of interviews and travel, an additional officer will be assigned to take care of administrative tasks. He will set up the "murder room," with its telephone lines, files, typewriters, radio communications to remote locations, as well as a host of assistants, file clerks, typists, and messengers. A good administrative officer will be able to organize a fleet of cars and drivers and a squad of officers for door-to-door interviews at a moment's notice.

The detective in charge of the investigation can range in position from staff sergeant to chief superintendent. But whatever his rank, he will devote all his energies — at times to the exclusion of food and sleep — until the killer is in his hands.

The partner's job is to back up his chief, take on some of the legwork and add his own special abilities to the investigation. There is a particular closeness in this team. Each has learned how the other thinks and, during an interview with the prime suspect, their teamwork will be as intuitive as the very best of bridge partners.

No matter how many police officers are involved in an investigation, the final responsibility rests with the two-man team. Through a combination of established routine, painstaking attention to detail and intuition, they attempt to track down the killer step by step. When the killer is finally brought to trial, the glamour of cracking the case rests with these detectives. Yet all along they will have been assisted by the more anonymous members of the murder squad — the forensic experts.

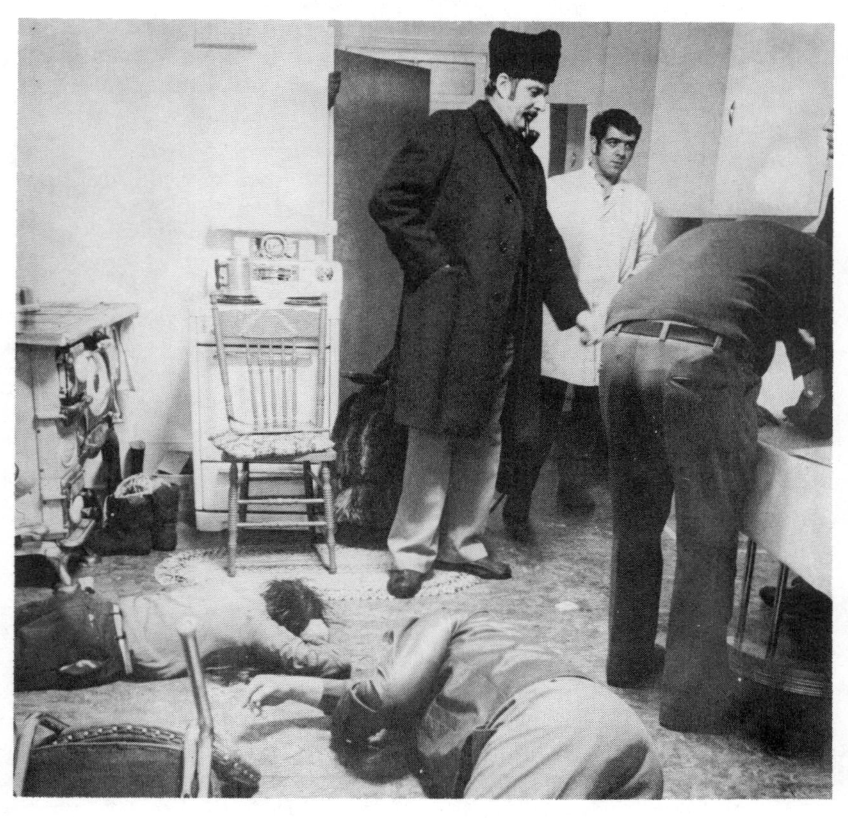

The murder scene, December 18, 1974 — Quebec Provincial police search a house in St. Joseph du Lac following the discovery of five bodies.
CP Photo

The Private Eye

The defence in a murder case will often call in a private eye to check alibis or investigate witnesses. For the most part, however, the private investigator's caseload is fairly mundane, involving insurance claims and divorce proceedings. Insurance companies often hire a private eye to produce evidence to prove, for example, that a severe back injury or whiplash is faked. A typical trick is for the private eye to station himself in a parking lot and observe the victim through the telescopic lens of his camera — after first pouring a can of motor oil around the front of the victim's car. The "insured" man approaches his car, sees the leaking oil and quickly bends down to look under the engine. This activity is recorded on film and sent to the insurance company as evidence of a faked claim. Another ploy for diagnosing phony back injuries is for the detective to arrange an early morning dumping of snow in front of the victim's driveway, and wait until his subject comes out with a snow shovel.

Although private detectives are seldom employed to catch a killer, they may be asked to find loopholes in the prosecution's case against a client. A good defence lawyer will employ a private detective to check into the background of prosecution witnesses or revisit the scene of the crime and confirm important details, for on occasion his detective work can yield a new interpretation of the police findings. Often this is because the police have uncovered a good lead too early in the investigation. The police pull out all the stops to follow a particular line of enquiry, to the neglect of all other possibilities. By contrast, the private detective takes the time to investigate every alibi and lead, as well as to explore inconsistencies in a witness's story.

In one Canadian case, for example, the accused had been identified by a witness one night in a parking lot. The private eye reading the statement wondered how the witness had been able to recognize anyone at 3 a.m. It was said that sufficient light came from a large illuminated billboard and a nearby hotel. The detective's investigation, however, showed that the lights in the hotel were out by that time and the billboard's time switch cut out at 2 a.m. The witness's story was shaken and the defence version of the incident assumed greater credibility. In another case, a private investigator visited the scene of a killing and discovered that a new door had been fitted to the apartment. With the aid of the janitor, the previous door was traced and found to contain marks of forced entry. As a piece of physical evidence, the door gave credibility to the apartment dweller's plea that the shooting had been done in self-defence.

Scene-of-the-Crime Officers

The police officers who search for "clues," or evidence as it is more generally called, are the identification officers or scene-of-the-crime officers. They will have already completed their initial police work as regular officers before opting to be trained in the skills of collecting evidence, lifting fingerprints and photographing evidence.

This forensic team generally consists of a photographer, a fingerprint officer and one or more experts trained to gather hairs, dust and fibres, and to search for tool, tire and bullet marks and signs of entry.

The final, scientific analysis of forensic evidence is not necessarily carried out by this team. Many clues are sent to a central forensic laboratory where specialists in a variety of fields can bring together all the techniques of modern science to the analysis of a single hair or a solitary drop of blood.

Dog Detectives

Police dogs are often used to search the scene of a crime that may involve large areas of difficult terrain. The dogs are trained to search for a body and to trace out the path left by the killer. On a dry or slightly humid day with little wind, the scent left by a human being can linger for up to twelve hours.

Police dogs are also able to pick out anything that has been touched by the killer or his victim; for example, a knife, jacket or handkerchief. From the smell of burnt powder, the animals will also find spent cartridges in the undergrowth, and concealed firearms.

The Police Photographer

The first member of the murder squad to explore the crime scene is a photographer. Before anything is touched and before the body is moved, a complete photographic record is made.

The photographer begins with a series of colour and black and white shots of the entire scene from a variety of different angles. If possible he will reshoot the same scenes under different lighting conditions because the appearance of an object can change under varying light. An indication scale is included in these shots, such as a ruler, a penny or, if the murder was committed outdoors, a police car may be included in the scene.

After each photograph has been taken the officer makes a record of shutter speed, aperture, time of day, and an indication of direction. To avoid confusion, he adds a brief description of the scene together with a simple sketch of what has been photographed.

After shooting the overall scene, the photographer moves towards the body, which is shot from several different angles before it is moved or the clothing touched. Then he focuses on close-ups of the detail of the crime scene, including weapons, bloodstains, torn drapes, broken glass, and the like.

It will be many hours before the photographer is free to leave the crime scene for he must also record the location of each fingerprint before it is "lifted" and transferred to a fingerprint card.

Months later at the trial, these photographs may provide a vital link in the prosecution case. To maintain continuity between the crime scene and the prints produced in court, a strict routine must be followed. For convenience in court, contact prints and enlargements will be used, but the negatives are considered "physical evidence" and they leave the photographer's custody only on receipt of a properly signed and dated form. If the defence can show that the negatives were ever out of the photographer's hands in an irregular fashion, or that the numbering of the prints and negatives does not tally with records in the photographer's notebook, then all the photographic evidence may be ruled inadmissible.

Police photographer at a murder scene.
London Metropolitan Police

Artistic quality is the least of a police photographer's worries when he is called out in the early hours of the morning. When photographing a corpse, particularly in a sex murder, he must take care to avoid "unnecessary exposure" of the sexual organs. A photograph taken in an improper manner may be ruled "inflammatory" by the judge and not admitted as evidence.

Approaching the Body

After the photographer has finished with the overall shots of the crime scene, the police doctor examines the corpse. The faster the doctor can reach the body the more accurate will be his estimation of time of death. Nevertheless, he will avoid a careless approach to the corpse for this could disturb vital evidence.

The detectives who are at the scene first examine the possible approaches to and exits from the scene, keeping in mind the following questions: How did the victim arrive? Was the victim followed by the killer or did they arrive together? Where did the killer leave? Did the killer run away or did he first drag the body some distance away?

The path taken by the killer and his victim probably contains important evidence such as hairs, dust, dropped articles, and fibres torn from clothing. Because the probable route is to be left undisturbed for the forensic team, the detectives deduce the least likely route and use it to approach the body. It is often marked out in tape, and the remainder of the crime area is considered sterile until it has been combed by the forensic experts. A second area is also marked off, to be used as a collection area where officers can gather to discuss their forensic samples.

The Pathologist

If police are in luck, the pathologist who performs the autopsy will be a specialist familiar with the advances in forensic science. But in a small town or country area the police may have to rely on the services of a hospital pathologist whose daily work consists of the study of tissue samples sent in by doctors and surgeons and of post mortems of hospital deaths.

The experienced forensic pathologist sees up to a thousand cases a year and has accumulated knowledge of tens of thousands of autopsies behind him. His laboratory will be up to date with the latest scientific equipment and a staff of technicians to assist him.

An expert pathologist performs such an autopsy in a methodical and painstaking way. Months later he will be able to make a positive identification of samples taken from a body and offer his expert opinion on the cause of death.

By contrast, the pathologist who does only occasional police work may be forced to use old-fashioned equipment in the confines of an inadequate mortuary. Under such circumstances mistakes are sometimes made: a body may be stripped and washed before the police arrive; vital evidence may be mislaid and samples improperly labelled or incorrectly preserved for the forensic laboratory.

But even the most experienced pathologist has made a mistake on occasion. One who became quite famous forgot to take a blood sample during the autopsy. His assistants realized what had happened but were too frightened of the great man's biting tongue to mention the omission.

The Police Doctor

The term "police doctor" is something of a misnomer, for the doctor himself is not a member of the police force but a local practitioner called in by the police on murder and assault cases. His training may include university courses in forensic medicine and spare-time reading of forensic journals, but essentially he is an ordinary doctor who uses his medical judgment for the benefit of the police.

The doctor begins his examination with his eyes alone. He notes the general condition of the body, its position, any gross injuries, the appearance of the face and — a particularly important clue — the onset of "lividity"; blotchy areas on the skin caused by dilation of blood vessels after death.

The exact location of lividity can give an important insight into the circumstances following the murder. Lividity appears where the skin is not constrained by tight clothing or by resting on the ground. Therefore, if the body has been moved after death by the killer or an accomplice, this lividity will appear on the "wrong" areas of the body and tell the doctor that the corpse has been tampered with.

The next step is for the doctor to touch the body. If the flesh is warm it is probable the murder will have occurred within the last ten hours, but if the body is cold and stiff, then death occurred between twelve and thirty hours earlier.

The detectives will naturally press for the cause of death and an accurate time for the murder, but here the experienced doctor will be cautious. He knows the textbook formula for the time of death has to be circumscribed by a wide latitude of uncertainty. He will give his opinion on the effects of bullet wounds and bruises as the cause of death, but caution the police that the final answer must wait until the autopsy.

After the doctor completes his initial examination, the scene-of-the-crime officer searches the body for hairs and dust before turning the body over to the doctor again. To find a more accurate time of death, the doctor loosens the necessary clothing and inserts a thermometer into the rectum of the corpse to determine the internal body temperature. He also makes a note of the temperature in the room and, if he is careful, repeats these readings in another half hour.

The Time of Death

The plot of a classical "country house" murder story often revolves around the location of each suspect at the moment of death. In real life, however, it is not easy to establish the exact time of death.

Body temperature and the extent of *rigor mortis* are by no means infallible indicators of time of death. Other means may serve to pinpoint the time more accurately — a broken wristwatch, for example, or a passerby who heard a shot or saw the killer running from the house. But even these indicators leave room for doubt. The watch may have stopped before the murder was committed, and witnesses sometimes become confused in their reports. The victim of Jack the Ripper's last murder was reported to have been seen five hours *after* her actual time of death.

A Galling Error

John George Haigh, the acid-bath murderer, believed that he had performed the perfect crime. After each killing, his victims were dumped into a drum of sulphuric acid until all that remained was a mass of sludge.

Yet even sludge can tell a story to a skilled scientist. Chemical analysis showed that the killer's workshop contained 475 pounds of human fat and three gallstones. Using a technique known as the peciptin test, forensic scientists showed the gallstones to be human in origin. Later a doctor came forward to testify that one of his missing patients suffered from gallstones. Haigh made his biggest mistake in not leaving the bodies in the acid for a sufficient time. In one of the drums, an acrylic plate from a set of dentures was found and later matched to a patient by a dental surgeon. Had Haigh waited another day or two, the plate, along with the remains of the victim, would have been gone forever.

Temperature

Warm-blooded animals generate heat by breaking down carbohydrates in their food and "burning" sugars to produce energy. At death, this process stops and the body begins to cool to the temperature of the surrounding environment.

The rate of cooling depends upon the quantity of body fat and of clothing, and the arrangement of the limbs. Cooling is also affected by the external temperature, draughts, rain and strong winds. A careful doctor therefore makes notes of the body's position, the amount of fatty tissue, thickness of clothing, and weather conditions. He repeats his readings after half an hour and then estimates time of death.

Roughly speaking, the adult human body maintains its normal temperature for the first hour or two after death and then begins to cool at a rate of about 2½°F (about 1½°C) each hour. After about six hours, this rate of cooling slows down to 1½ to 2°F (1°C) an hour. Within twelve hours the body feels cold to the touch and at the end of twenty-four hours the internal organs will have reached the temperature of the external surroundings.

But the accuracy of this estimate varies, depending upon the circumstances and the time elapsed between the murder and the doctor's examination. If the doctor arrives at the scene immediately after the crime and no one has touched the body, then it will be possible to estimate that death occurred, say, half-an-hour previously. If there is a delay in calling the doctor or if the body has been moved, the inaccuracy in estimating the time of death may vary by several hours.

In his book, *Forensic Medicine,* Dr. Keith Simpson mentions a couple who died within minutes of each other in a suicide pact. The body temperatures of the corpses, however, differed by 3°F. An inexperienced doctor may have deduced that one of the partners died an hour later; in fact, one of the corpses was more heavily insulated by clothing than the other.

Thin people cool faster than fat people. A body stretched out in death will cool more rapidly than one curled up or hunched against a wall. A corpse that has been dumped in a river will lose heat rapidly and feel cold to the touch after only five or six hours. All such factors make the estimation of time of death a tricky matter.

In determining how many degrees a body has cooled it is usually assumed that the person who died had a normal body temperature. But the victim may have been suffering from a fever or he could have struggled violently, both of which would have raised the body temperature at the time of death.

Finally, of course, there are gruesome cases in which a body feels warm days after death. The cause — a colony of maggots inside the body that eat the flesh and generate their own heat.

Blood Eliminations

Bloodstains, like fingerprints can be helpful in eliminating suspects from a murder victim. For example, during an assault the victim may have scratched an attacker on the face and blood may be found under the fingernails. If this blood group does not match that of the prime suspect he will be eliminated from the investigation.

At present it is not possible to prove that two samples of blood actually come from the same person but, as certain combinations of blood groups can be as rare as one in 50,000, they will certainly add to the weight of evidence in a case.

Rigor Mortis

Another myth perpetuated by the police doctor in detective fiction is that the time of death can be accurately established through the onset of *rigor mortis*. In actual fact stiffness of the limbs begins anywhere from six to twelve hours after death.

Following death, chemicals in the muscles break down and act to stiffen muscle fibres. First the face, then the arms, trunk and legs stiffen until, after about twelve hours, the whole body is fixed in its position of death. About a day later, this stiffness starts to wear off and the body becomes flexible again. Again, these time intervals can vary widely.

By noting body temperature readings and the progression of *rigor mortis*, the doctor will be able to give the murder squad an approximate time of death within a latitude of two days.

Organ Samples

Organ samples from an autopsy are sent to the forensic laboratories for analysis and detection of poisons. Certain poisons tend to accumulate in specific organs.

Poison	Concentrates in
Barbiturates	*liver*
Metallic salts	*kidneys*
Aspirin	*urine*
Arsenic	*hair and fingernails*
Lead	*bone*
Chloroform	*fatty tissue and brain*
Carbon monoxide	*blood*

The Victim's Last Meal

During the autopsy it is a routine matter to remove and examine the stomach. If the pathologist is in luck, the stomach may contain the identifiable remains of the last meal eaten by the dead person. In some cases a friend or relative of the victim may recall a meal they had together. If this memory agrees with the analysis of the stomach contents, it is clear that the murder must have taken place before the victim had a chance to eat again.

If the time of this last meal is accurately pinned down, its condition in the stomach will help in determining time of death. There is a well-defined process of digestion inside the stomach before food passes into the intestines. The pathologist can estimate how much of this process took place before the victim died. As with temperature and *rigor mortis*, however, the actual time taken for digestion varies from person to person and can be affected by worry, anger, fear and tension. If a victim had been in a threatening situation soon after eating his last meal, the stomach contents could rest undigested for several hours until the killing took place.

Decomposition

As the body begins to decay, tiny bubbles of gas form in the blood and give rise to a marbling appearance in the veins of the neck, shoulders and groin. The presence of marbling and a greenish tinge to the skin indicate that the corpse is several days old.

About two weeks after death the internal organs in the corpse start to decay and the abdomen bulges with gas. Over the following weeks, depending upon the outside temperature, the intestines, heart and liver decompose, followed by the lungs and brain. Finally, the kidneys and uterus decay.

The Top Ten Post-War Poisons

Barbiturates
Aspirin
Lysol
Cyanide
Corrosive acids
Morphine
Nicotine
Liniments
Phosphorus

The actual time taken for all these processes of decomposition depends upon external conditions. A body that has been dumped in a field in the heat of summer will decompose much faster than one left in the basement of an unheated house.

Several months after death, the body organs will have decayed and all that remains of the flesh will be a form of slime. The skeleton itself begins to break apart, and in some cases, a chemical change occurs in the body fats. A hard waxy "soap" takes the place of the fat and the bones become covered with this stiff white substance called *adipocere*.

Even after several months a few bones and pieces of decayed clothing can still yield a surprisingly detailed picture of the murder.

Removal of the Corpse

By now the "removal service" will have been called; generally they are the employees of a local undertaker who take the body to a pathology laboratory for an autopsy. Before the body is removed, the identification officers make another careful search of its clothing and the surrounding area. Each piece of evidence is photographed and placed in a pillbox or plastic bag labelled with an identification code, together with the time, date, location, and signature of the police officer.

The corpse itself is then wrapped in a plastic sheet to prevent contamination of potential evidence with foreign dust and hairs, and placed in a "coffin shell."

The ground beneath the corpse now becomes the focus of attention because dust or fibres may have been trapped under the body. In an outdoor killing the state of the ground beneath the body can give a clue to the time of death. Dry earth, for example, could fix the crime as happening before a rainstorm or snowfall.

While the body is on its way to the mortuary the forensic experts start their more detailed examination of the crime scene. They continue until not even Sherlock Holmes himself would be able to find another clue.

The Right to Remain Silent is Questioned

Following a lengthy investigation into the mysterious deaths of a number of babies at Toronto's Hospital for Sick Children, nurse Susan Nelles was arrested in March, 1981 and charged with murder. Later, an Ontario provincial Court Judge found that there was no evidence to link the nurse to the deaths and she was released.

In November, 1982 Nelles filed an $850,000 malicious prosecution lawsuit against her two arresting officers, the Toronto Police Chief and the Attorney General of Ontario. In their defence, lawyers argued that Nelles was "the author of her own misfortune" by remaining silent during police questioning. The defence claimed that remaining silent "is the right that applies to the criminal trial...but...was a factor which these police officers were entitled reasonably to take into account." The defence went further and suggested that the nurse's insistence on having her lawyer present during the questioning made her "guilty of negligence, which caused her to be arrested and prosecuted."

Clues at the Crime Scene

The character of Sherlock Holmes is generally acknowledged to be based upon a particularly observant professor of medicine, Dr. Joseph Bell, who deeply impressed Conan Doyle during his student days. Bell took pride in astounding the medical students with precise deductions as to the occupation of his patients. His astonishingly successful conclusions were based upon careful observation and logical deductions — two attributes that became the trademark of Doyle's greatest creation, the consulting detective, Mr. Sherlock Holmes.

A C.I.D. officer finds fibres at the scene of a crime.
London Metropolitan Police

When Holmes arrived at the scene of a crime, he fell to his knees and, like an aristocratic bloodhound, moved off on the scent. Holmes based his deductions on a spot of mud on a clean carpet, a scratch on a casement window or a pinch of tobacco ash. Even if a room were combed by the police, Holmes could still find another clue that put him on the track of the criminal.

In the modern police force, the scene-of-the-crime officer is the equivalent to Conan Doyle's creation. He knows that a single chip of paint will identify the make and model of the getaway car, a sliver of glass can place a suspect at the scene of a robbery, a blood stain or cloth fibre can trap a killer or identify a corpse.

The first hours spent at the scene of a murder may provide the evidence necessary to trap a killer because modern forensic science can often produce a complete picture of a murderer — his stature, age, colour of hair, make of car, clothes, and, thanks to the power of fingerprints, a name on a police record.

The officer trained in forensics begins his search by photographing (if this has not already been done by a photographer) and collecting any evidence that may deteriorate. A drop of blood is lifted with an eye dropper and squirted into a vial containing a saline solution. Dried stains are scraped into a pill box and, to establish a comparison standard, some of the surrounding material is scraped into another box.

As each piece of evidence is collected, the officer records it in his notebook; these records are important because he may have to identify a sample months later in the courtroom. If chemical tests are to be carried out, comparison samples of soil, vegetation, dust, paint, and fibres are also collected to ensure that any surrounding material does not give a spurious result to a sensitive chemical test.

After collecting and recording perishable objects, the officer turns his attention to the other major pieces of evidence. Each item is photographed from several angles, then fingerprinted and the prints are photographed and transferred onto cards. Written notes are made about the objects, which are then placed into a box or plastic bag.

The Thames River Police

By the end of the eighteenth century, British importers, whose cargos were unloaded from the River Thames, suffered annual losses as high as 500,000 pounds. To combat river crime, the Marine Police were created in 1798. The force used rowing galleys to patrol the river and visit the various docks.

In 1839, with the amalgamation of the various London police forces (with the exception of the City of London Police), the Thames division of the Metropolitan Police replaced the Marine Police. Today the division is staffed by regular police officers who have volunteered to work on the river and take courses in seamanship, rivercraft and port law. Senior officers carry a Customs and Excise warrant that gives them the power to board and search vessels for contraband. One of the division's less pleasant tasks is the recovery of some sixty corpses a year from the river.

The Murder Weapon

If a gun is found, it is lifted by the trigger guard or checkered part of the grip to leave fingerprints undisturbed. A careful officer will loop a string through the trigger to lift the gun for examination. Unlike the television detective, he does not poke a pencil down the barrel; this could damage ballistic marks inside the gun.

The position of the hammer and safety catch is noted, as well as whether the gun is loaded or has a live charge in the chamber. The serial mark on the gun is recorded and the officer adds his own initials to the gun. Any ammunition is marked on the base or nose to avoid disturbing ballistic marks.

Latent fingerprints are developed, photographed and transferred from the gun to a card, together with the gun's serial number to guarantee identification. Once the examination is complete the gun is placed in a bag and sent to the ballistics laboratory for testing. If the weapon is loaded, it is placed in a bag marked "Caution, Loaded Firearm."

Knives, axes, hammers and other murder weapons are handled in a similar manner to avoid disturbing latent fingerprints and to ensure later identification.

Casts and Clues

The scene-of-the-crime officer then concentrates on the probable route taken by the killer as he entered and left the area. This region is combed for traces of glass, paint, hair, fibres, and dust. Each fragment is placed in a box or bag and labelled, along with comparison samples. The carpet or floor is swept or vacuumed and the dust placed in sealed bags.

Finally the doors and windows of the murder room are examined for tool marks, signs of entry, fragments of torn clothing, and blood stains. Any marks produced by a jemmy or axe are cast in plastic and the casts sent to the laboratory. Later, if a tool is discovered, it can be connected with the scene of the crime by microscopic comparison of its edge and the marks recorded in the plastic cast.

If the murder took place outdoors, plastic casts are made of all tire marks and footprints. The police also search the undergrowth for torn and broken twigs that may have trapped tiny fibres of the killer's clothing or strands of hair. Soil and vegetation samples are also removed for analysis as they can contain microscopic particles that match those found on a suspect's clothing.

After the whole area has been searched, swept and vacuumed, the fingerprint experts begin to work with their brushes and powders. Although a fingerprint may be the most important clue to a killer's identity, the fingerprint officer cannot be allowed to contaminate forensic evidence with his powders until every piece of evidence has been collected.

In addition to such obvious items as the murder weapon and ammunition found at the scene, the officer may remove doors and windows that show tool marks, light fittings, large ornaments, and even sections of a wall — anything, in fact, that may be needed as evidence in court. For it would be unfortunate if the police had to return several days later only to find the room in which a murder took place redecorated and the carpet and drapes returned fresh from the cleaners.

By the time the fingerprint officer and the photographer are ready to pack up their equipment and leave, over twenty-four hours of continuous policework may have taken place.

Footprints

As long ago as 1786 police in Scotland made plaster casts of footprints taken at the scene of the murder of a young woman. One of the suspects was found to be wearing boots whose soles exactly matched the casts, and he was convicted.

Today the examination of footprints has become a fine art. With a holographic technique, it is possible to measure the displacement of carpet fibres made by a shoe to within 1/100,000 of an inch. The technique can also be used on a wood floor to detect the shape of the shoe or foot that compressed the wood fibres.

By measuring the rate of return of the fibres to their original state, scientists believe that one day it will be possible to calculate the exact time a foot touched the floor.

Chapter 2

FINGERPRINTS

What Makes a Fingerprint?

Charles Darwin pointed out that our remote ancestors swung from trees and, indeed, the palms of our hands contain the record of this early life — "friction skin." Unlike the skin on the remainder of the human body (with the exception of the soles of the feet), hands are covered with a pattern of ridges that give an effective gripping surface.

Over three thousand years ago the Egyptians, Babylonians and early Chinese realized that this convoluted system of lines was as individual as a human face or voice. They used hand and fingerprints pressed into clay tablets to guard against forgeries and to prove authorship.

In the centuries that followed, palmists and chiromancers turned their attention to recurring patterns in the lines of the hand which, they believed, told the story of human personality. Today, doctors have developed a system of diagnosis based upon certain characteristics in the human hand, and detectives use fingerprints in tracing criminals.

A fingerprint, or even a palm or footprint, is a foolproof method of identification. A face can be altered by plastic surgery or dyes but there is little a criminal can do to change his fingerprints. Each finger is unique and its impression may be left behind each time we open a door, drink a cup of coffee, answer the telephone, or write a letter.

Modern police forces have tens of thousands of fingerprints on file, and within minutes the details of a particular print can be transmitted across the world. Today, computers hasten the process of searching for a particular print; within seconds a suspect can be placed at the scene of a murder on the evidence of an invisible smear of sweat.

Modern crimes are often solved on the basis of a single fingerprint, or even a fragment of a print. In some cases whole towns have been fingerprinted in an effort to track down a killer. Fingerprints are also used to determine the identity of a victim. A headless body washed up on a beach or a mangled torso may provide no other means of identification than its fingerprints.

Before Fingerprints

In the nineteenth century a cat burglar or a pickpocket who had been released from prison needed only to grow a beard or dye his hair to take on a different identity in a new town. Beyond a written or photographic description, the police could rely only upon such lucky accidents as birthmarks, surgical scars and tattoos to make a positive identification. Early "mug shots" show that experienced criminals were skilled in distorting their faces in front of the police camera.

As police forces expanded and their methods became more scientific, it was natural for them to search for some foolproof method of identifying criminals. In France, Alphonse Bertillon, chief of criminal identification for the Paris police, believed he had the answer. Alphonse had the advantage of being the younger brother of the eminent statistician Jacques Bertillon who had developed the mathematical study of social factors such as causes of death, changes in population growth, divorce rates, and the incidence of alcoholism.

Alphonse had seen the power of his brother's statistical methods applied to whole populations and it gave him the confidence to develop a new science of his own. He called it "anthropometry" or "Bertillonage." Bertillon argued that whereas two people may have the same height, weight or chest measurements, it is highly improbable that they have a combined series of measurements exactly the same. Bertillon proposed that fourteen different measurements be made of each criminal, including his height; length of ears, nose, fingers, arms, legs, and feet; and the circumference of his head and chest. In combination, this set of measurements should be unique and impervious to change.

Anthropometry was slow in gaining ground at first, but during the last two decades of the nineteenth century police forces in Europe and North America purchased the Bertillon measuring equipment and kept files of measurements of their criminals. The system enjoyed only a brief lifespan, for in 1903 an American criminal named Willy West was discovered to have identical Bertillon measurements to one William West. At first it was assumed the two men were, in fact, the same person, but their fingerprints did not match. William and Willy not only had the same name but, coincidentally, similar anthropometric measurements.

The Fingerprint System

In 1858, Sir William Herschel, working for the British government in Bengal, made use of thumb prints as a means of identification on official documents. In England, Sir Francis Galton, the founder of the science of eugenics, (selective breeding), had made an exhaustive study of the complex patterns of ridges on the finger and calculated that the chance of two people having the same fingerprint would be sixty-four billion to one.

By 1901, Scotland Yard adopted a classification system of fingerprints developed by Edward (later Sir E.R.) Henry, Inspector General of the Bengal police, which was based on Galton's earlier system. With minor modifications this system of print indexing is used throughout the world today. In South America, Juan Vucetich, head of the Statistical Bureau of the La Planta police in Argentina, independently developed his own system, which was adopted in Buenos Aires in 1894.

The Henry system is based on three main components of a fingerprint pattern — the arch, loop and whorl — which are further subdivided into a plain arch, tented arch, ulna loop, radial loop, plain whorl, central pocket loop, double loop, and an accidental. A modified terminology is used in the United States.

The system uses all ten fingers in its classification. Each finger is given a number or letter according to which characteristic it contains. By counting those fingers that contain whorls, central pocket loops, double loops, and accidentals, the analyst can assign the print one of 1,024 primary classifications. The print can be further classified by ordering the various pattern types of each finger until the number of possible variations runs into many thousands. Finally, fine details of the pattern, such as the number of ridges in a loop or whorl, are grouped together to form a subsecondary classification.

In less than ten minutes the expert will have classified the fingerprint into a formula or index number. This index number is used to place the print card in the print file. In searching for a killer, the police can telegraph this number across the world. If a card bearing the same number turns up, then the print is examined under magnification to obtain positive identification.

In most crimes the killer does not leave a complete print of all ten fingers behind so the Henry System does not apply. Instead, individual fingerprints from the crime scene are compared with those of the suspect.

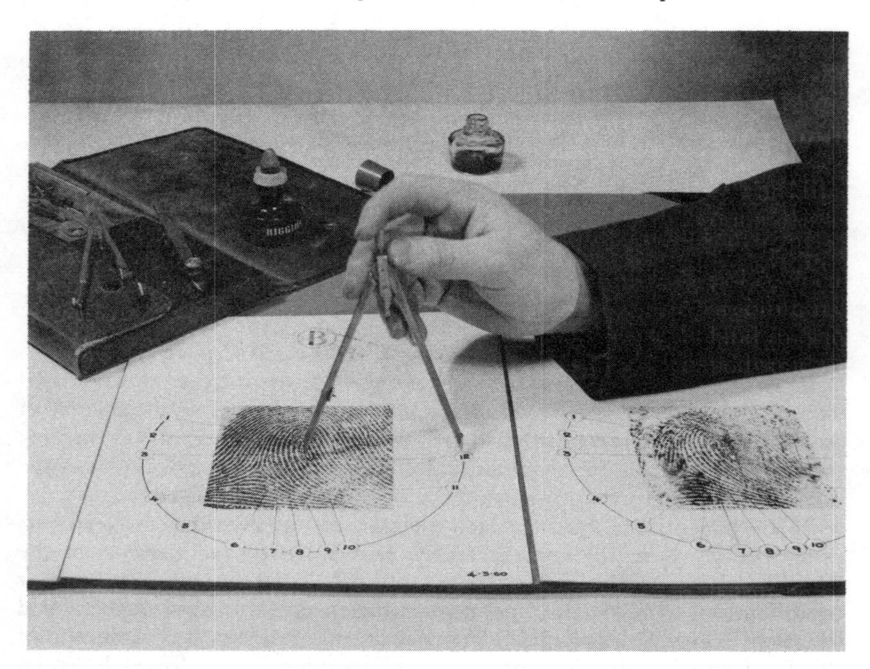

A comparison chart between two fingerprints is drawn up.
R.C.M.P.

In the first decades of the twentieth century most police forces admitted the usefulness of fingerprints as a means of identification. As more and more crimes were solved using fingerprint evidence, the police realized the importance of keeping up-to-date fingerprint files. In the near future, however, automatic scanning systems attached to computers will probably replace human classification systems, and computers will scan their files to make accurate print comparisons within seconds.

Prints on Computer

The computer is ideally suited to the tedious business of classifying and filing fingerprints.

In Canada, the Royal Canadian Mounted Police have been converting their fingerprint files to videotape records and computer-coded binary digits. Each print in the existing file is being photographed and stored in sequence on a two-inch videotape which will then be available for instant replay. The print expert sits at a screen and calls up patterns from the videotape records.

The next step in the automation process has been to eliminate the human expert from the routine print-comparison process. The videotape is subjected to an electronic analysis that breaks down each print into sixteen shades of grey and scans this pattern to determine overall details — ridge line counts and so on. Finally, the print is stored in a computer file as an array of binary digits.

The computer can scan its files and compare them with a print from the crime scene in a very short time — between twenty seconds and two minutes. The two prints are then displayed on a video screen for the human expert to check. As an added precaution, the computer also displays twenty-five similar prints from its files at which point the final assessment is made by a fingerprint expert.

To guard against loss by fire or criminal tampering, two copies of the fingerprint file are kept in a main building, and a third is sealed in a vault in another building some distance away.

The Making of a Fingerprint

A killer's hand, smeared with the victim's blood, may rest for a moment against a wall and leave a perfectly visible print of each finger. In other cases, paint, oil or ink that stain a killer's hand leaves a clear impression that can be photographed and studied by the police.

At most crime scenes, however, fingerprints are invisible and, like the unseen image on a photographic film, await development. It is the identification officer's powders and brush that develop these fingerprints.

If you examine your own finger through a lens you will see the ridges in greater detail. Each ridge contains tiny pores through which the skin breathes and secretes its sweat. It is this almost invisible layer of sweat that is left behind when a finger touches something.

During a break-in or a violent attack, the criminal is often in a state of tension and his hands are more sweaty than usual. In addition, if he has recently touched an area of his head that contains sebaceous glands — his forehead or chin — the grease from these glands will also be on his fingers. As soon as he touches anything, invisible impressions are left of his fingers. Such fingerprints can be developed months or even years later with the use of chemical reagents.

Prints on the Corpse

Recent work in England indicates that it is possible to obtain fingerprints of a murderer from the body of the victim. In the mortuary, the areas in which fingerprints are believed to be present on the corpse are dusted with a fine powder of lead. The body is then x-rayed and, if the pathologist is lucky, a clear fingerprint will be revealed.

Lifting a print

The fingerprint expert begins his examination of the crime scene by attempting to retrace the path taken by the killer. Along this path he looks for the best fingerprint surfaces: flat, smooth areas such as walls, desk tops, glasses, car doors, envelopes, and papers. Obvious loca-tions, such as a telephone receiver or doorknob, may contain the killer's prints but the build-up of grease and dirt on much-handled objects usually obscures any latent (or hidden) prints.

Poroscopy

Each ridge of a fingerprint contains its own unique pattern of sweat pores. In examining a greatly enlarged photograph of a fingerprint fragment, it becomes possible to compare and identify its patterns of pores with those on the suspect's print. A chart can be drawn up showing points of comparison in the pore structure of the two prints.

Poroscopy has been used only in rare cases and its general acceptance by the courts has not yet been established.

The identification officer sometimes examines a surface using angled light from a flashlight. In this way a clean glass or polished ashtray may show a clear print to the naked eye; but in most cases the print is barely visible and must be dusted with powder before it can be examined. On a light-coloured surface the officer uses a powder of black graphite and, for good contrast, talc or white lead is used on dark surfaces. First he spins the fingerprint brush between his hands to clean and splay out its fibres. Then he pours the powder onto a piece of paper and dabs the tip of the brush lightly into it. Using light, even strokes, he brushes the powder over the latent print. As particles of the fine powder stick to the sweaty impressions, the outline of the print shows up, and the brush is swept along the contour lines to provide greater emphasis. With luck, a perfect print appears.

The next step is to preserve the fingerprint as a permanent record that can later be produced in court. To ensure that continuity is preserved between the print at the crime scene and the evidence that is presented at a trial, the identification officer makes a circle around the print with a grease pencil and adds his initials, the date and any classification marks. The whole identification is then photographed with a fingerprinting camera.

Next a piece of transparent adhesive tape is placed over the area of the fingerprint and smoothed out. If the object is small enough, for example, a glass or a cigarette lighter, it is put in a bag for protection, but in most cases the print is transferred by carefully peeling off the transparent tape and sticking it onto a fingerprint transfer card. The card will now carry an impression of the fingerprint plus the identification marks made by the officer. These marks will correspond exactly with those shown in the photograph at the crime scene.

Member of the N.Y. City Crime Scene Unit dusts a car for fingerprints.
Spring 3100 Magazine, N.Y. City Police

Letters and Documents

The wise burglar wears gloves when he is out "on a job" but even the most careful of criminals sometimes slips up. He may take off a glove before opening a letter, for example.

Paper is an absorbent material, so there is little use in dusting an envelope or cheque for prints. Instead, a chemical reagent, such as ninhydrin, is used that produces a vivid colour when it comes into contact with sweat. Another technique is to blow fumes of iodine across a document. Fingerprints show up as a purple-brown image which must be quickly photographed as it has a tendency to fade.

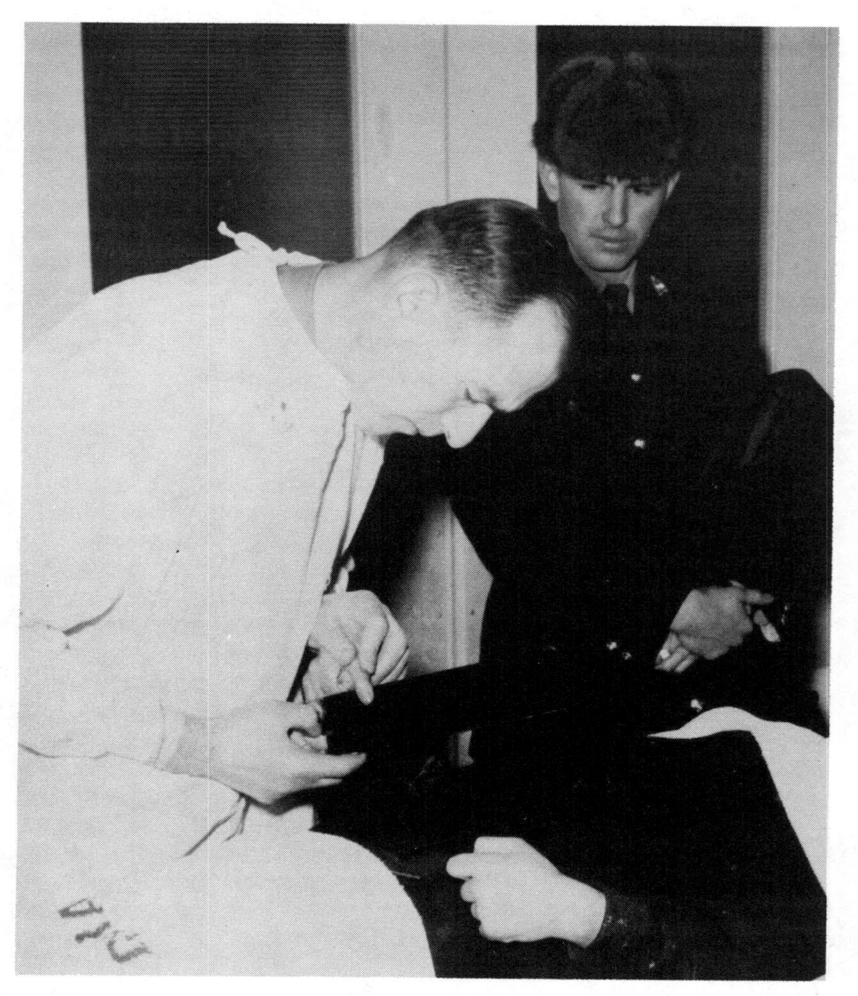

Fingerprints are taken from a corpse.
R.C.M.P.

In the case of a letter with fingerprints that are months or years old, a method known as "vacuum deposition" can be used. The paper is placed in an apparatus next to a metal wire and air is pumped out until the paper is under a vacuum. The wire is then heated until metal atoms "boil off" and condense on the paper. The atoms have a tendency to stay away from the ridges of the fingerprint and collect in other areas. After sufficient time has elapsed, a "negative" picture of the fingerprint will have formed as a fine metal coating on the paper.

Forensic Deductions

In The Hound of the Baskervilles, *Sherlock Holmes deduced, on the evidence of a walking stick left by his visitor, that the owner was an amiable, unambitious, absent-minded doctor of thirty who had a favourite dog.*

Such deductions are not always confined to fiction. In one real-life case, pathologist Edward Heinrich examined a pair of denim overalls and concluded that their owner was between twenty-one and twenty-five years old, weighed 165 pounds, was less than five feet ten inches tall, had medium-light hair, light-brown eyebrows, a fair complexion, and small hands and feet. Furthermore, said Heinrich, the owner had neat habits, worked as a lumberjack with fir trees and was left-handed. These amazing deductions, based on the overalls alone, were later proved correct.

Fingerprint Headaches

In most cases, fingerprints are developed with the use of dusting powders or iodine fumes, but on occasion the odd case turns up for which special methods must be used. A killer may, for example, throw his gun into a nearby lake or river where it lies awaiting the police dragnet.

It is popularly thought that an object that has been left in the rain or recovered from under water will be useless as far as fingerprints are concerned. This is not always so. If the article is carefully dried, it may still be possible to develop a latent print provided that the killer's hands were contaminated with grease or chemicals.

A variety of reagents may be used to bring up the fingerprint pattern. Because ninhydrin reacts with the amino acids in sweat, it is often used. Ninhydrin dissolved in acetone is sprayed over the object and allowed to evaporate. The object is then heated until a reddish-cream print emerges. In other cases silver nitrate solutions are used to develop stubborn prints.

In Canada, the Ontario Provincial Police and the National Research Council are developing a laser technique for raising the prints on articles such as plastic bags and rubber gloves and porous surfaces, which have traditionally been thought to be impossible surfaces. The method is based on the theory that most of us come into contact with traces of chemicals in our daily lives — ink from typewriters and newspapers, motor oil from a car, paint, and household chemicals.

Many of these chemicals glow brightly and "fluoresce" when exposed to laser light, an effect similar to that produced by a false tooth or a detergent-washed shirt in ultra-violet or "black light." The article containing a latent print is placed under the laser and, if fingerprints are present, a glowing image appears.

In the end, it is often the nature of the surface that defeats the fingerprint expert. A chequered grip on a gun, a pair of leather gloves, a roughly finished wall all may contain a hidden print but the texture of the surface itself will break up the print, making it impossible to identify.

The Black Museum

London's Black Museum is more properly entitled the Prisoner's Property Office of the Metropolitan Police. Few members of the general public ever see beyond its locked doors, unlike other museums.

Exhibits in the Black Museum range from hangmen's nooses and poisoner's vials to the victims' last remains and killers' guns. Notable attractions include the spade used by Dr. Crippen to bury his wife, a bathtub used by George Joseph Smith to drown one of his wives, a bottle bearing fingerprints that was found in the Great Train Robbery hideout, and a match-box containing a single pubic hair from the home of multiple killer John Christie.

Elimination Prints

If a murder takes place in a room used by many people — in an office, for example — dozens of prints may be developed and lifted at the crime scene. From among these, the police must locate the killer's prints.

The walls and desks in the room may contain prints of the murdered man, his secretary, visitors, cleaners, and colleagues. The first task of the police, therefore, is to take a set of "elimination prints" from everyone who entered the office on the day of the murder.

Detectives visit everyone connected with the victim — his family, friends, neighbours, office staff, and business associates. In each case an interview is carried out and a short statement taken down. The person being interviewed may be asked to be fingerprinted. In most countries, fingerprints cannot be demanded from a person unless a charge has been made or an arrest has taken place, so the police are diplomatic in their request, pointing out that a set of elimination prints will save the person a great deal of time and public expense. The prints are destroyed when the case is closed or they may be returned to the donor.

To make a fingerprint, most police forces use a pressure sensitive paper or the time-honoured ink pad. In the latter, more messy but traditional technique, the fingers of each hand are first cleaned and then pressed down onto a pad containing printer's ink. Each finger is then rolled onto a card bearing the person's name. A complete hand print is also made by pressing all the fingers onto the card simultaneously.

One final set of prints must be taken and eliminated from the enquiry — those of the dead victim. The identification officer who attends the autopsy in order to collect additional evidence, takes a set of fingerprints from the corpse after the preliminary examination of the body.

Making an Identification

If the prints found on the murder weapon and those of a suspect have the same Henry classification, this does not automatically mean that they came from the same person. Identical classification simply means that the two prints show a remarkable coincidence in their features. For the purposes of legal identification, the two prints must first be scrutinized in minute detail.

The experienced print expert can tell if two prints match as easily as most of us recognize the face of an old friend. If he thinks they do, his next step is to justify his initial assessment by establishing points of comparison between the two prints. These points of comparison involve tiny details in each print: a sudden break in a line, the forking of a line, or an isolated dot or ridge. Like moles or birthmarks, these features are unique and can be used as identification marks that will be acceptable in courts.

The fingerprint officer makes up a comparison chart which contains a blown-up photograph of each print together with a list of the points of comparison. Various courts require different levels of proof. In Britain, sixteen individual points of comparison are normally required; in the United States twelve points are acceptable.

Months later the identification officer will enter the witness box and testify that a fingerprint found on an item matches that of the accused. In addition to producing his comparison chart, he must testify to every link in the chain of evidence. On oath, he will swear to developing the latent print at the scene of the crime, to transferring the print onto a card and to comparing this print with one taken from the accused.

Fingerprint Fragments

Not every killer obliges by leaving a tidy set of prints near his victim. In some cases the hand that made the print shook with fear or anxiety, and in others only the tip of one finger touched an object. The killer may have grasped a rough-textured surface or one smeared with grease. The killer's glove may have had a small rip in one finger, which left only a tiny print fragment.

The problem is how to begin to decipher a fragment, for the normal Henry classification methods cannot be applied. The first step is to decide which finger made the print. By experimenting with his own hand, the expert deduces which finger was involved. Next he studies the fragment and makes a guess regarding the overall pattern to which it belongs. He may decide, for example, that certain lines are the start of an arch or the outer lines of a whorl. Using this trial pattern, he makes a tentative classification. If such a classification corresponds to that of one of the suspect's, the officer compares details in the fragment with those in the suspect's print. A points-of-comparison chart is made up for a print fragment, just as it is for a regular fingerprint. In extremely difficult circumstances, the science of poroscopy may be resorted to.

Fingerprint Forgeries, Past and Future

Ever since fingerprints became a potent weapon in the fight against crime, the underworld has dreamed of turning the tables with print forgeries. So far no criminal has advertised his success in breaking the problem of his telltale fingerprint patterns.

Early attempts to avoid detection involved burning the fingertips or treating them with acid. For a time the damaged fingers carried scar tissue but in the end, when the detail reappeared, unfortunately for the criminal, the new pattern was an exact replica of the old.

In 1919, George J. Lacey, a superintendent in the Houston Identification Bureau, attempted to change his print pattern — for scientific rather than criminal motives. Lacey burned his right thumb with a hot iron until a blister formed. He then cut off the raised skin to ensure that his thumb print was completely destroyed. At first his thumb was covered by a scar, and over the next two months Lacey took prints of his thumb to check for the returning detail. As he expected, the new thumb print was identical to the original, even down to a minute dot between two ridges.

If acids and hot irons fail to work, then what about modern science? Could a transplant produce a new pattern?

One small-time American criminal named Ruscoe Pitts went as far as having the skin stripped from each finger and replaced by tissue grafted from his chest. To achieve this transplant, his hand was taped to his bare chest while the grafts developed. Pitts gained new finger skin but not a new set of prints, for unlike the hands and feet, the skin of the chest does not carry a pattern of ridges. Pitts' new fingertips were smooth and therefore obviously false.

It was even possible for a fingerprint officer to make an identification of Pitts in spite of his featureless fingers. Old skin around the site of the graft showed sufficient ridge detail for the officer to be able to piece together a points-of-comparison chart with the previous set of prints.

Faced with the impossibility of changing their prints, some criminals turned to the scheme of leaving a set of dummy or forged prints at the scene of the crime. Such forged impressions were supposed to confuse the police or point the finger of suspicion at another criminal. Craftsmen constructed fingerprint stamps which could be pressed onto an object to give the appearance of a real print. To the casual observer the prints looked like the real thing, but on closer examination the absence of pore details showed them to be false.

Today, a killer determined to leave a false set of prints at the scene of a murder could proceed in the following way: skin would first be peeled from the fingertips of a corpse or living "volunteer"; at the crime scene the killer would wear fine surgical gloves and carefully wrap the skin around his own fingertips. The forged prints left in the room in blood or grease would show all the characteristics of a real print and create a false trail leading the police away from the identity of the true killer.

Intelligence agencies and large organizations engaged in fringe activities have greater resources at their disposal than the everyday criminal. Would it ever be possible for them to develop new prints for their agents?

There is no reason why fingertip skin cannot be transplanted from one person to another, thereby providing new prints. The major problem is one of tissue rejection, but with the use of modern immuno-suppressant drugs, the rejection reaction can be prevented. An agent would have to weigh the advantages of a totally new identity against the problems of taking immuno-suppressant drugs.

At present, a fingerprint stamp does not produce an image of sufficient detail to fool an experienced fingerprint officer. But a more superior stamp could possibly be developed in the laboratories of an intelligence agency somewhere in the world. The advantages of placing a foreign dignitary, politician or businessman at the scene of a crime or scandal would be enormous, politically speaking, for certain authorities. If forged prints could be developed for such important personages, then their "identity" could be transferred to compromising documents and the like.

It is not beyond the realm of possibility that a set of artificial fingerprints could be manufactured using a modern synthetic material. Worn as gloves and smeared with sweat, amino acids and grease, they would provide the victim's "prints" during a staged break-in by intelligence agents.

The Canadian City Police Hierarchy

Chief of Police
Deputy Chief
Staff Superintendent
Superintendent
Staff Inspector
Inspector
Staff Sergeant
Sergeant
Constable

Chapter 3

THE AUTOPSY

The Autopsy

The second major source of forensic evidence in a murder comes from the victim's body itself. The investigating detective and the identification officer usually attend the autopsy, which is delayed until the murder squad has completed its investigation at the crime scene.

In the event of a "smoking gun" murder, at which the police arrive within minutes of the killing and an arrest is made at once, the police need to be armed with as much information as possible before they begin their interrogation of the prisoner. In a crime of this nature the detectives will probably request an immediate autopsy so that they can be fully briefed before they face their prime suspect. In the majority of cases, however, the detectives will have been working steadily for twenty-four hours by the time they arrive at the mortuary. The questions they want answered are:

Who is the victim?

How did he die?

Can the time of death be narrowed down still further?

Problem of Identification

The official identification of a corpse is an important first step in a murder hunt. More often than not, the prime suspects in a killing are the victim's close relatives, friends and business associates. If the murderer is one of them, and if he can conceal the victim's identity, he can also conceal his relationship with the victim.

When the corpse cannot be immediately identified, the police must rely upon the combined talents of the pathologist, the fingerprint expert and the forensic scientist to piece together the history and personality of the unknown victim.

If the killing took place in his home or office, a member of the family or a friend will make the official identification at the mortuary. A body found in a motel room or in a remote location proves more of a problem. Without a wallet or name tags on the clothing, the police may have to circulate a photograph in newspapers and on television.

If identification through missing-person files or photographs placed in newspapers draws a blank, the police must proceed with a process of deduction. First the body and clothing are examined. Does the body show any curious birthmarks or distinctive tattoos? Is there any jewellery that could be identified, or a watch with a repair mark scratched inside?

Clothing can provide an indication of the victim's status and income; and cleaners' tags, tailors' marks or even the weave of cloth can lead to a record in a receipt book. Even a fragment of clothing, hanging onto a skeleton, has been traced to a particular bolt of cloth. Armed with the manufacturer's list of retailers, the police can then go from store to store with a photograph of the deceased or a description deduced from his remains.

If there is no clothing, the corpse itself can yield information about the sex, age, weight, height and hair colour, even if it is in an advanced state of decomposition. A tattoo, for example, can be traced to a particular artist, and nail scrapings, stains on fingers and the state of the hands can suggest a particular occupation — fiddle player, dark room assistant, auto mechanic, house-painter, carpenter, printer, and so on.

Operation scars also provide a useful form of identification. The case for the Crown in the Crippen murder hung on the identity of the dismembered corpse found under Dr. Crippen's coal cellar. Sir Bernard Spilsbury, the noted pathologist, maintained that a patch of skin found on the body contained the scar of an abdominal operation similar to that performed on Belle Crippen. He dramatically produced the specimen for the edification of the jury.

Sir Bernard Spilsbury

Sir Bernard Spilsbury was one of the world's most famous pathologists and a star performer in court. His successes included the identification of Dr. Crippen's wife, Belle, and of the bodies in the "Brides in the Bath" murders.

After the Crippen case of 1910, Sir Bernard's reputation as a pathologist rose to a point where he was considered almost infallible. He was not impervious to high drama and would sometimes suddenly produce an exciting piece of forensic evidence for the court. To some lawyers, Spilsbury's stature had its drawbacks; he transformed the position of impartial medical adviser into that of an authority who could sway opinion and influence juries. On one occasion, the counsel addressed the great man as "Saint Bernard."

Spilsbury was an aloof sort of person who found close personal contact distasteful. He also maintained a certain rigidity of mind. Yet, as a pathologist he was brilliant, his deductions were masterful and he laid the groundwork of much of modern forensic science. Spilsbury is credited with the invention of the murder bag — the collection of tools the police carry to the scene of a killing. His interest in the physiological mechanism of death led to his conducting a campaign to have the hangman's "drop" extended to ensure that death was immediate.

In the early 1930s Spilsbury's star fell into decline. His findings were often challenged by a younger generation of pathologists — Francis Camps, Donald Teare and Keith Simpson — known as "The Three Musketeers." And in one case he received a severe mauling at the hands of Sir Patrick Hastings, counsel for the defence. In his later years Sir Bernard became something of a recluse, but he continued to appear in court as a forensic witness even after his official retirement in 1934.

One evening in December, 1947 he entered his laboratory at University College Hospital, London, where it was not unusual for him to spend the night hours pottering about. This time, however, the pathologist did not reappear. When a fireman burst through the laboratory door he discovered Sir Bernard lying dead at his bench. He was dressed in his business suit, his lab coat still hung up. Several Bunsen burners were turned on but the gas had not been lit. The great pathologist had gassed himself.

The whole body of the victim is also x-rayed in search of broken bones or evidence of an operation that might be traced to medical records. If the autopsy reveals a recent illness, this information might jog the mind of a local doctor. In general, however, operation scars and evidence of disease are unreliable as doctors keep their files under the names of their patients rather than their diseases or surgical procedures. It is difficult for a doctor or hospital to recall an appendix operation or a broken leg, particularly if the event occurred ten or twenty years before.

Teeth provide the police with a much better chance of identification as all dentists keep records and charts of their patients' mouths, together with sets of dental x-rays. Indeed, dental identification dates as far back as the fifteenth century. Faced with an unknown corpse, the police will generally circulate dental x-rays to local dentists and beyond, through advertisements in dental journals. Even a toothless skull can yield an identity: pockets of decay in the jaw and evidence of old extractions can be used to build up a picture of a past dental history.

But what about fingerprints? If they are a surefire way of identifying a criminal why are they not used to put a name to a corpse? The problem is that provided the victim has led a respectable life, his or her prints will not be on police files. Government employees, airline workers and the staff of security minded corporations may have their fingerprints on file, but the majority of the population does not.

Prints do prove valuable if a corpse has the general characteristics of a person reported missing. Fingerprints obtained from the body are compared with those found in the home of the missing person. Even if months have elapsed between the discovery of a corpse and the murder, it is still possible to find a print at the back of a cupboard or on an object at the bottom of a drawer. The matching of such prints is taken as legal identification even if visual recognition is impossible.

If the victim has spent several hours in the water or has been deliberately disfigured, with a head that has been badly mutilated, it may still be possible to obtain identification. Once the skull has been reconstructed, a skilled pathologist can build up a "face." By superimposing a photograph of the missing person and checking for an exact fit, it is possible to associate a name with the body.

Scattered bones can also be made to talk. By fitting each bone to its neighbours, fragments of the skeleton can be reconstructed. Using precise measurements of the length and width of each bone, it is possible to estimate the height, weight and even sex of the victim.

Bones also give some evidence of age. Teeth, particularly if they belong to a body aged twenty and under, are an accurate indicator of age. In middle age the bones of the skull give some idea of the maturity of the corpse, as do the frailty of bones and changes in the jaw structure in old age.

The Autopsy Begins

Before the pathologist takes his knife to the corpse, the clothing is carefully examined.

In a hit-and-run accident a search is made for paint chips, oil smears and slivers of glass. All evidence is collected and labelled; dry stains are scraped into pill boxes or left on the clothing for later analysis. Each item of clothing is then vacuumed and the removed dust is placed in another sample bag. This clothing will later be examined by the forensic laboratory and then stored until it is produced as evidence in the trial.

Using a powerful light, the pathologist can then begin his detailed examination of the naked body, working his way down each side, beginning at the head and ending at the feet. He makes a note of bruises, wounds and scratches, and takes photographs of the corpse and close-ups of wounds and identifying marks.

He next takes samples of hair from the head, beard and pubic area, together with swabs of the mouth, throat, anus and vagina. Nail scrapings are collected and the hands fingerprinted. The fingerprint officer may use his ink pad at the mortuary to record the prints or he may cut off the corpse's fingers and take them back to his office.

Before the pathologist makes his first incision, he classifies surface wounds as being fresh or old and makes a note of any defence wounds on the victim's hands and arms that would indicate a struggle with the assailant. In a shooting death, the victim's hands are swabbed in order to be tested for firearm residues.

The next stage of the autopsy involves the excision of wounds and scars that may later be produced in court. In a sexual murder the pathologist removes bite marks that might be matched with the impression of the accused's teeth. By cutting around rather than into these wounds made by a knife or bullet, the entry and exit marks of the weapon are preserved. In a shooting death the bullets are carefully removed for ballistic comparison. Although this may seem a simple matter to the layman, digging for a missing bullet can take the pathologist considerable time.

The surface examination of the body completed, the pathologist turns to the internal organs. With a sweeping cut from throat to pubis, the pathologist peels away the outer layers of skin and fat to expose the main organs. At this stage, the pathologist is at an advantage if the victim's medical case history can be obtained. Recent complaints of stomach cramps and headaches, for example, would suggest poisoning and direct the pathologist's attention to the general state of certain internal organs.

A successful pathologist has a high level of suspicion and the experience of diagnosing thousands upon thousands of unnatural deaths. Even if the cause of death appears obvious — a shooting or a drowning — he keeps an open mind so as not to be misled by his initial diagnosis.

The relationship between the organs is preserved by removing them in groups. In a case of poisoning the pathologist extracts the cheeks, tongue, throat, and stomach as a complete system. Each organ is removed and weighed and a written record made of its appearance and characteristics. Small pieces of the organ are taken from representative areas, together with blood and fluid samples and prepared as stained sections for mounting on microscope slides. Under high magnification, these samples may yield additional evidence of disease or damage.

The organs are then preserved in containers and sent to the forensic laboratory for additional tests. Even with a known cause of death the forensic laboratory makes a routine organ analysis for common drugs such as barbiturates, alcohol, arsenic and cyanide. If the pathologist suspects that poison was involved in the death, he requests an additional analysis for a much wider spectrum of drugs and poisons.

Even after all these tests have been completed the organs are retained, because months later the pathologist for the defence may wish to examine them in his own laboratory.

With the body organs removed, the pathologist turns his attention to the brain. After sawing through the skull he folds back the tough protective tissues around the brain and looks for evidence of cerebral bleeding and compression. As with the other organs, the brain is removed, weighed and placed in preservative.

The autopsy completed, the coroner releases the body for burial unless it is to be preserved for the defence pathologist who may want to undertake his own post-mortem.

Bruises

Careful examination of any bruises on the body will indicate how long they were made before a killing and the type of instrument used. The impact from the steering column of a car or a blow from a belt buckle, shoe or whip leaves a characteristic mark on the body that can be matched with the object used. A reddish bruise changes to deep purple within a week and then moves through, green and yellow to brown. By the end of two weeks to a month, the bruise will have vanished. Microscopic examination of the bruise tissue will supplement these findings.

Stabbings and Suicides

When a corpse bearing stab wounds on the throat, chest or wrist arrives at the mortuary the pathologist must decide whether death occurred by murder, suicide or accident. The position and shape of the knife wounds enables an experienced forensic doctor to deduce the type of knife used and the nature of the attack.

Where murder is suspected, the pathologist looks for defence wounds on the hands and arms made as the victim attempted to ward off the attack. These wounds take the form of deep cuts on the arms and slashes across the palms of the hands. If they are absent, bruises on the arms may indicate that the victim was restrained or held during the attack.

If there are no defence wounds or restraining bruises, the pathologist will examine the overall pattern of the stab wounds. A suicide victim often sits in a comfortable chair, loosens the clothing around the throat, takes the knife in his right hand (assuming he is right-handed) and makes the first tentative cut. He places his knife just below his left ear and makes an exploratory weak cut. The second cut is firmer and deeper and sweeps around, ending just below the right ear. The person is now bleeding, but because the throat was stretched back for the first cuts, his knife will not have penetrated deep enough to sever the massive carotid artery; death will not be instantaneous. By contrast, murder is hurried and violent, with straight, rather than curved, slashes at the throat and other parts of the body.

Suicide by cutting the wrists also follows a deliberate pattern. A person who wishes to stab himself in the heart will first lift and part his clothing and then drive the knife into his chest just below the breast bone.

A knife attack that is not made upon the elective suicide sites of wrist, throat or heart — or that appears frenzied and unplanned — comes under immediate suspicion. To the experienced pathologist, a suicide attempt is surrounded with such a ritual that it can never be mistaken for murder.

Staining of the Mouth and Throat

Hydrochloric acid	*Grey-black*
Sulphuric acid	*Grey-black*
Nitric acid	*Brown*
Caustic soda	*Grey-white*
Carbolic acid	*Grey-white*
Lysol	*Brown-leathery*

Drownings

Every year a large number of people are dragged from under the water. Some are the victims of swimming and boating accidents; others chose water for their suicide. There is a third category of aquatic dead — the dumped corpse and the deliberately drowned.

To the pathologist, water is a world of its own in which bodies cool and decay at different rates from those on land, and serious bruises and wounds have nothing to do with death.

A person who falls from a boat or develops cramps will gulp mouthfuls of air and water as he struggles. The lungs and throat become filled with a froth of bubbles, and the remaining air in the lungs is trapped and forced deeper. In death the lungs are swollen and pressed hard against the rib cage, froth fills the nose and throat, and changes occur to the heart and bloodstream. A previously murdered corpse dumped in a lake or pool shows none of these characteristics.

If a person has drowned in a lake or river the pathologist will find particles of silt and weed in the lungs and microscopic creatures, called diatoms, in the bloodstream. The "diatom test" will prove whether the victim was alive when he hit the water; if he was, these tiny creatures will be found in his brain, kidney and bone marrow. A person drowned in a bathtub or swimming pool and later dumped in a nearby river would show all the signs of drowning, but the absence of diatoms in the blood and organs would be a sure sign of foul play.

If the body has had time to drift downstream, the characteristic silt and weed found in the lungs and stomach give a clue as to where the drowning took place. In addition, at the moment of death, a drowning person will literally "clutch at straws." Weeds, overhanging branches, even fibres from the killer's coat, can be found locked in a cadaveric spasm.

In drowning, the composition of the blood changes in the chambers of the heart. As the lungs fill, their fine blood capillaries take in water so that the blood that returns to the heart is considerably diluted. A comparison of blood in the right and left chambers of the heart may indicate that a fresh water drowning has taken place. In salt-water deaths, different changes take place.

The killer who drowns his wife in the bathtub and then dumps her body out at sea will be caught because of the expertise of modern pathology.

A body's temperature drops faster in cold water than on land and so the police doctor takes the temperature of both the water and the body into account, using a different cooling formula than that for bodies found on land in determining the time of death. The amount of fat on the victim's body and the thickness of clothing affect his estimation, as they would on land.

Following a day's immersion in water, any fleas that were originally on the body would be dead. But after only twelve hours under water, it should still be possible to revive them.

In cold water the processes of decomposition are slowed and the formation of gases in the stomach can take several weeks instead of days. But once the body has become bloated with gas, it floats to the surface where it can be spotted. By this time its skin will have become wrinkled and sodden, with the hands and feet beginning to peel.

Post-mortem injuries on bodies dragged from the water are common, for the corpse may wash against a dock, drag across sharp rocks, be sliced by a ship's propeller, or attacked by small animals. Although it is sometimes difficult to distinguish individual post-mortem wounds from those made during the murder, their overall distribution provides a clue for the pathologist.

Underwater injuries after death tend to occur on the head, shoulders and knees. Specific injuries concentrated in other regions will arouse suspicion.

A corpse trapped under water by weeds and rocks suffers considerable decomposition. Hair and fingernails peel off and the flesh is eaten by fish. After several months a chemical reaction takes place which transforms the body fat into a hard waxy substance that coats the bones and body organs.

The Diving Reflex

Whales, dolphins and seals are, like human beings, mammals and air breathers. How, then, are they able to dive beneath the sea and remain submerged for several minutes without oxygen?

The answer lies in a partly understood mechanism known as the "diving reflex," which diverts the blood supply from the skin and body organs to the brain and heart. During submersion, breathing stops and other body processes are suspended so that vital stores of oxygen in the blood can be used to supply the heart and brain.

A residue of this reflex is present in human beings, particularly in young children, who will stop breathing and swim about under water if they are, for example, thrown into a swimming pool. It is the sudden shock of cold (or hot) water on the face that will trigger the reflex and stop the breathing.

A fall into icy water may trigger the "diving reflex" and throw the victim into a state of suspended animation. If the body does not quickly surface, then a form of "dry drowning" results in which no water is present in the lungs. Like the vagal reflex, the diving reflex is another of those only partly understood mechanisms that can result in sudden death.

Dry Drownings: The Brides in the Bath

A husband may claim that his wife collapsed and fell in the bathtub. The pathologist who finds no froth in the mouth or lungs will immediately become suspicious. This faked suicide is an example of murder by "dry drowning."

The first publicized case of dry drowning was the trial of George Smith, the wife murderer. Sir Bernard Spilsbury showed that Smith "drowned" his wives without any struggle by suddenly grasping their legs while they were in the bathtub, forcing their heads back under water. Drowning did not occur by the inhalation of water but by a reflex known as vagal inhibition.

The vagus is one of the most important groups of nerves in the body. Known as the tenth cranial nerve, it runs down the neck and branches into the heart, lungs and digestive system. One of its many tasks is to regulate the heart beat; if the vagus is accidentally stimulated it can slow or stop the heart.

On rare occasions a man may place his hands, in play, around his girlfriend's neck only to have her drop dead at his feet. Pressure on the vagus stopped her heart. In rare cases a doctor's hypodermic has stimulated the vagus and caused the heart to stop.

In a "dry drowning" a similar situation occurs. The victim is suddenly forced under water. Water rushes into the mouth and hits the back of the throat, stimulating the vagus nerve and stopping the heart. The victim dies without a struggle or outward signs of violence, and no water enters the lungs as it does in a normal drowning.

A Few of the Major Human Blood Groups

Group	**Discovered**
ABO	*1900*
MNSs	*1927*
P	*1927*
Rh	*1940*
Lutheran	*1945*
Kell	*1946*
Lewis	*1946*
Duffy	*1950*
Kidd	*1951*
Diego	*1955*
Yt	*1956*
I	*1956*
Xg	*1962*
Dombrock	*1965*

Hangings

Judicial hangings involve a fracture of the second cervical vertebra, with a disruption of the nerve centres that control breathing and heart beat. This almost instantaneous death is achieved in a whiplash effect as the knot in the noose, placed under the left side of the jaw, throws the head back and snaps the spine.

By contrast hanging in a suicide or murder is a more gradual affair. Death does not, in fact, normally occur through compression of the airways but by obstruction of the blood supply and what may be a gentle loss of consciousness.

If a rope or wire is used, its abrasions will be left on the neck, but a towel or other soft material may leave no such marks. Tiny hemorrhages in the eyeballs and face, congestion and a protruding, darkened tongue are all indications of hanging.

Most probably it is the detective rather than the pathologist who will distinguish suicide from murder by examining the general circumstances and the condition of the crime scene. In addition, the detective will ask himself if a suicide would have placed himself in a particular position or been able to tie the rope around his own neck.

Sexual Deaths

On occasion, the police are faced with a highly bizarre death in which the body is found bound and hanged, with the head tied in a plastic bag. This need not be some sadistic gangland revenge but the tragic acting out of a sexual fantasy. Bondage, combined with restriction of the blood supply in a mock hanging, plus an elaborate ritual can be the means to a heightened release in individuals (generally men) who may otherwise lead a normal life.

Strangulation

Manual throttlings are never suicidal. Their trademarks are injuries to the neck, small cuts caused by the fingernails and defence wounds and bruises. In some cases, a killer may tighten a telephone cord, belt or rope around his struggling victim, but it is rare that such a killing would be confused with suicide.

Poison

Outside an industrial plant or the chemist's laboratory, death by poison, other than by an overdose of a prescribed drug, is a rare occurrence today. Once, however, murder by corrosive acids, lysol or cyanide was the choice of the squeamish who wished to polish off a spouse or rival without violence.

In investigating murder by poison the police must rely upon the pathologist and his forensic laboratory to provide an identification of the chemical used. Although there are a large number of poisons, they can be grouped together into common families.

The Corrosives

Common acids such as sulphuric, nitric and hydrochloric, together with caustic soda, bleach and phenol, have a burning and eating action in contact with human flesh.

The act of drinking a corrosive is a ghastly business since the fluid attacks the face and mouth and causes considerable burning in the throat. The victim experiences intense pain and vomiting as fumes from the poison are inhaled into the lungs.

Death occurs in a few hours or in several days, depending on the speed with which the stomach is eaten away and internal bleeding takes place. Often irritation of lungs by corrosive fumes leads to pneumonia and finally death through the collapse of the circulatory and respiratory systems.

The first clue to death by corrosive poisoning is the characteristic burning of the face and mouth. The colour indicates the type of corrosive used and this can later be confirmed by an analysis of the stomach contents.

The Heavy Metal Family

Arsenic, along with cyanide and strychnine, are the "classical poisons" used by Victorians and Edwardians to eradicate troublesome relatives and spouses. The metal belongs to the family of poisons known as the "heavy metals," all of which have a similar action on the body.

Antimony mimics arsenic in many of its reactions. It was used by George Chapman to remove two wives and a mistress at the turn of the century.

Thallium, another heavy metal, was employed by Graham Young, the St. Alban's poisoner, to polish off his workmates, and by the fictional Zachariah Osborne in Agatha Christie's novel ahe Pale Horse.

To this list of heavy metals can be added mercury, copper, iron, tin, barium, zinc, and bismuth.

Arsenic

Arsenic is a member of the "heavy metal" family that includes antimony, lead and thallium. Its cumulative, slow action makes it an ideal poison to administer in small doses over a long period. In popular fiction, it is the means of revenge for old ladies and meek, harassed husbands.

Oxide of arsenic is virtually tasteless and can be baked into pies, sprinkled over food and added to medicine with no fear of detection. Within half an hour of eating the poison, the victim will experience stomach pains and, if the dose is large, vomiting, diarrhea, cramps, and twitchings. The symptoms of a small dose of arsenic soon wear off and leave a general feeling of weakness. They are often mistaken for stomach flu or food poisoning.

When arsenic is given over a long period, the victim slowly declines in health, loses weight and hair, and experiences numbness in the hands and feet. In the end the victim dies. Provided that the suspicions of his doctor have not been aroused, a death certificate indicating neuritis — a general deterioration of the nerves — will be issued.

If an autopsy is ordered, even years after burial, arsenic would not be difficult to detect. Decomposition of the body would have been slowed and certain changes would have occurred in the internal organs and skin.

Confirmation of arsenic poisoning comes with the analysis of tissue samples. The metal accumulates in hair and fingernails, and samples sent to the forensic laboratory will detect even the minutest trace. By estimating the quantity of arsenic in a known sample it is then possible to calculate the amount of poison accumulated in the body at death.

Strychnine

Strychnine was the poison chosen by the infamous Dr. William Palmer to dispatch his relatives and friends. Extracted from the seeds of the *Nux vomica* tree, it is intensely bitter and must be masked by strong-tasting foods before it can be fed to an unsuspecting victim.

The poison is rapidly absorbed by the stomach, from where it passes on to the central nervous system. Within minutes the victim feels restless, excited and suffocated. To a great extent, the course of the poisoning mimics the symptoms of tetanus or lockjaw. As the nervous system becomes progressively poisoned the slightest noise or vibration triggers a violent spasm in which the chest locks and the spine bends until the head and the heels touch the floor. During each spasm, breathing stops but the mind of the victim remains perfectly clear, and his face is locked in the terrible grimace known as *risus sardonicus*. After each fit the body relaxes in a state of exhaustion until the next attack begins. Fully conscious, the victim experiences convulsion upon convulsion until death by exhaustion or suffocation is the only release.

Provided the pathologist does not confuse strychnine symptoms with those of tetanus infection, poisoning is immediately indicated.

Cyanide

Prussic acid, or hydrocyanic acid, is the most dramatic of poisons. The victim can literally drop dead while still clutching his poisoned drink.

Cyanide enters into chemical combination with oxygen-releasing haemoglobin in the blood and prevents the blood supply from releasing oxygen to the tissues. A victim of cyanide poisoning is immediately starved of oxygen. The speed of death varies with the kind of cyanide used. With cyanic acid, death is instantaneous but if salts of cyanide are administered, such as sodium cyanide, poisoning takes a longer time. First the salt must be broken down by acid stomach juices so that free cyanide can be released and absorbed into the blood. Victims with severe stomach disorders may be unable to break down the stomach salt and thus have a chance of surviving a poisoning attempt.

In cyanide poisoning the pulse becomes weaker as the respiration speeds up. Cyanhaemoglobin in the blood makes the victim's skin a bright pink, and the breath carries the odor of bitter almonds.

During the autopsy a pathologist will be alerted by the bright pink appearance of the body organs and the persistent smell of bitter almonds in the tissues.

Carbon Monoxide Poisoning

Before natural gas was introduced into domestic homes, coal gas, which contains five to ten per cent carbon monoxide, was often used for cooking and heating.

Carbon monoxide is also present in car exhaust fumes and during incomplete combustion of kerosene and paraffin stoves. Being colourless and odourless, its undetectability, except by scientific tests, makes it especially dangerous.

Carbon monoxide combines with haemoglobin in the blood to form a stable compound that prevents the take-up and release of oxygen by the blood stream. With as little as one per cent monoxide in the atmosphere, the blood rapidly becomes affected and death can result within five to ten minutes. Over a two-hour period death can occur when the concentration in the air is as low as one part per thousand.

The symptoms of carbon monoxide poisoning vary as the concentration in the blood complex increases. Given sufficient time, even the lowest amounts of carbon monoxide in the outside atmosphere will build up in the blood and result in death. With a thirty per cent concentration the tissues begin to become oxygen-starved and the victim feels dizzy. At forty per cent concentration, coordination begins to fail. By now the victim will realize that he is being gassed but he is too weak and confused to act. At fifty per cent speech is slurred and the victim begins to vomit. Above this concentration death is fairly rapid.

The pathologist detects carbon monoxide poisoning by the pinkness of the face and internal organs. The blood refuses to clot and when subjected to a test known as Kunke's Tannic Acid Test, it forms a dark brown precipitate.

Poison Analysis

Common poisons can be detected by specific chemical tests. Today, the production of sophisticated modern drugs, insecticides, weedkillers, and industrial chemicals have increased by thousands the possible number of poisons a killer can use.

One technique used by forensic scientists to determine a poison is to take an infra-red spectrum of body samples and compare the results with known poisons, using a computer search program.

Guns and Bullets

Both the bullet and the wound itself give vital clues about a shooting death. By examining bullet entrance-and-exit wounds a forensic pathologist can deduce the range and angle of fire. This may prove that a suspected suicide did not fire the gun or that an accused person could not have fired and hit his victim from the position described by witnesses.

Range of Fire

Hot gases, sparks and unburned powder leave the muzzle of a gun upon being fired, along with the bullet. Contact wounds, produced when the gun is pressed close to the victim's body, show deposits from this discharge. The entry wound is jagged with skin, and the clothing around it is burned and stained by the hot gas. The flesh itself may bear the imprint of the gun muzzle.

The pathologist photographs the area of the wound and makes chemical tests for powder residues. If the murder weapon is later located, test shots will be fired from various ranges in an attempt to duplicate the pattern of powder burns.

The impact left by a gun varies with the range at which it was fired. At a range of between a few inches and six feet the flesh is still tattooed by powder but the area of burning is less severe. A bullet that leaves a rifle barrel spins for several feet before it settles down to a smooth flight. Even at a range of up to 100 feet, the bullet moves with a "tailwag." Entrance wounds from a medium-range shooting have a jagged nature as a result of tailwag but show no powder burns. A bullet fired at long range from a high-speed rifle has a perfectly smooth flight and leaves an entrance hole scarcely bigger than the projectile itself.

Direction of Fire

To determine the direction of fire the pathologist ascertains the entrance and exit holes and the position of the victim when he was shot. In close-range shooting the presence of powder burns indicates which wound is made by the bullet's entrance. With a high-speed bullet, however, the entrance and exit holes may appear identical except for the "ring of dirt" around the entrance wound. This is caused by grease on the bullet that is rubbed from the projectile as it enters the body.

Shotgun Wounds

A shotgun produces a different wound from a rifle or pistol, since it fires a cartridge of small lead balls that spread out to cover the target — generally birds or small game. At very close range the shot will not have had time to spread out and a spherical wound will result. At around three feet for a sawn-off shotgun, or further for a standard model, the balls begin to spread out and give rise to a peppering of shot around the main wound. Gunshot wounds at longer range cover the body with small puncture wounds that form a characteristic pattern. Unless a shotgun shooting is done at very close range there are unlikely to be any exit wounds.

Ballistic Fingerprints

The barrel of a modern pistol or rifle contains spiral grooves and ribs (called lands) that bite into the bullet and cause it to spin for a more accurate flight. Each bullet bears the impression of a gun's lands which, together with other characteristics are as unique as fingerprints.

A bullet recovered from a shooting will reveal both the calibre of the gun and the number of lands inside its barrel. Cartridges recovered at the scene of a crime help the police pin down the make of gun because each weapon has a characteristic cartridge ejection pattern.

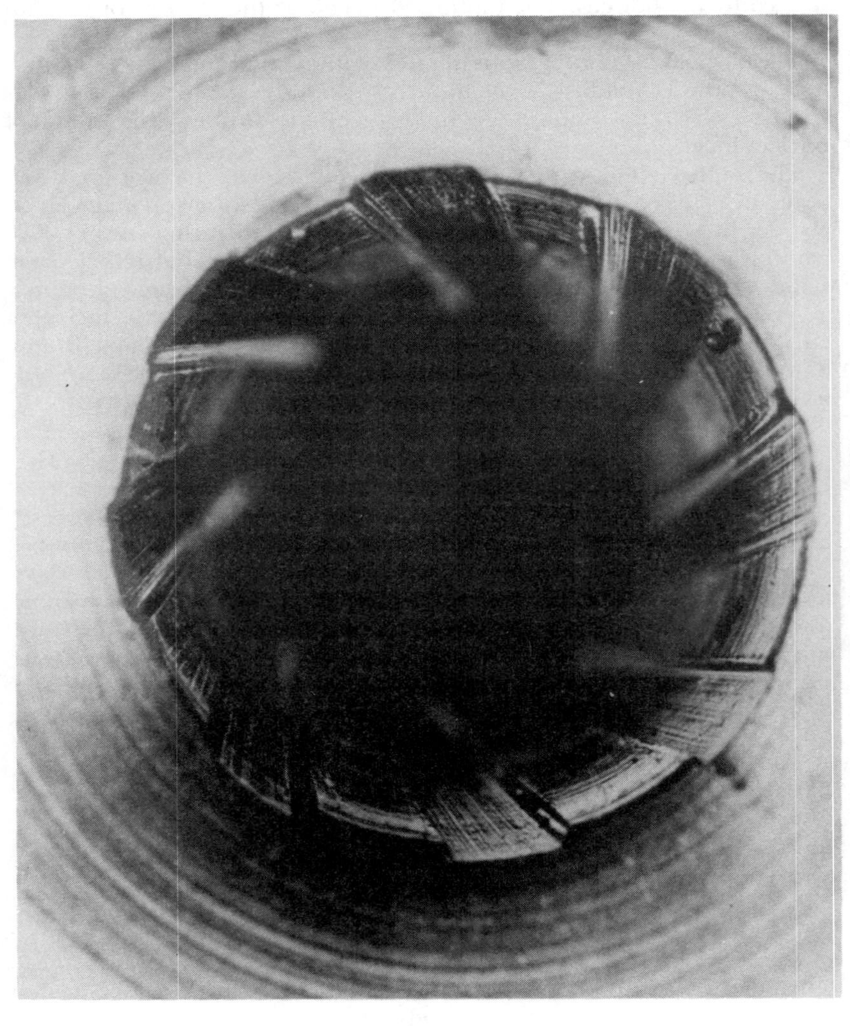

Riflings inside a barrel.
R.C.M.P.

Comparison test on two bullets.
R.C.M.P.

Chapter 4

FORENSIC TREATMENT OF CLUES

Stains on the Clothing

Following an arrest, the suspect's clothing is sent to the forensic lab for testing. During their search for hairs, dust and fibres, scientists will also look for stains, particularly blood, that can be matched with the victim's. If the serologist discovers a faint red stain, his first step will be to spray on a solution of luminol. If the stain gives off a faint blue luminescence, he can be fairly sure it is animal or human blood. To confirm his finding, a filter paper is rubbed onto the stain and treated with benzene in an acid solution. In the case of a bloodstain the haemoglobin will release oxygen and turn the benzene a brilliant blue.

Neither of these tests is conclusive, and so an additional test is carried out, such as the Takayama or Memochromogen. Following these tests, the serologist will determine if the blood is human or animal and which blood groups it contains.

The colour of a blood stain can give some indication of its age. Although the present method of analysis is not particularly reliable, it is possible to distinguish between a stain several days' old and one made months ago.

Are Bloodstains Infallible?

Blood tests are not always accurate. The standard Benzene test, which should differentiate blood from other stains, will occasionally confuse blood with vegetable stains.

The classification of blood groups from a drop of a killer's blood may not be reliable if he has recently received a blood transfusion.

When it comes to the blood stains on a corpse, it is possible for changes to occur in the blood after death because of bacterial action. Such a process affects the antigens in a blood sample and can give incorrect results for blood groupings.

Blood Groups

When a sample of blood arrives at the forensic laboratory it will be classified according to the various blood groupings. It will be matched to the familiar ABO blood group as well as to each of over forty additional blood groups. With the aid of this exact classification it becomes possible to pick out a suspect from amongst hundreds or even tens of thousands of individuals.

Blood groupings need not even rely upon a blood sample for some of them can be identified in saliva, semen and body tissue. If a blackmailer happens to secrete a particular blood group in his saliva then this can be detected in the envelope he has licked and sealed.

Antibody Profiles

Blood groupings constitute only one area of blood identification. Even more revealing are the thousands of microscopic "visiting cards" called antibodies. Antibodies are produced by a healthy body to fight pollens, disease viruses and bacteria. Antibodies specific to a particular pollen will persist in the body years after the source of irritation has been removed and so can give a clue to a suspect's past history. For example, ragweed antibodies in the blood of a murderer in Britain would indicate that the killer had lived for a time in North America (ragweed does not grow in Britain). Other antibodies present might suggest that the killer kept a cat or worked with horses.

Antibody profiles can also indicate that a person has lived in an area where specific epidemics have occurred. And, since certain diseases are caught at different ages, an antibody profile can give some indication of the killer's age.

Forensic scientists anticipate that one day, by means of antibody tests, a single drop of blood will give a complete profile on a killer.

Positive Identification from Blood

One day it may be possible to make a total identification of a killer from a single drop of his blood. At present, the occurrence of key drugs and chemicals in the blood is an important clue to identity.

A heavy smoker's blood, for example, will contain continine and thiocyanate in even the smallest sample. Chemicals and their by-products can be analysed to show whether the killer took aspirin, barbiturates, morphine, or birth control pills. Combined with an antibody profile, bloodstain analysis can provide an important clue to a killer's way of life.

Paint Flecks

A fleck of paint found on the clothing of a hit-and-run victim can lead the police to the killer's car. The chip is sent to the laboratory where a thin vertical section is made. Under the microscope this section may be found to consist of several layers of paint: primer; undercoats; and top coats. By comparing these layers with a car manufacturer's specifications, the police hope to discover the make, model and year of the car.

In most cases a manufacturer will retain the same primer and undercoats from model to model but their chemical composition will vary as the company obtains its fresh supplies throughout the year. The top coat itself is generally blended for a particular model year.

In addition to visual matching of paint layers, a series of laboratory tests can be used to compare tiny chips.

Oil Stains and Fragments

The victim of a hit-and-run driver will often have oil stains on his clothing. Gas chromatography and other analytic techniques can be used to compare the stains with oil from the suspect's car.

Positive identification of a car can also be made by matching glass fragments, chrome trim, plastic lens, broken antennas, body filler, and large paint flecks found on the roadway near the accident.

Wood Samples

Sawdust found in a suspect's pockets, or wood fibres adhering to his clothing can place the suspect at the scene of a crime. It is possible to identify different species of wood according to their cellular characteristics and determine whether wood fibres at a murder scene are identical to those found on the suspect.

A murder committed during a bank robbery can be particularly revealing, for a mixture of wood fibres is often found on the safe-blower's clothing. Between the inner and outer steel jackets of a safe is a layer of insulation consisting of fireproofed sawdust. When the safe is blown, some of this dust is driven into the criminal's clothing. A comparison test can therefore place him at the scene of the crime.

Fibres and Pieces of Cloth

A fragment of cloth hanging from the torn nail of a victim or clutched in a drowned man's hand can provide yet another path to a killer's identity. If the sample is large enough to identify the weave and pattern used in the garment, the original bolts of cloth can be traced through the manufacturer's records to clothing stores and the record of sale. Once the killer's clothing is recovered it might be possible to see whether the fibres and pattern match those of the ripped garment.

A single fibre is more of a challenge to the forensic scientist. Through a microscope he can identify the fibre as coming from cotton, wool, linen, or a synthetic material; however, in addition to the colour and texture, this may be all that the laboratory can deduce. When it comes to matching a single fibre with those from a suspect's clothing, the lab must resort to an analysis of the chemical composition of the cloth. With an infra-red spectograph, a single strand of synthetic fibre can be made to show its detailed chemical composition, which can then be compared with fibres from the sample of clothing.

Exotic Poisons

Exotic poisons, such as extract of rare sea urchin or deadly mushrooms crop up in fiction and it is not beyond the bounds of possibility that such chemicals have already been used by scientifically minded killers, or intelligence agencies to dispatch unwanted spies. Although poisoners tend to stick to tried and trusted recipes, in the history of murder, several out-of-the-ordinary substances have been used to remove a victim.

- *Dr. Crippen used hyocine hydrobromide, a drug sderived from the deadly nightshade group of plants to kill his wife.*
- *Kenneth Barlow injected his wife with a dose of insulin and precipitated a massive forensic investigation into the cause of her death.*
- *Ricin, enclosed in a tiny metal pellet, was used to kill the Bulgarian broadcaster Georgi Markov.*
- *Dr. Carl Coppolino was accused in 1966 of murdering his wife Carmela and Col. William Farber, using succunylcholine chloride. Coppolino, an anesthesiologist, knew that such a drug would totally relax the muscles until breathing stopped and yet be undetectable in an autopsy. An added bizarre element in the case was the claim by Col. Farber's wife that Coppolino had hypnotized her in order to assist in the killings.*

A Strand of Hair

Forensic scientists are not yet able to pinpoint a killer from a single strand of hair but they can at least narrow down their range of suspects.

From its shape and appearance a single hair can be identified as coming from the head, eyebrow, armpits, or pubis. A cross-section helps to indicate race. Caucasian hair, for example, tends to be oval in section whereas that of Mongolians is generally circular. The hair of each race also exhibits particular characteristics and distribution of pigments.

Examination under the microscope indicates whether the hair has been dyed, permed or otherwise treated cosmetically. Microscopic analysis also yields information on the structure of a hair, such as the size of the medulla, or inner core, and characteristics of scales on the cuticle or outer layer.

There is at present no fool-proof method of identifying hair samples but it has been estimated that, using a microscope, an experienced officer will make a sufficiently good identification that the chances of error are 4,500 to 1 for scalp hair and 800 to 1 for pubic hair.

Paraffin Gloves

A sensitive test for firearm powder is given by neutron activation analysis. Molten paraffin is poured over the suspect's hand and allowed to cool. The resulting wax "glove" is peeled off and placed in a nuclear reactor where it is bombarded with neutrons.

Trace elements present in the gunpowder and transferred from the hands to the paraffin gloves become radioactive inside the reactor. Back in the laboratory the gloves will give off radiation characteristics of each trace element in the gunpowder. A comparison can then be made of the radioactivity from the paraffin gloves with that from the gun's cartridges.

Slivers of Glass

A brick thrown through a window does not drive all the glass forward; some of it shatters backwards and lodges in the brick-thrower's clothing. A forced entry through a broken window invariably leaves fragments of glass in the thief's clothing that are not removed by casual cleaning.

Several characteristics such as thickness, colour, fluorescence, refractive index, density, and chemical composition can be measured and used to classify a sliver. This information may help in tracing the fragment to a factory or home that has been glazed by a particular firm.

However, most window and container glass is manufactured by a continuous melting process, during which raw materials are added and molten glass constantly removed. The characteristics of a "batch" of glass can, therefore, change with time — all of which makes it very difficult to identify the origin of a particular sliver.

Ballistic Comparison Tests

In order to prove that the suspect's weapon is identical to the one that fired the murder bullets, the police first make ballistic comparison tests.

Each gun barrel is finished with a fine honing and polishing. During this process, scratches are produced on the lands. After repeated firings, additional scratching from imbedded dirt makes the gun barrel unique; therefore every bullet fired from it will bear the same pattern of tiny impressions, which can be observed under a microscope.

The ballistic expert fires a test round from the suspect's gun into a tank of water or a layer of wadding. The bullets are recovered and one of them is mounted on the stage of a comparison microscope side by side with the bullet taken from the shooting. When adjusted, the microscope brings together the two images like two pieces of a jigsaw puzzle. If the expert is convinced that both bullets were fired from the same gun, an enlarged photograph is made of each bullet and a points-of-comparison chart is drawn up for use in court.

Murder outdoors may involve frogmen and tracker dogs in the search for evidence.
London Metropolitan Police

Chapter 5

DETECTIVES AT WORK

The Detective Begins

After the autopsy has been performed, the forensic results from the crime scene are sent to the detectives. The second phase of the murder hunt begins.

Like the forensic scientist, the detective proceeds in a logical and methodical way, except that he deals with people and emotions, and not in the physics or biology of matter. He must be sensitive to the promptings of intuition and ready to adjust his theories to new information. The forensic evidence gives him a clear picture of how the crime was carried out. The next step is to narrow down his list of suspects until he has the killer in clear focus. In the final hours of his investigation, he will tighten the noose of evidence around his suspect's neck and then make his arrest.

The interval between the detective's arrival at the scene of a crime and his arrest of the killer can take anywhere from hours to weeks or even years. Each murder differs in its individual peculiarities but certain murders fall into ready classification.

The "Smoking Gun" Murder

A great many murders are committed on impulse by a close relative or friend of the victim. It is common for the police to be called to the scene of a murder only minutes after it has occurred, and so the term, "smoking gun" murder.

The circumstances are obvious to the police the moment they arrive. "Verbals" and spontaneous utterances are particularly significant, for the first words spoken by a suspect, confronted at the scene of a murder, can mean the difference between a verdict of murder, manslaughter or justifiable homicide.

If it is obvious who the killer is, the officers at the scene make an immediate arrest and take their suspect to the station for questioning. Here the arresting officer can either interrogate the suspect at once or allow him to stew in isolation for the next few hours. The detective in charge weighs this choice carefully. On the one hand, immediately after a murder, the accused is in a state of confusion and more likely to blurt out a full confession. He will have had little time to invent and rehearse a story. On the other hand, if the detective waits a few hours he will have reports on the forensic evidence and the autopsy. Armed with the background facts to a killing, he can walk into the interview room with a considerable advantage over his suspect. If the accused attempts to invent a story, he could be trapped into a lie. With a full forensic report in his hands, it is probable that the detective would have a more complete picture of what occurred at the time of the murder than even the man who committed the crime.

Once a detective is convinced that the accused committed the murder, he is under obligation to lay a charge. At this point the interrogation ends.

The police also hope for a statement or confession signed by the accused. In the police cell, a man may agree that he has committed murder but later on when he stands in the dock supported by his lawyer, he may make a different plea. A signed confession, however, is difficult to deny at a later date.

The Police Press Release

It is police policy when dealing with the media to omit specific details of a murder or other serious crime. For, when certain details of a murder are known only to the police and the killer himself, it is possible to cross-check confessions and the leads supplied by informers.

It is not unusual for a person to walk into a police station and make a complete confession to a murder. In most cases it is easy for the police to decide that their visitor is a crank or harmlessly mad. Whereas the confession may be fervent and determined, the actual details of the crime appear hazy. "I can't actually remember what she was wearing but I must have killed her...I'm sure I did it," is the type of statement made by the unbalanced. Specific questions on the part of the police such as "Where did you hide the gun?" "Was the woman in bed when you stabbed her?" "Did you move the body afterwards?" "How many shots did you fire?" will be sufficient to tell the police whether a confession is genuine.

When the real killer comes to make his statement after an arrest, inclusion of details known only to the police will strengthen its authenticity and give additional ammunition to the prosecution.

The Routine Investigation

Even when the prime suspects of a murder are close at hand, some killings reveal no obvious suspect and their solution lies in routine investigation.

In such cases, the detectives and the scene-of-the-crime officer hold a conference in which they attempt to reconstruct the murder and the events that led up to it. Suspects are suggested and possible leads mapped out. In their search, the details of the last twenty-four or forty-eight hours of the victim's life are determined, and everyone who came into contact with the dead person is questioned and a statement taken. In all probability, the killer will be one of the people interviewed, although he may not be a prime suspect initially. (His first statement usually provides useful ammunition when he is later arrested.) Parents, relatives, business associates, and friends all add their pieces to the jigsaw of the last day in the murdered man's life. Meetings are cross-checked and times confirmed until the police will have pieced together the complete story of the dead man's last day. Each meal, every meeting, the route he took to work, and the stores he entered will be described in the police interviews. Somewhere in this mass of words, the detective hopes to find a weak link — a time that does not cross-check, an alibi that seems shaky, a possible motive, some old argument or sexual jealousy uncovered.

Through patience and attention to detail the detective attempts to uncover some discrepancy. From this routine beginning the first leads are born.

London's Flying Squad

At the end of World War I, a top-level meeting was held at Scotland Yard to devise new ways of combatting crime. Senior detectives argued that a mobile squad of police should swoop down on criminals all over Metropolitan London. As a result of the discussions Detective Inspector Walter Hambrook was chosen to lead C.8, the eighth branch of Scotland Yard's Criminal Investigation Department.

In those early days the squad did not so much fly to the scene of a crime as gallop. They used a horse-drawn phaethon and a covered wagon hired from the Great Western Railway to reach the scene of a crime. Later, C.8 obtained two Crossley Motor Tenders once owned by the Royal Flying Corps (WW I's equivalent to the RAF). A team of policemen driving around London in air force trucks could hardly escape comment and W.G.T. Crook, crime reporter for the Daily Mail, *dubbed them "The Flying Squad."*

By the early 1930s, the Flying Squad was using a number of powerfully tuned undercover vehicles — delivery vans, post office trucks and the like — which were capable of speeds of over 100 m.p.h. Drivers became experts in high-speed city chases after training at the Brooklands race track. The top floor of Scotland House, a building adjacent to Scotland Yard, had been turned into a communications room to deal with "999" emergency telephone calls; it was clear that a mobile force of detectives, free to operate anywhere across London, had become a powerful weapon against crime. During World

War II, when police forces returned to the bicycle, or tramped their beats on foot, the Flying Squad was issued a special ration of gasoline. Using a fleet of Rovers, Humbers and Jaguars, eight mobile teams patrolled the city at the height of the bombing.

In the war period each Flying Squad team consisted of eight or nine detectives plus their drivers. Their main function was to break up the black market underground which had sprouted when consumer goods and food became scarce. By the end of the war, the Flying Squad had become established as one of the most effective police squads in the country, and not long after similar mobile units were set up in big cities all over the world.

Somewhere along the way, Cockney rhyming slang converted the "Flying Squad" to "Sweeney Todd," which became shortened to the "Sweeney."

The Corner Store Killing

The most difficult murders to solve are those in which there has been little planning. A murder committed during a corner store hold-up or a mugging can be a nightmare for the police. The main problem is the lack of connection between killer and victim, for these crimes are often committed on impulse, and the location chosen haphazardly.

Most murders are solved through interviews with a limited number of obvious suspects — relatives, business partners, neighbours. But if there are no such suspects, no eye witness or forensic evidence, the police can only fall back on a *modus operandi*. Criminals tend to follow set patterns in their crimes. One enters private houses at night, another breaks into banks, a third passes dud cheques, a fourth holds up small stores using a knife, and so on. Like members of small specialized unions, criminals tend not to cross the demarcation lines between the various classes of crime.

If there have been several similar hold-ups in the area, the police will have good reason to suspect that the killing was done by the same gang. If so, systematic checking of criminal records and the movements of likely suspects will result in an arrest.

Many petty crimes are committed as much for the thrill as for gain. Bank robbers, for example, often boast of the excitement of entering a vault without a single alarm being tripped and then walking out, loaded down with bank notes. Cat burglars are known to delight in entering the room in which their victims are sleeping.

If a small-time hold-up ends in murder, the chances are that at some point the criminal will boast about it. To fellow drinkers in a crowded pub, or in private to a girlfriend, he will hint at getting away with murder. News travels fast underground and soon an informer will telephone the police with news to sell. Often a corner store murder or a similar killing that has remained unsolved for months can be finally cracked through the help of an informer.

Sex Killers

Like the corner store killer, a man who rapes and murders for sex is particularly difficult to track down. The victim is usually chosen at random from prostitutes, who walk the city streets at night, or women waiting at a bus stop. The killer bides his time, strikes quickly and is gone with little to connect him to his victim. Even if a fingerprint is discovered, it may be of little use. Often, the habitual rapist or sex murderer appears perfectly respectable in his everyday life and his fingerprints are, therefore, not on file.

As a matter of routine the police will search the files of psychiatrists and mental hospitals in the area, and check the movements of known sex offenders. Neighbours in the area will be questioned in the hope that someone saw the killer lurking about on the night of the murder.

In some cases it is the killer's perverted psychology that traps him. His sexual disorder may, for example, extend to the need to steal the underclothes from his victim, or he may have a history of taking underwear from bedrooms and clothes lines. He may also be known to local prostitutes because of his sadistic desires. At times, the sexual murderer feels the urge to return to the scene of the crime, or taunt the police with letters. Each time he commits an additional criminal act or draws attention to himself, his chance of being caught increases.

Crime in Rural Areas

Homicide in a small village has a different flavour from that in the big city. Country people live in a close community where gossip is rampant and private lives are common knowledge.

After a rural homicide the police gain a wealth of vital information from their routine interviews. Any strangers in the area will have already been noticed and their movements discussed. A change in habit of one of the locals will have been the subject of gossip. As the case progresses, the police learn of arguments and jealousies stretching years back. Such detailed knowledge about one's neighbours occurs more rarely in a city setting.

Gossip and motive will lead the police to a prime suspect, whose movements during the day of the murder may have taken place under the eyes of watchful locals. Armed with statements from neighbours and subsequent forensic evidence, an arrest is usually possible.

The Power of a "Snout"

A "stool pigeon", "grass", "snout", "shopper", or police informer can give an important lead in a murder case. Throughout the world, police depend upon such a body of informers to supply them with regular information on everything from murder to petty break-ins.

Many police forces keep an informer's fund which pays anywhere from a few dollars to thousands for a piece of information. To some this smacks of corruption but others are willing to adopt a flexible attitude. These informers' payments are unlikely to appear on anyone's income tax form, and receipts are not generally given by snouts. So such payments are difficult to trace.

The snout, or grass, belongs to the world of crime. He may be engaged in small-time robbery or in fencing stolen goods. In any case he has an ear for the latest underworld gossip. The grass generally has a special relationship with one particular detective and gives information to no one else. The motivations behind such a relationship are complex. Sometimes the detective may be the same man who once arrested the snout and sent him to prison; yet an element of respect is present and the snout perceives the policeman as straight and fair-dealing. In other cases the snout is motivated by vengeance and jealousy of other criminals. Passing information raises the snout's self-esteem and self-importance — he can call for meetings at any time with a detective. The snout may also feel that the relationship holds the promise of protection or immunity in the future.

For his part, a good detective will be straight and honest in his dealings with a snout. All information will be paid for and no exaggerated promises made as to criminal immunity. A policeman who is trusted and grudgingly admired has no trouble in attracting informers.

Guarding the Supergrass

A "supergrass" or high-level police informer was responsible for arrests in the British Great Train Robbery. Today, Scotland Yard is taking steps to protect such informers. A new section, known as "Uncle," is staffed by experienced detectives whose responsibility is to provide a snout with a new identity. At a few hours notice a new passport, driver's licence, insurance number, and even a job will be tailored to fit a change of name.

Uncle borrows its techniques from the security agencies that have succeeded in protecting defectors and foreign agents who decide to "turn" and assist other governments.

Despite murder contracts, paying up to 40,000 pounds for the lives of supergrasses, the British police have so far been effective in protecting their sources of information.

The Prostitute and the Taxi Driver

Next to the snout, taxi drivers and prostitutes are the greatest source of information to the police since both groups often come into contact with the sordid underbelly of respectable society.

In many big cities a measure of police protection from harassment is offered to prostitutes in return for a supply of information. Once a working relationship is established, a detective can expect from a prostitute the latest news on the underworld or the sudden appearance of big money.

Where a sex killing is concerned, prostitutes are eager to talk — their lives may depend on it. It doesn't take long for word to get around about the respectable businessman who likes his women to dress up in school uniforms, or who pays good money for a girl willing to be beaten at so many dollars a stroke.

The Origin of the FBI

During the American Civil War, a police force was formed in the Treasury Department to investigate the production of counterfeit bank notes. After the war Congress was concerned about a federal secret police growing out of these Treasury Board detectives.

In 1901 Theodore Roosevelt was inaugurated following the assassination of President McKinley and pledged a nationwide fight against crime and a return to law and order. To accomplish this, he attempted to enlist the Treasury Board detectives but Congress, remembering its old fears, countered with a bill forbidding Treasury detectives to work for other government departments, including the Department of Justice. Roosevelt persisted and in 1908, against considerable opposition, he created a new national police force under Attorney General Charles J. Bonaparte called the Bureau of Investigation. It served the federal Department of Justice.

The Bureau was concerned with minor crimes such as the importation of obscene materials and liquor violations. But with the passing of the White Slave Traffic Act by James Robert Mann, its activities suddenly expanded. The Mann Act was designed to stamp out organized crime associated with prostitution and made it a federal offence to transport a woman across state lines for an immoral purpose. The crime came under the jurisdiction of the Bureau of Investigation.

The Bureau's budget received another boost in 1917 as the United States entered World War I. Its mandate was to protect security installations and keep enemy aliens under surveillance.

In 1924, a young lawyer, J. Edgar Hoover, who had created the national fingerprint collection, was made director of the Bureau. Under his leadership, the agency was shaken free of its previous political overtones and all its recruits became subject to training in law and modern police techniques. In 1935 the agency adopted its present title of Federal Bureau of Investigation.

A prisoner is photographed at Central Booking in the Bronx. The camera takes three simultaneous photographs.
Spring 3100 Magazine, N.Y. City Police

Underworld Argot

Just like any other profession the criminal world possesses its own unique jargon. Below are a few British underworld terms.

Bundler: sexual sadist
Busy: detective
Chokey: punishment cell
Iron: passive homosexual
Kite man: criminal who passes forged cheques
Lag: convict
Miler: experienced convict
Pater mender: safe-blower
Panman: forger
Pump: questioning by the police
Screwsman: burglar
Slapparat: masochist
Stir bat: method of conversing in jail without moving the lips
Stoppo lark: someone who organizes jail escapes
Wide boy: member of the underworld

Chapter 6

PULLING IN THE KILLER

When to Make an Arrest

A **detective does not always arrest his suspect as soon as he feels the case is cracked.** In some cases he may let the man know that he is under suspicion, yet leave him free to enter and leave his home.

Before arresting someone, a detective must be close to having a cast-iron case, for in most countries, the suspect must be charged or released within twenty-four hours of an arrest. The case must be closed within that time limit. There are, of course, several ways of circumventing this rule of Habeas Corpus. A suspect may be kept on a holding charge; that is, on a minor technical offence such as possessing a firearm or driving dangerously. Or the suspect may be released and then rearrested as soon as he leaves the police station for a further twenty-four hours. Bending the rules gives the police more time to interrogate a suspect but they then risk being accused of harassing the suspect at the trial. However, whenever possible the police keep the prime subject under surveillance until they have completed their investigation. Only after alibis have been checked and forensic evidence analysed will they make an arrest. Presented with a cast-iron case against them, most people will break down and confess.

An exception to this procedure occurs with a "runner." If the police suspect that a killer will go into hiding or escape the country, they will arrest him at once. The usual technique is to "catch him with the dew on him" by making an arrest in the early hours of the morning. At such a time the killer is disoriented and not in the best position to resist the effects of a pressing interrogation. Whatever happens, the police must be in a position to charge their suspect within the next twenty-four hours.

Warrants

As the net closes around a killer, the police must enter his home to search for evidence. To obtain a warrant for the search, the officer concerned must lay information before a magistrate, judge or justice of the peace. The information gives details of the suspected crime and indicates that the cause of justice would be served by a search of the suspect's premises and that the police have reasonable grounds to believe evidence will be found. The officer must swear to the truth of his information.

To be legally valid, the warrant or legal "instrument" must be specific in all its details, including the exact address of the building to be searched and a list of the evidence to be seized. The warrant is issued to a specific officer and is valid only for the day on which it is issued.

For certain offences, such as drug or excise violations, some countries issue a writ of assistance, which is a form of general warrant, giving police the power of search without the need to consult a magistrate. But to exercise the power of such a warrant the police must have reasonable grounds to suspect that evidence is being concealed in a given building.

Even with a search warrant the police are not supposed to break into a suspect's home. Before entering a house, they should first ask to be allowed in. Only if resistance is put up by the suspect can they use a reasonable amount of force to make their search.

Illegal Search

There are times when the police bend the law where searches are concerned. An illegal search can take place for a variety of reasons and in a variety of ways. The police may force their way into a home without a warrant, seize goods not named on a warrant or use a warrant worded in vague terms regarding the offence in question.

When evidence introduced into a case is obtained by illegal means, the defence lawyer will probably make a formal objection to the judge. In what is known as a "voir dire," the judge listens to arguments from the prosecution and defence on the admissibility of the evidence. In Britain and other Commonwealth countries, illegally obtained evidence will generally be admitted if it is relevant to the case. Precedents have been established in the United States, however, that rule illegally seized evidence is inadmissible.

Lawful Arrest

Not only can a police officer arrest someone committing an indictable or summary offence but in many countries he can arrest on suspicion of a crime, provided his suspicion is based on reasonable grounds.

Arrests are also made on warrants issued by judges, magistrates and coroners. Like search warrants they are specific in naming both the suspect and the offence of which he is accused.

The arrest must be made in a proper manner to ensure that it is legally valid. For example, if a policeman questions a suspect on the street and suggests he should come to the station to answer more questions, he has technically not made an arrest. If the suspect gives the officer a reason for being on the street he is free to walk away without answering any more questions. For an arrest to be valid, the suspect's freedom of movement must actually be "arrested." He must be told that he is under arrest and for what offence. If he then tries to walk or run away, the policeman can use reasonable force to restrain him and take him to the police station.

At the station the arrest is recorded, and the suspect is placed in a cell or an interrogation room. In most countries the suspect must be released within twenty-four hours or charged and "booked" for an offence. As soon as possible after a charge has been laid, the accused is brought before a magistrate, judge or justice of the peace and again formally charged with a particular crime. At this point he can request release on bail.

A Nickname Sticks

An experienced criminal may change his name, dye his hair and move to a new part of town, yet the police can still catch him. It is a curious fact that although a criminal will change his name, his nickname tends to stick.

An informer may not know the new identity of the suspect but he will still be able to report on the movements of the man's girlfriend or close relatives. No matter how often a crook changes his name and address, his daily routine or "modus operandi" usually remains the same.

The Interrogation

Although the detective has sufficient evidence to have made an arrest, he may not be totally convinced that his case is watertight. There may be weak links in the chain of evidence or aspects of the case which are still missing. The motive may be obscure or the question of self-defence and provocation cloudy. Enquiries from neighbours may have suggested an unknown accomplice or even a conspiracy. Key evidence may be missing such as the murder weapon, the get-away car, or the body itself. During the interview the detective must fill in missing details and secure the vital evidence in order to lay a charge. If he is in luck, he will also obtain a signed confession of the crime.

By the time the charge of murder is laid the police hope to hand the prosecution a cast-iron case. Their success or failure will depend upon the skill of the interrogator in getting the arrested man to condemn himself by his own words and in so doing, complete the case for the police.

The tactics employed to elicit information vary to some extent with the nature of the crime and the character and intelligence of the suspect. Before the interrogation some suspects will be left to stew for hours in the interview room, with a stern, silent officer on guard at the door. Others may be softened up by a long and tedious interview with a junior member of the team, who takes the suspect over the same ground over and over again. Some officers work in pairs, one aggressive and bullying, the other a sympathetic father figure. While one piles threat upon threat, the other suggests it would be best to get the whole unpleasant business over with as fast as possible.

No matter what tactics are adopted, the interrogation is governed by the Judge's Rules. These spell out the basic rights of the prisoner and the ground rules for the interrogation procedure. Basically, these general rules seek to maintain the dignity of each suspect. He should be free from the threat of physical torture as well as psychological torture — a concept difficult to define and more difficult to prove.

The Judge's Rules direct that reasonable concern should be exercised for the prisoner's physical comfort. The accused should not be kept without food and drink or prevented from going to the toilet during the questioning. If he feels ill, then a doctor must be called. If he is arrested at 8 a.m., he should not still be being questioned in the early hours of the following day, for this could be construed as mental stress.

There are times, of course, when these rules are bent or openly violated. Does the prisoner have any recourse? During his trial his defence counsel can request that a confession be ruled inadmissible. If the court believes the spirit of the Judge's Rules was violated in obtaining a confession, the confession may not be allowed to be brought up at the trial and the prosecution's case would be weakened.

But what if a brutal interview leads to the recovery of the body or the murder weapon? Is such evidence ruled inadmissible? In Britain and Canada, for example, physical evidence relevant to the case is admitted even when obtained by illegal means. In the United States, however, such evidence is generally ruled inadmissible. There, many police forces videotape the entire interview to discount any later accusation of intimidation.

Citizen's Arrest

In many countries the ordinary citizen possesses the power of arrest. If a passerby sees someone committing an indictable offence or if he believes a person to have committed a serious offence, then he has the power to arrest that person and take his prisoner to the nearest police officer. (An indictable offence is a far more serious crime than a traffic violation or letting a dog run free.)

To keep within the letter of and spirit of the Judge's Rules, most police forces take pains to preserve a record of the accused's movements while in custody. Continuity of supervision is maintained so that every minute of the time spent under arrest can be accounted for. If there is a gap in the record, then the accused could always claim that he was abused or threatened by a third party. All meals, drinks and visits to the toilet are noted, as are the length of rest periods and the duration of questioning.

The interview or interrogation room is small. Its only furniture consists of a small table and three chairs, one for the suspect, one for the detective and the third for a police stenographer. The atmosphere is close and the prisoner is isolated, out of touch with his friends and family.

The next few hours can be stormy and emotional. A curious rapport can develop between the men who sit on opposite sides of the table; it can be as intense as a love affair or as dependent as the relationship between parent and child. A skilled detective has an intuitive feeling for his suspect. He looks for strengths and weaknesses, hopes and fears. He can detect the arrogance that will trap a killer and the terror that may lead him to confess.

The prisoner need not say anything during the interview. He can keep his mouth shut for the next twenty-four hours and do nothing to assist the police. Such a strategy may seem infallible in theory but in practice is incredibly difficult to maintain. Most of us have a need for human contact, an obligation to reply to small talk and a compulsion to fill the gaps in a conversation. When offered a drink or a cigarette, it is hard to say nothing. Once the first trickle of casual chatter begins, the skilled interrogator will keep the conversation flowing until the suspect finds himself speaking about his involvement in the crime.

An experienced crook will be on his guard but a respectable businessman is simply out of his depth and may find himself bombarded with the following proddings:

"Sure you can phone your wife. Just tell us a little more first."

"Look, if you've got nothing to hide then why won't you talk to us."

"What do you need a lawyer for? If you help us, then we'll help you."

"If you come clean and tell us what we want, then we won't be as hard on you when we get to court."

"Look, if you don't say anything, people are going to get angry. They're going to think you've really got something to hide."

Who Kills Whom?

Recent statistics on murder show that eighty per cent of victims are known to their killers and thirty per cent of murders are within the family.

Thirty-eight per cent of killings involve guns, twenty-three per cent are beatings and twenty-two per cent stabbings.

Eighty-six per cent of murderers are male as are sixty-six per cent of victims.

Eighty-three per cent of Canadian murders were resolved by arrest or by suicide of the suspect.

The detective knows that a prisoner with a religious background will yearn for the relief that comes after confession. If guilt has been weighing on a killer already exhausted by the hunt, he may by only too ready to talk. Once in captivity, he may want to have done with the whole thing. In such cases the detective may appear an open, honest human being who will listen with compassion and understanding.

In other cases, the suspect may be hard and clever, determined to outwit his interrogator with a fabricated story. The officer, armed with all the facts in the case and earlier statements made by the prisoner, will try, by going back over old ground, to lead the suspect into a lie. Once he realizes that he is trapped, the killer may become angry and even afraid. Pushed further, his thinking may become confused as he tries to hang on to the threads of his story.

Some interrogators favour the direct approach. Rather than manipulate the suspect or trap him in a lie, the detective demonstrates the scientific infallibility of the forensic evidence, the power of witnesses' statements and the strength of the police case. He puts all his cards on the table, points out that the suspect stands no chance of escaping the charge and suggests that the interview be concluded in an amicable and unemotional manner. It may happen that, like two doctors discussing an interesting diagnosis, killer and interrogator will run over the details of the case, filling in odd points and confirming others. At the end, a statement is typed up for the accused to sign.

The hardened criminal is wise to most of an interrogator's approaches and will probably remain stubborn and uncooperative. It is then that the detective may decide to bend the rules. He may try a little gentle negotiation — an agreement not to oppose bail, a discussion of the possible mitigating circumstances, the chance to see his wife or girlfriend — in return for a little cooperation. Or, angry and tired, he may tell the suspect that they will "throw the book at him." If all else fails, he may even resort to physical intimidation.

Television and Crime

Does television contribute to crime? David Berkowitz, the "Son of Sam" thinks so. Berkowitz killed six women and wounded seven other people during his rampage through New York City in 1976 and 1977, for which he was sentenced to thirty years in prison.

Writing to the Buffalo News *in April, 1980 from his cell in Attica prison, Berkowitz complained about the coverage of crime on television.*

> *Sometimes it becomes difficult if not impossible to feel guilt and remorse when people are always trying to exploit my crimes by making them seem thrilling and exciting while at the same time reducing the victims to mere objects.*
>
> *Society will have to contend with plenty of Sons of Sam in the future. Why? Because any individual with death and destruction on his mind will always be guaranteed plenty of publicity and a willing audience when he turns to anti-social acts for recognition or whatever else.*

The Third Degree

It is an unfortunate fact of life that, throughout the world, individual police officers use physical force to extract information and confessions from witnesses and suspects. Whether brutality is common, or happens only in isolated incidents depends, in the last analysis, upon the attitude of the community. In "civilized" societies, generally, violence and intimidation are confined to dealings with the "criminal class." The businessman who has swindled his partners out of several million dollars, or the bank manager who shoots his wife will be treated with politeness, whereas the petty thief with a string of convictions behind him or a child molester are likely to get a beating.

An experienced criminal treats the police interrogation as another part of the game. He will not allow himself to be trapped into any admission of guilt nor does he feel sorry for his misdeeds, like the middle-class offender. Sometimes it is these very attitudes of sarcastic indifference that trigger violence in officers. In other cases it may be the nature of the crime itself, such as the sexual murder of a child, that angers police officers.

The tactics of intimidation appear to be similar all over the world:

- An arrested man "stumbles" and trips while being helped from the police cruiser. He "falls" downstairs while being shown into the cells.
- During an arrest the suspect is pushed from behind into the arms of an officer. This will be classed as an attempt to resist arrest and the officer will use "reasonable force" to quell the violent prisoner.
- During an interrogation the suspect is goaded into making an attack on the questioner. The moment he reaches forward to swing at his tormenter's face, a colleague will run forward and "restrain" the prisoner.
- At times all pretence is dropped and the prisoner is simply beaten up. Sometimes punches are given through a heavy telephone directory held against the side of the head to avoid leaving bruises.

On the other side of the coin, there are cases where the defence uses a cry of "police brutality" simply to discredit officers on the case. Prisoners in a cell will go to considerable lengths to inflict wounds upon their bodies as evidence of a "beating." Occasionally, an arrested man may himself start a violent attack on his interrogator.

For some police officers, threats of violence or a little "softening-up" of a hardened criminal is an unavoidable part of their job. For others, such an attitude smells of incompetence and failure. Many experienced detectives favour a combination of good police work and a measure of psychology in the interview room to establish a case. For them, even the slightest bending of the rules is the first step to corruption, ending with the general discrediting of the police force.

The Violent Cop

Violent cops soon get known throughout the force. They lean on witnesses and rough up suspects in an effort to close a case as quickly as possible. Some are over-eager; others are violent by nature. To their colleagues they are an embarrassment, for in many cases they will feel obliged to lie to protect a violent cop.

If a prisoner complains that he has been beaten, a police enquiry is set up. And, depending upon local rules, the officer in question may be suspended for the duration of the enquiry. The enquiry itself is normally carried out by senior police officers, who report to a board consisting of the police chief and government or civilian representatives. It can vary from a purely internal investigation to a full enquiry by an independent body. Penalties for police brutality range from a simple warning to dismissal with the records being turned over to the prosecutor's office.

Homeowners vs. Burglars

The homeowner who is overzealous in his attempt to defend his property from robbers could end up in trouble with the police. Although courts recognize the right of citizens to exercise reasonable force in their own self-defence, protecting their possessions with guns and booby-traps is penalized. For example, in 1971 the Iowa State Supreme Court upheld an award of $30,000 in damages to a burglar who had been injured in a booby-trap when he broke into a farmhouse. In 1974 a homeowner was convicted of assault when a rigged gun shot a teenager who was stealing from a garage. In 1976 two burglars were seriously injured in Aube, France when a booby-trapped radio exploded. One later died and the other was partially blinded. The homeowner was given an eight-month suspended sentence and the surviving burglar a two-month suspended sentence.

I Want to Make a Phone Call

In the best police-fiction tradition, an arrested person is entitled to one phone call. In practice there is no such golden rule and the Judge's Rules must be interpreted as they apply to each arrested person. Generally, the police give an arrested man the opportunity to call his lawyer, contact his wife or even pass on necessary instructions to a business partner. If his lawyer or wife does not answer at once the arrested man will be allowed to make additional calls.

In certain cases the police can use the phone call as a matter of negotiation or reward for cooperation. In extreme cases the police may forbid any contact with the outside world — for example, if they feel a phone call could be used to warn an accomplice or obstruct the investigation.

Police Forces in the U.S.A.

It has been established that the United States has 40,000 separate police forces which range from highly sophisticated organizations to small two-man volunteer forces. The partial list below shows something of the general structure of the network.

The federal level includes the FBI, Bureau of Internal Revenue Police Force, Secret Service, Narcotics Bureau, and the Post Office.

The state and municipal levels include the state police; sheriffs, deputies and county forces; police forces in over 1,000 cities and 20,000 townships; police serving villages and boroughs; and police associated with parks, bridges, railways, universities, etc.

Each force has its own area of jurisdiction and it is not unusual for a particular crime to attract the interest of more than one force when responsibilities overlap. Under the federal constitution, individual states have the power to enact and enforce laws; however, where federal offences are concerned, a body such as the FBI enters the investigation.

As a hypothetical example, suppose a civil rights worker is found dead on the campus of a city university, with narcotics in his pocket. The investigation could involve the FBI, the Narcotics Bureau, state police, sheriff's office, city police, and campus police, all of whom may pursue different lines of investigation in their attempt to lay charges, which can also be different. Each force has the power to question the witnesses, seize evidence and send it for analysis, arrest suspects, and place witnesses in protective custody.

Get Me My Lawyer

In most countries a person has the right to legal representation. This means he should be able to consult a lawyer who is unimpeded by the police or the state in the preparation of his case. But whether this right extends to having his lawyer present during that part of the interrogation that occurs before a charge is laid is not well defined.

When the police believe that a lawyer would complicate their enquiries they may not allow the arrested man to seek legal advice. However, the suspect can counter by exercising his right to silence until his lawyer is present. Once the tide of an interview has turned from a simple enquiry into an accusation, however, the suspect has the right to consult a lawyer, according to the Judge's Rules.

A skilful lawyer who hears that his client is in custody will probably demand to speak to his client and to the arresting officer. With the right combination of indignation and hints of harassment, he will generally get what he wants. Supported by his lawyer, the accused will be more confident and less likely to confess. The lawyer may advise him not to answer certain questions, and demand that his client be either charged with a specific crime or immediately released.

Scotland Yard

In the early nineteenth century the London police had their headquarters in a house at 4 Whitehall Place. The rear of the building overlooked a small street called Scotland Yard, and soon the officers were using the latter name in preference to their official address. As the Metropolitan Police grew in size, a new headquarters was needed and in 1890 New Scotland Yard was opened. Ironically, the granite used to build it had been quarried by the convicts of Dartmoor Prison.

Today the headquarters of the Metropolitan Police are in a modern building, the Commissioner's Office near St. James's tube station, but the familiar name — New Scotland Yard — is still used by Londoners.

Laying a Charge

At some point in the interview the detective will be convinced that he has the right man. Once he believes that the evidence clearly establishes guilt, then he is duty-bound, by the Judge's Rules, to administer the formal caution and tell the prisoner that he will be charged.

Before laying a charge, the detective may arrange a quick meeting with the prosecuting counsel, particularly if several people are involved in the murder, in which case, the question of conspiracy or being accessories before and after the crime will involve tricky legal points. If, for example, there is a question of one of the conspirators giving evidence in return for immunity from prosecution, the police must bow to the advice of the prosecutor; or, the nature of the charge itself may not be clear. A police officer may feel that a killing was committed in self-defence, or that the murderer acted under extreme provocation, and be willing to charge him with manslaughter. The prosecutor, however, may prefer a "blanket charge of murder," since it will give him more room to negotiate with the defence outside the court.

After the charge has been administered the detective can, in theory, relax, his responsibility being over. If he questions his prisoner again, there is the danger that the defence will plead harassment. Any further interview will be to clear up minor inconsistencies in his statement or to resolve some ambiguity. According to the Judge's Rules, the inquisitorial phase, as questioning, must end with the charge.

The caution is standard: "John Doe, I must warn you that anything you say may be taken down and used in evidence." Note that the important words are "in evidence" and not "in evidence against you" that is so popular with television detectives.

The charge itself is made verbally and is later written into the charge book at the police station. As soon as possible after being charged, the prisoner is brought before a magistrate or justice of the peace who formally charges him. The charge must be specific and refer to a particular section of the criminal code with an indication of time, place and details of the crime.

The British Police

Unlike many other countries, Britain does not possess a state or national police force. With the exception of London's Metropolitan Police who are directly responsible to the Home Secretary, the forty-six police forces in the United Kingdom come under the jurisdiction of Chief Constables. (In Ulster, however, the Royal Ulster Constabulary has something of the character of state police and is under the authority of the British Home Office.)

Appointed by the Home Office, each chief constable can be fired by the Home Secretary, but he is otherwise independent of direct political influence. The force itself must be certified by the Inspector of Constabulary. Half the salaries are paid by the state and half by the local government. Each region has its own forensic laboratories and pathologists, with a back-up of scientific advice and experts from the Home Office. In troublesome cases, the chief constable of a particular area can request the assistance of New Scotland Yard's "Murder Squad" or the Fraud Squads operated by the Metropolitan Police and the City of London Police.

The backbone of these forces is the "bobby" or constable on the beat. In the past, each constable was assigned a small area — his "patch" or "manor" — to patrol each day. In this way he became known to the locals and got first wind of any gangs or underworld activity in his area. Through daily briefings the Station Sergeant would build up a general picture of petty crime, movement of suspects and activities of gangs in the area. This information proved invaluable to the CID in the solution of robberies and murder cases.

As cities grew in size and complexity, the bobby on the beat became less efficient. In 1966, he was replaced by a system called "Unit Beat Policing" in which teams are assigned, on a shift-work basis, to each area. Each team consists of two bobbies, who live in the area and devise their own "beat." They are backed up by a detective and his driver. In addition, a central collator sifts through reports brought in by the teams and devises a daily bulletin of incidents.

Like the bobby on the beat, Unit Beat Policing is intended to combat crime by preserving a measure of contact between the working policeman and the public who live and work in his "manor."

The Statement

Before questioning the police will keep a written record of questions and replies and may ask the killer to sign this official account of the proceedings. In other cases, an officer may suggest that the murderer should write out a confession. No one is under any obligation to make such a statement to the police; indeed if it is to go unchallenged by the defence, it must be given voluntarily and without coersion or promises or favors from the police.

The statement will by typed out by a police officer and then signed by the killer. It must always be in his own words for, if it is couched in legal terms or uses police jargon, the court may declare it inadmissible. To remain within the spirit of the Judge's Rules, a wise police officer will repeat the official caution before allowing the statement to be made.

The British Special Branch

The activities of the British Special Branch lies between police detection and intelligence work. Unlike MI5 *and* MI6 *intelligence services, Special Branch officers are policemen — but hardly average policemen for they are not concerned with day-to-day crime.*

The Special Branch was formed in 1884 to combat attacks by Irish dynamiters believed to present a threat to the British. Since that time the force has evolved into an intelligence organization with a focus on sedition, treason, riots, and violations of the Official Secrets Act. In addition, the Special Branch keeps its eye on certain aliens who enter the country and takes responsibility for the protection of visiting dignitaries.

The force has a somewhat delicate standing as no formal mandate has been passed in Britain for the operation of a secret or political police force. Yet the Special Branch must infiltrate suspect organizations (often political) and gather information during demonstrations and public meetings. It also investigates companies involved in special government contracts.

Ironically, during the past few years the Special Branch's greatest concern has centred on the area for which it was originally created almost 100 years ago — the investigation of Irish terrorists.

The French Police Force

France, the country of Georges Simenon's creation, Maigret, boasts two national police forces: the Police Nationale and the Gendarmerie Nationale, augmented by the municipal Gardiens de la Paix and the Sûreté Urbaine.

The Gendarmerie Nationale is a semi-military organization under the jurisdiction of the minister for armed forces. Its men are quartered in barracks and so are responsible for guarding main roads and rural areas.

The Police Nationale is subdivided into "départements," each of which is commanded by a prefect. Formed in 1966 through a merger of the Paris Préfecture and the Sûreté Nationale, it is responsible for intelligence activities and public safety. In addition, this judicial arm of the police is responsible for police force training and regulation.

At the local level, the Gardiens de la Paix help solve crimes whose detective work is performed by members of the Sûreté Urbaine.

Police in Italy

The Guardia de Publica Sicurezza is part of the armed forces. It is responsible for law and order, the prevention of crime and the collection of evidence.

The Corps of Carabineri is a national police force responsible to the Ministry of the Interior and to the Ministry of Defence. It investigates crimes and reports to the judiciary.

The Guardia di Finanzia is concerned with smuggling and tax-evasion crimes.

The Vigili Urbani comprises the municipal police forces.

London Metropolitan Police

Commissioner
Deputy Commissioner
Assistant Commissioner
Deputy Assistant Commissioner

Chief Superintendent	*Detective Chief Superintendent*
Superintendent	*Detective Superintendent*
Chief Inspector	*Detective Chief Inspector*
Inspector	*Detective Inspector*
Sergeant	*Detective Sergeant*
Police Constable	*Detective Police Constable*

Blood Groups and Paternity

Blood groupings are often used in disputed cases of paternity. While a particular grouping cannot prove *the identity of a father, they can certainly establish instances in which a man could not have fathered a particular child. Children listed in the right hand column could not have been produced by parents having blood groups listed on the left. For example, a child with blood group A having a mother of group O could not be fathered by a man with blood group O.*

Parents	**"Impossible" Children**
O & O	*A B AB*
O & A	*B AB*
O & B	*A AB*
O & AB	*O AB*
A & A	*B AB*
A & AB	*O*
B & B	*A AB*
B & AB	*O*
AB & AB	*O*

The Yorkshire Ripper

Sonia Sutcliffe, the killer's wife, became the prime target of reporters. According to an article in the British Sunday Times *(May 3, 1981), the* BBC *negotiated with her for six hours in an effort to obtain an interview. The* News of the World *was supposed to have offered her 110,000 pounds, and other papers simply promised to top anything their rivals offered.*

Sutcliffe's friend, Garry Jackson, had a photograph of the killer when he worked as a grave digger and this was sold for 350 pounds. Another friend, Trevor Birdsall, was signed up for an exclusive story with the Sunday People.

Sutcliffe's parents were also a target. The Daily Mail *is said to have offered Peter's father up to 10,000 pounds for a story, and paid for the family to stay in the Stirk House Hotel.*

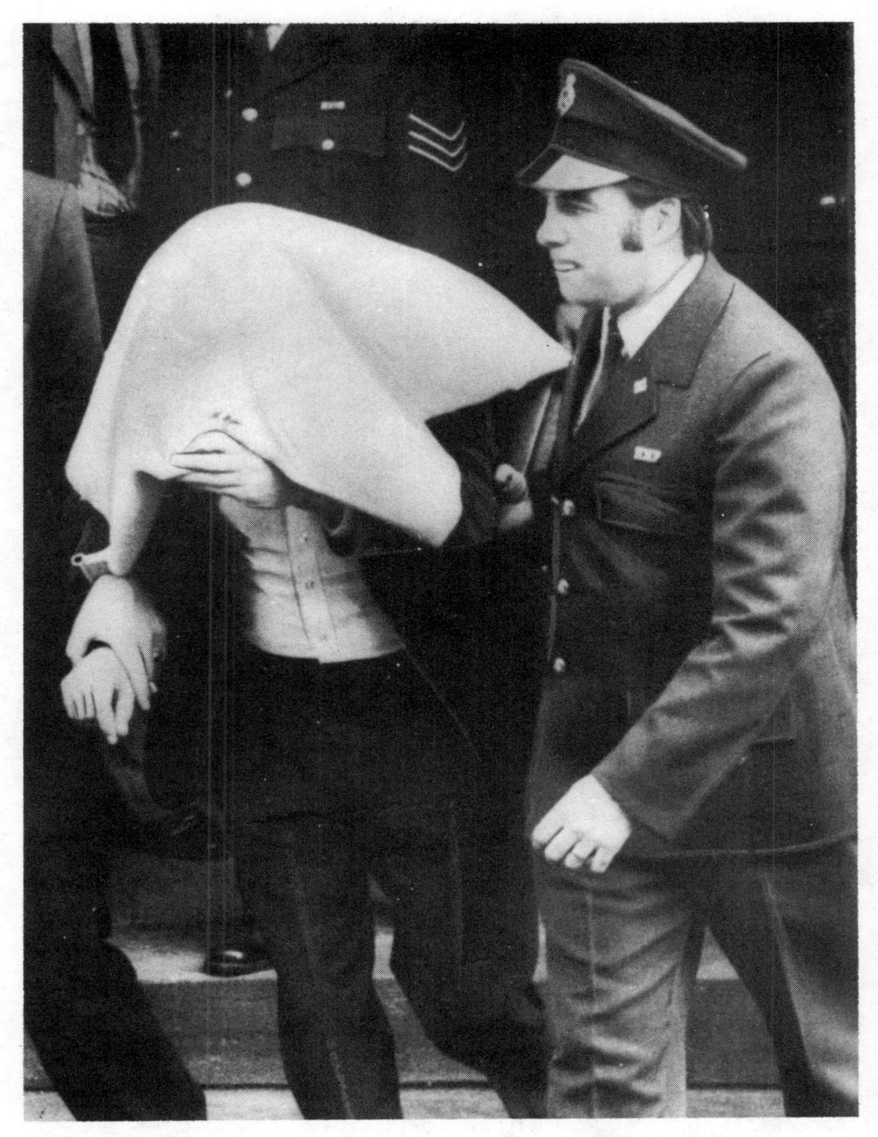

Peter Sutcliffe, head covered, leaves the Dewsbury Magistrates Court, Friday, February 20, 1981. Security was strict at the hearing, the road outside was blocked at both ends and everyone entering the court was searched by the police.
Syndication International

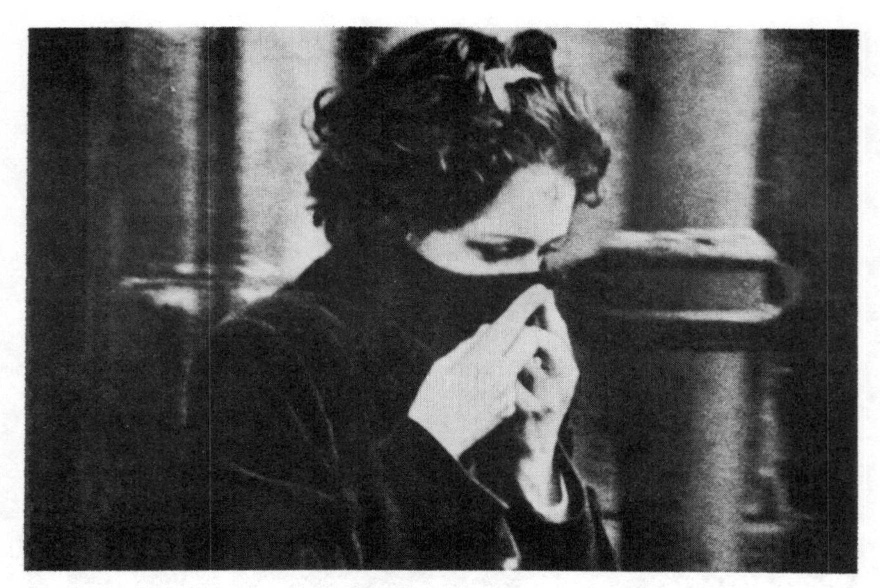

Thirty-year-old Sonia Sutcliffe tries to hide her face as she leaves the court following her husband's remand on a murder charge. During the trial which followed, Sutcliffe's friends and relations were pursued by certain members of the British press who outbid each other to obtain exclusive stories. This practice was later strongly condemned by the British Press Council.
Syndication International

Police watch over Sutcliffe's home in Bradford following the Ripper's arrest.
Syndication International

Peter Sutcliffe sitting in the cab of his lorry. The photograph was used as part of sales drive to boost the company's image.
Syndication International

Before each murder Peter Sutcliffe would spend weeks cruising the red light districts of England's northern towns and carefully selecting the location for his crime. His victims were mainly prostitutes who were first stunned by hammer blows and then stabbed in the abdomen, chest and throat. Sutcliffe appears to have had a shoe and brassiere fetish; on occasion he would return to the scene of the murder to gloat over the body.

Olivia Reivers, 24, (left) was with Sutcliffe in his car when he was arrested on January 5, 1981. Minutes earlier Denise Hall, 19, (right) had turned him away feeling instinctively suspicious about his behaviour.
Syndication International

No. 1 Wilma McCann 28, mother of four and part-time prostitute. Murdered in Leeds, October 1975.

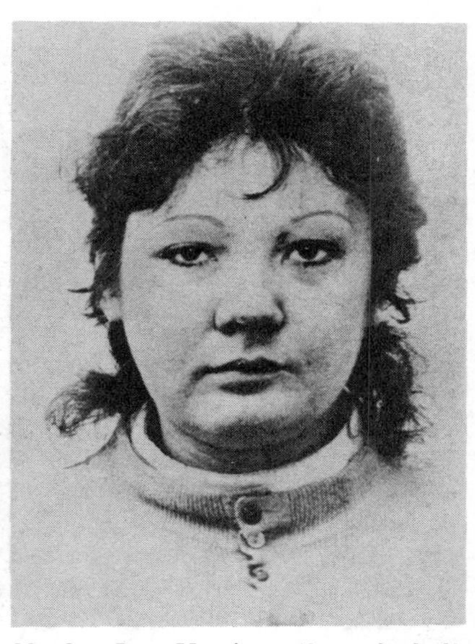

No. 2 Joan Harrison, 42, an alcoholic. Murdered in Preston, November 1975.

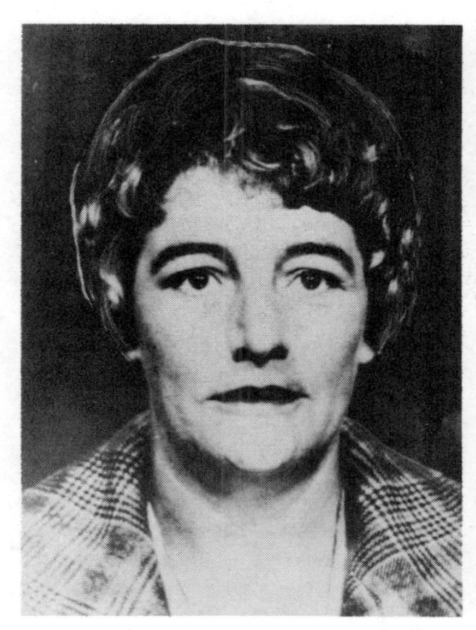

No. 3 Emily Jackson, 42, had recently turned to prostitution. Murdered in Leeds, January 1976.

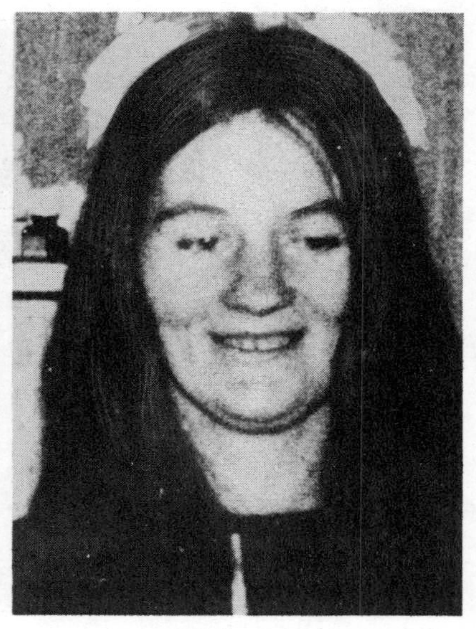

No. 4 Irene Richardson, 28, mother of two, unemployed and virtually homeless. Murdered in Looed, February 1977.

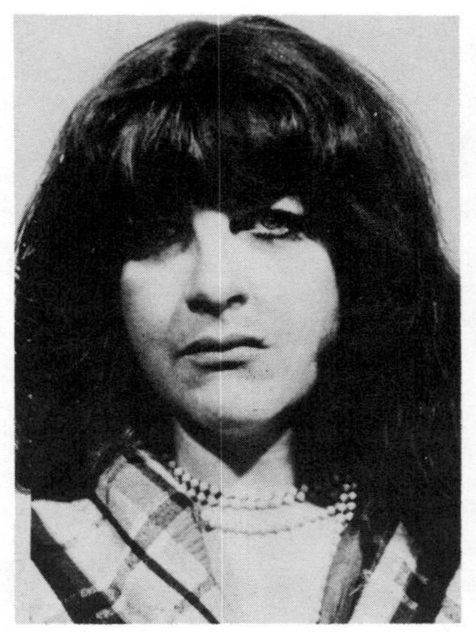

No. 5 Patricia Atkinson, 33, murdered in her apartment after apparently taking Sutcliffe home with her. Bradford, April 1977.

No. 6 Jayne McDonald, 16, murdered in Leeds, June 1977. The first victim not involved in prostitution.

No. 7 Jean Royle, 21, mother of two and a convicted prostitute. Murdered in Manchester, October 1977.

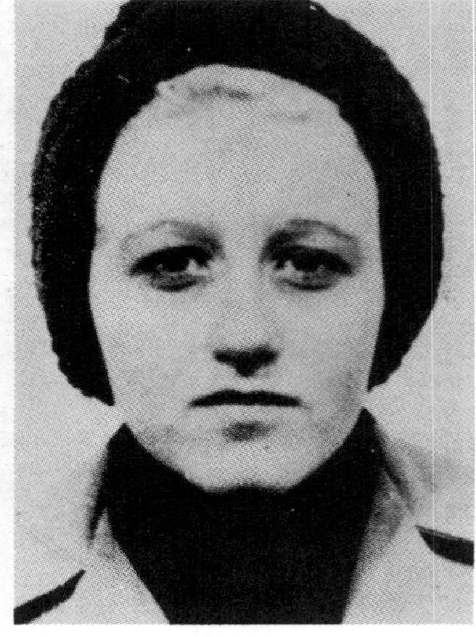

No. 8 Yvonne Pearson, 21, mother of two and convicted prostitute. Murdered in Bradford, January 1978.

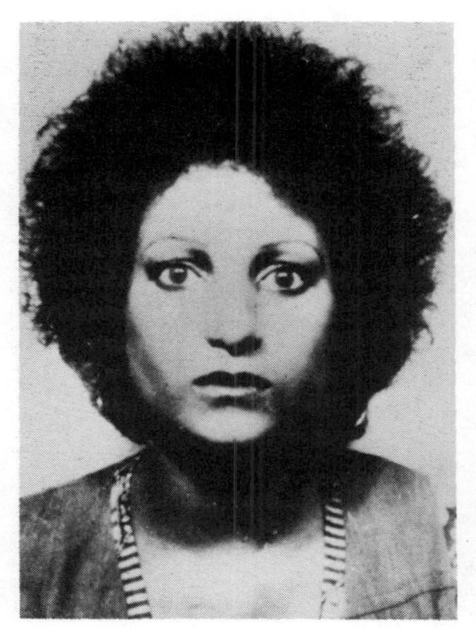

No. 9 Elena Rytka, 18, an active prostitute. Murdered in Huddersfield, February 1978.

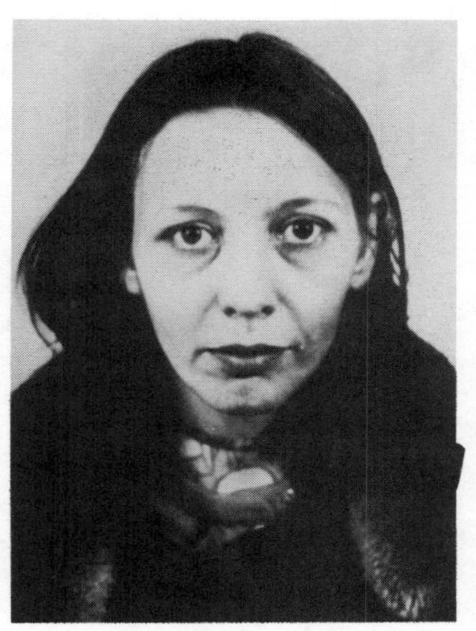

No. 10 Vera Millward, 41, a convicted prostitute and mother of seven. She was murdered in Manchester in May 1978.

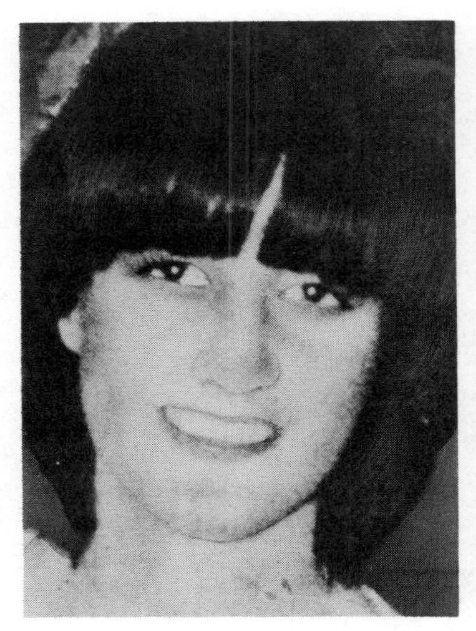

No. 11 Josephine Whitaker, 19, murdered in Halifax, April 1979. The second victim not involved in prostitution.

No. 12 Barbara Leach, 20, a student, not involved in prostitution. Murdered in Bradford, September 1979.

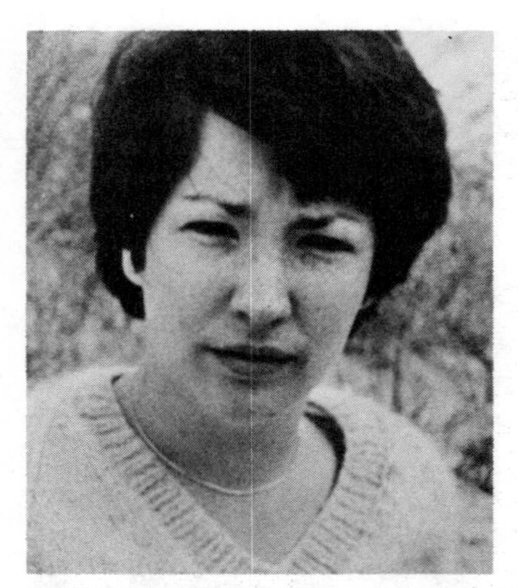

No. 13 Sunday school teacher Jacqueline Hill. Murdered in Leeds, November 1979.

Olive Smelt, a victim who escaped on August 15, 1975. Mrs. Smelt was attacked from behind while walking home at night. She spent several weeks in hospital as the result of her injuries.
Syndication International

When every lead draws a blank the police will resort to any help to catch a killer. Clairvoyant Simon Alexander with Detective Inspector Len Bradley and Detective Suphdon Glendill at the scene of Jayne McDonald's murder — one of the Yorkshire Ripper's victims.
Syndication International

Chapter 7

THE TRIAL

Origins of the Trial

Some formal means for resolving disputes between parties and for punishing offences against the state is practised all over the world. At one time, the simplest and most direct method was to allow the parties to fight it out until one was killed or begged for mercy. This trial by battle lies at the origin of many of the world's present legal systems. Today, adversaries joust before a judge with weapons of words and precedent in place of sword and mace.

An alternative to trial by battle was trial by ordeal, in which the accused person was, for example, made to plunge his hand into hot liquid or was submerged under water. The court held that the accused, if innocent, would come through the ordeal unscathed.

Towards the end of the Middle Ages in Europe the practice of compurgation gained favor. Here each party presented witnesses to the court. The witnesses did not testify to what they had seen, as in a modern trial, but, under oath, to the truthfulness of one of the parties. The verdict in such a trial depended, to some extent, upon the number of witnesses willing to swear to the uprightness of one of the parties. The remnants of trial by compurgation have come down to us in the form of character witnesses, who testify not to matters of fact but to the previous good character and honesty of the accused person.

Before the development of central governments that draw up laws for a whole country, the practice of the courts tended to reflect local needs and customs, and civil courts existed alongside those administered by the church. With the coming of centralized rule, these individual practices were combined into a formal constitution that ensured that all citizens benefitted equally from the law.

In Britain it became the practice for the courts to appoint a jury of local citizens to advise the court on customs and practices in the area. Out of this system evolved British Common Law, honored by tradition and practice as opposed to an act of parliament or a written constitution. The legal descendants of British Common Law are to be found in the United States and in many countries of the Commonwealth. Individual laws may differ and local courts may vary in custom, but on major points the laws operate in essentially similar ways. The procedure of the trial, which is discussed in this book, is based on such a system.

In England in the Middle Ages an accused person, charged with certain offences, would have his lands forfeited and his children made destitute after his execution. Since his chance to a fair trial was not good, his only hope lay in refusing to plea. Without such a plea the court could not proceed and the suspect's lands were secure. The court was, however, allowed to apply pressure in the hope of obtaining a plea. Under a *peine forte et dure* ruling, heavy weights were placed upon the accused's chest until he was willing to answer the court. If the accused died under this torture, no plea was entered. However, his lands would remain untouched. By 1772 English law was changed and a refusal to plea was taken as "guilty." In 1827 this position was again reversed and today a refusal to plea is taken as "not guilty."

Until the eighteenth century throughout Europe, the courts were often biased against the accused. The trial was held in the absence of the accused who was not even allowed to read the testimony against him, consult counsel or put questions to witnesses. By 1708 the accused in an English court was given ten days to prepare his case and was allowed to have a list of witnesses for the Crown. By 1836 the accused could retain counsel. But it was not until 1898 that he could enter the witness box to speak on his own behalf.

In France the practice of the court evolved into an inquisitorial system. Through the person of the judge the court attempted to arrive at a true account of what had taken place. By contrast, British law retained something of the character of the trial by combat. In the accusatorial system the court hears arguments from both sides regarding guilt or innocence. Its business is not so much to determine truth, as in the inquisitorial system, but to establish proof.

Escobedo and Miranda

Escobedo and Miranda are not a nightclub flamenco act but two important decisions handed down by the United States Supreme Court. In essence, the two decisions rule that statements made to the police by the accused are admissible as evidence only if certain safeguards have been taken. An accused person who has been taken into custody must be warned that he has the right to remain silent, that any statement he makes can be used in evidence and that he has the right to an attorney. If a suspect in custody wants to consult an attorney, then no further questions should be asked. If the suspect agrees to be interrogated but later says that he does not wish to answer further questions, then the interrogation must cease.

In arriving at their Miranda decision, the Supreme Court examined several police manuals on interrogation and, noting their increasingly "psychological" tone, commented: "Even without employing brutality...the very fact of custodial interrogation exacts a heavy toll on individual liberty and trades on the weaknesses of individuals."

The Supreme Court emphasized that government must "accord to the dignity and integrity of its citizens" and that the privilege of United States citizens against self-incrimination must be guaranteed.

The police, for their part, have argued that to restrict their activities during interrogation to such an extent would seriously hamper their efforts to fight crime. Unless they are able to lock horns with killers and established criminals during an interrogation, the police feel that many guilty persons will walk away scot free.

The Charge of Murder

For the crime of murder to have occurred, or any other crime for that matter, the law demands that two elements should be present — the *mens rea* (guilty mind) and the *actus reus* (criminal act).

Mens Rea

The first element in committing a crime is the intent. A person who accidentally sets fire to a house during a robbery, for example, does not possess the *mens rea* for arson. Nor does a person who commits murder during an epileptic fit or who injects a fatal drug, not knowing it to be poisonous.

Actus Reus

For a crime to take place some physical action, or *actus reus,* must also occur. It is not sufficient to wish someone dead or injured — the act must be carried out. An act of murder that misfires can result in a lesser charge of attempted murder.

Partners in Murder

In some cases more than one person is involved in a murder. In law the partners in crime are classified according to the principal offender (the person who commits the killing); the abettor (who gives advice on how to carry out the deed); and the procurer (who obtains help for the principal to perform the killing). All the partners are considered equally guilty of the crime. A murder need not even have been planned. For example, if a group of men plan to rob a bank and one of them shoots a guard, each member of the gang can be charged with murder.

Conspiracy

If several people gather together to plan a murder or to hire a killer, the *actus reus* is the agreement and planning itself, not the fatal deed. Even if no killing takes place, all are guilty of conspiracy to murder. For the charge to stick, the police must show that actual discussions took place and there was a firm intention to carry out the deed.

The Power of the Judge

The judge is a symbol of supreme authority in the court for he sits as representative of the monarch or the power of the state. During the course of a trial his power is formidable for, at his discretion, anyone can be held "in contempt of court" and kept in jail for an indefinite period without appeal.

Such a figure is not without influence upon the jury and many lawyers have had occasion to worry about the abuse of this power. It is not unknown, for example, for a judge to make dismissive movements with his hands while counsel is stressing a point, or even to raise his eyebrows in disbelief while the accused gives evidence. During his summing up, the judge's body language and tone of voice may prejudice the jury towards some aspect of the case. A smile or a shrug when mentioning a particular witness may give the jury the impression that certain evidence in the case should not be credited.

In an appeal, the summing up of the trial judge is subject to a detailed examination. If he erred on a point of law or was unfair in presenting evidence, then a verdict may be reversed. However, courts of appeal deal only with written records in which there is little evidence of a judge's "theatrical" performance during the course of the trial.

Provided that his remarks have been fair and his rulings technically correct, there would be little grounds for a defence lawyer to claim that the judge was biased against his client.

Accessory After the Fact

A person can be charged if he gives assistance or shelter to a killer, knowing that a murder has taken place. A mother cannot shield her son, but husbands and wives can offer each other protection without fear of the law. In some countries the law allows a wife to assist her husband's friend, yet a husband cannot shield his wife's friend if that friend is involved in murder.

Going to Trial

After being cautioned and charged the accused person is brought before a magistrate or justice of the peace. An "information" is sworn out by the detective, which gives details of the facts in the case. The accused man need not make a plea at this point but may ask to consult a lawyer. The magistrate for his part will direct the accused to appear before a judge at a preliminary hearing of the evidence. He will arrange for the accused to have legal counsel and will hear an application for bail.

If the offence is not serious then the accused may have to appear a second time to decide at what level the trial should be held. For example, an accused person may elect to appear before a judge and jury in a lower court, or before a judge in a higher court.

The Judges' Rules

In 1918 a committee of British judges devised a set of rules to guide the police in gathering evidence, in interrogations and in the treatment of accused persons. Called the "Judges' Rules," they are not, in fact, enforceable by law but outline rules of procedure for the police. The testimony of a police officer who violates the letter or spirit of the Judges' Rules may be declared inadmissible by the court.

In 1964 the Judges' Rules were revised and are now referred to as the "New Rules." The New Rules clarified existing ambiguities. For example, the old rules required a person in custody to be cautioned before being questioned. But, the police asked, when is a person technically "in custody"? Does being at a police station during an enquiry constitute custody? Under the New Rules, a person must be cautioned before questioning only after he has been charged with a specific offence or told that he will be prosecuted.

While the New Rules are specifically designed for British police forces, similar guidelines exist for police in many other countries. The Canadian police operate somewhere between the new and old rules; while in the United States, a series of Supreme Court decisions, such as Escobedo and Miranda, have restricted the activities of police in a way similar to the Judges' Rules.

The Preliminary Hearing

The preliminary hearing is a formal pre-trial, at which a judge decides whether the prosecution has sufficient grounds to ask for a full trial. It begins with a reading of the "Information" of indictment, a legal instrument that lists the specific charges against the accused. If the "Information" is vague or ambiguous in its wording the defence will move to have the charge quashed at this point.

The prosecution then presents his case and may call on witnesses. Each witness is examined by the prosecutor and cross-examined by the defence as in a normal trial. During the proceedings, the accused may make a statement and in many countries he need not take an oath at this stage. His defence can present witnesses or simply sit tight, listening to each of the prosecution's witnesses and searching for weak points in the case. The pre-trial is a chance for the defence to examine the prosecutor's case, the strength of his witnesses and the power of any forensic evidence. Appraised of the prosecution's case the defence will spend the weeks before the trial checking the witnesses' backgrounds, lining up experts to examine the evidence, and planning his own tactics. To the accused his lawyer may not appear to be doing much work, simply sitting and listening while the prosecution makes all the points. But unless the defence feels that he can have the case dismissed at the pre-trial, he may decide to remain silent, and allow the prosecution to reveal his hand with the hope of turning the tables on him at the trial.

By the end of the hearing, the judge will either dismiss the charge or send the accused to trial. In exceptional circumstances higher authorities can make a direct indictment, even when the charge is dismissed at pre-trial.

The Charge

The opening lines in a British court drama are read by the Clerk of the Court. In the trial of Donald Hume they were as follows:

"Brian Donald Hume, you are charged that on 4 October last you murdered Stanley Setty. How say you, are you guilty or not guilty?"

After pleading "Not Guilty" the jury was sworn in and addressed by the Clerk:

"Members of the jury, the prisoner at the Bar, Brian Donald Hume, is charged with the murder of Stanley Setty on 4 October last. To this indictment he has pleaded Not Guilty, and it is your charge to say, having heard the evidence, whether he be guilty or not."

The Plea

Depending on the nature of the court the trial begins with a reading of the "Information" or the bill of indictment to the prisoner. At this point he must make his plea of "guilty" or "not guilty." If the accused chooses not to speak, an automatic plea of "not guilty" is entered. The defendant's lawyer may instruct his client to plead not guilty to the charge as read but guilty to a lesser offence or to make a special plea of insanity or diminished responsibility.

Following a plea of guilty the judge will hear the facts of the case, together with arguments from the defence and the prosecution, before passing sentence. He may also request that a medical or psychiatric examination be carried out before sentencing. If a plea of not guilty is entered, the trial will proceed and a jury is chosen.

The jury consists of twelve men and women chosen to represent the views and beliefs of the society that judges the accused person. The jury at a murder trial are in fact a "petit jury" as distinct from a Grand Jury, which operates in an entirely different legal framework. (The Grand Jury does not try cases like a petit jury, but is a group of laymen called upon by a court to investigate certain legal matters, call and interrogate witnesses and issue a report or make a formal charge.)

The members of the jury are chosen from among a panel of voters who are commanded to appear in court on a particular date. Certain individuals are excluded from the list, such as law students, clergymen, police, the insane, and people who have served time in prison for certain offences. Objections can be made to each potential jury member by the defence or prosecution if he or she appears biased or holds beliefs that could prejudice the case. If a jury person has read about the case in the newspapers or discussed it with his friends he will probably be rejected unless he convinces counsel of his open-mindedness. In certain countries only a limited number of objections can be made and each objection must be for a good reason. In other jurisdictions an unlimited number of objections can be made without giving any logical reason.

Some prosecutors believe that there is such a thing as an "ideal jury" — that is, one more likely to convict an accused person. In some cases this ideal jury consists of lower-middle class people with stable homes and steady jobs. By contrast, the defence prefers educated and imaginative people who would be sympathetic to arguments about the accused's state of mind and capable of following the subtle testimony of expert witnesses. A case of rape, however, is more likely to secure a conviction with a jury of women and young people.

The attempt to pick up an ideal jury represents the first skirmish between the rival counsels.

Plea Bargaining

Before the bill of indictment is read and during a recess in the trial, it is not uncommon for the two adversaries, prosecutor and defender, to walk down the corridor, heads together, the best of friends. They may be discussing the weather or the influence of the judge's digestion on the strictness of a sentence. They may equally well be engaged in plea bargaining.

To the accused and the police, the business of plea bargains seems a sordid and furtive business, but to the legal profession it is a perfectly respectable way of getting business done in the shortest possible time.

An artist's impression of the Old Bailey and the exhibits table with its awful contents during the trial of Peter Sutcliffe —"The Yorkshire Ripper."
Syndication International

Plea bargaining takes place informally and in the absence of the accused. On occasion, it will take place in the judge's chambers and the judge himself may become involved. A wise judge, however, listens to both sides without giving guarantees, reserving his judgement for the open court.

Most lawyers agree that plea bargaining is an effective way of cutting down on time and costs in court. Even something as elementary as agreeing to accept the prosecution's arguments on the identity of the murder weapon or on the time of a murder is a form of bargaining, for it avoids the time taken in calling of supportive witnesses.

The basis of a plea bargain is the age-old art of negotiation in which both sides bandy strengths and weaknesses in the hope of arriving at the best possible compromise. The defence, for example, must weigh the possibility of conviction on a serious charge against the tactic of pleading guilty to a reduced charge. The prosecutor may estimate his chance of losing the case and decide that it is better to ensure a conviction to a lesser crime. In the end, the defence may agree to plead guilty to a lesser charge and the prosecutor to drop the major one, or the prosecutor may agree to ask for a lighter sentence.

As in all negotiation the personalities of the parties play an important part, and a variety of curious motives will influence the outcome. The defence lawyer may be convinced of his client's innocence, but he may also dislike the prosecutor. The prosecutor, on his part, may be worried about the effect on his career of losing this particular case, or he may be in conflict with the judge. If one side has kept a few cards to his chest — concealing the weakness of one of his witnesses or his inability to dispute certain forensic evidence — then he may strive for a better deal by appearing to bargain from a position of strength. In most cases an inexperienced prosecutor has little hope against a cunning defence counsel. Where justice is concerned the ability to hire a top lawyer certainly helps.

Solicitors and Barristers

There are several differences of procedure between the courts in Britain and the United States, particularly when it comes to obtaining legal representation. In Britain a murderer will retain the services of a solicitor who takes statements, investigates legal precedents and builds a general picture of the case. Armed with this information, the solicitor approaches a barrister who is an expert in similar cases and will plead the client's case in court.

During the course of the trial the barrister is "briefed" or instructed by the solicitor who, in turn, speaks with his client. The whole arrangement is not unlike that of the British medical system in which the consultant surgeon, an expert in operations, sees his patient as a square of skin and intestines in the operating theatre while the diagnosis and medical interview is carried out by the patient's doctor.

By contrast, in the United States a killer will contact the top lawyer in his city and ask him to take on the case. The lawyer, and his assistants, will listen to the client, prepare the groundwork, talk to witnesses and argue the case in court. In complex trials, more than one lawyer may spread the workload, one questioning the expert witnesses and the other addressing the jury. Similarly, a British murder trial is dominated by a "leader" or senior barrister, with more routine cross-examinations conducted by his junior.

Both systems have their advantages and disadvantages. The British would argue that a barrister, serving at one of the Inns of Court, comes to know the intimate details of court procedures and the idiosyncracies of individual judges. An American lawyer would argue, however, that his overall handling of the case gives him a more rounded approach, and he is better able to serve his client by taking responsibility for all aspects of the defence.

The Trial Begins

With the jury sworn in, the trial now begins with the prosecution outlining the argument against the accused and presenting the facts surrounding the murder. Next, he fills in the details of his argument. Each witness is called to the stand, put on oath and taken through an "examination-in-chief" by the prosecutor, who confines himself to simple questions. These are chosen to keep the witness to the main thread of the story. During an examination-in-chief questions must be carefully phrased, for the counsel is not allowed to make suggestions to witnesses, influence their answers or lead them to a particular conclusion.

To establish links in the chain of evidence the prosecutor will call on a series of witnesses. For example, one witness may testify to seeing an abandoned car with the accused standing near it, another to taking the car to the police station by tow truck, a third to having examined the car and extracted samples of human hair and fibres of cloth. An expert witness may then testify to examining the fibres and matching them against samples supplied by the police. To complete the links in the chain, the arresting officer may testify that he took clothing from the accused's home and sent it to the police laboratory.

In some cases the defence may cut across this parade of witnesses by admitting the truth of certain evidence.

Each witness is allowed to testify only about his direct experience — what he heard, saw, touched, smelt, or felt. He cannot give evidence about what he suspected, guessed or learned from someone else. An exception to this rule is the "expert witness" — a doctor or forensic scientist who can offer an opinion or conjecture based upon his experience and his examination of the evidence.

Hearsay evidence is not admitted in court. A witness cannot repeat gossip or overheard conversations but he can testify, for example, that he overheard the sound of people talking, or that he heard a shout. An exception to this rule is the "verbal" or spontaneous statements made to the police immediately after the crime or during the arrest.

If one of the prosecution's own witnesses becomes evasive in giving evidence he will be ruled a "hostile witness." A relative or close friend of the accused who finds himself in the position of giving evidence for the prosecution may prove uncooperative or even refuse to make a statement. Once such a witness is ruled hostile the prosecutor is allowed to change the tactics of his examination-in-chief and probe and cross-question the witness to get at the truth.

Each witness must be unrehearsed and, for this reason, he cannot read from notes or a script made by himself or the counsel. Notes made at the time of the event, however — from a policeman's notebook, for example — are allowed in the box.

During an examination of witnesses, the opposing counsel may object to the tone of the questions or even to the admission of physical evidence or a written statement. In such cases a trial-within-a-trial takes place. In what is known as a "voir dire" the prosecutor and defence present arguments to the judge in the absence of the jury. The judge listens to both sides and then makes his ruling. He may decide that a particular piece of physical evidence cannot be admitted in evidence or that a written statement or confession cannot be read out in court. In some cases he will tell the jury that they must ignore the statement previously made by a witness — a difficult task at the best of times.

After the examination-in-chief is finished the defence counsel rises to cross-examine the witnesses. His approach will depend on the importance of the evidence and the background of the witnesses. In some cases the defence counsel may accept statements as they stand; in others he may suggest an alternative interpretation to the witnesses' statements. He may attempt to shake a witness's testimony with regard to an exact time or identification or he may introduce evidence indicating that the witness has poor sight or hearing. Finally, there are cases in which the honesty and objectivity of a witness may be questioned. Research done by a private detective may reveal that a witness is having an affair with the accused's wife, or that he stands to make money from a newspaper article if a murder conviction is obtained, or that he has previously committed perjury.

With an "expert witness' for the prosecution, the defence lawyer will choose his tactics carefully. If the expert is sloppy, the defence will seize on minor matters such as undated forms or unsigned reports to erode the impression of authority made by the witness and to throw doubt on his testimony. In some cases the best he can hope for is to have the expert qualify the force of his conclusion.

Following the cross-examination the prosecutor attempts to repair any damage to his case by a re-examination in which he stresses the main points in the witness's story.

Once the prosecution has completed its case against the accused the defence begins its argument. He can adopt a variety of methods. He may move to have the charge dismissed on the grounds that no proof for the crime has been offered. He may do his best to discredit the prosecution's case and call witnesses of his own to testify on expert matters. In some cases the defence will suggest a totally different interpretation of the facts or present an alibi. Finally, in those cases in which guilt is obvious, the defence must resort to a plea of extenuating circumstances or provocation.

No matter what approach the defence counsel takes in terms of tactics, the way he is allowed to proceed with his case is similar to that allowed the prosecution. The defence will call witnesses and, during the examination-in-chief, attempt to present his client's case in the best light or throw doubt on the prosecution's argument. The prosecutor has his chance to attack the testimony during the cross-examination and the defence will then attempt to repair any damage during the re-examination.

In exceptional circumstances either side can recall a witness and subject him to questioning. The recall of a witness cannot take place simply because counsel forgot to ask a question or did a bad job on the first occasion. Witnesses appear a second time only if new evidence has emerged in the trial upon which they can give testimony.

After the last witness has been called the prosecuting and defence counsels make their final address to the jury. In the past, this was a time for high drama featuring descriptions of the victim's orphaned childhood or the killer's wasted life. Today, counsel is more likely to run over the main points of the case in a calm manner and emphasize the logic of his arguments.

The Old Bailey

At the beginning of the thirteenth century the New Gate, set into the walls of the City of London, was used to hold felons. Newgate Prison, as it came to be known, was expanded and rebuilt several times in the centuries that followed. On one occasion, money was provided by the executors of the estate of Mayor Richard Whittington — "Dick Whittington." It became London's major prison for felons and debtors, and by the nineteenth century over 600 men and women filled its cells, victims of the epidemics that swept through the confined quarters.

The prison laid much emphasis on the life beyond. There were two church services each Sunday in the chapel and executions outside on a movable scaffold called the "New Drop."

The Bailey was built next to Newgate prison to try the "vilest and most evil villains." It is said that the smell which reached the Bailey from the nearby cells of Newgate was so foul that nosegays of herbs were carried by the justices, and flowers were strewn over the floor. The accused were led from the cells and placed in the dock — a wooden frame with a mirror suspended from above to reflect every movement.

In 1907 a new court was opened in London by King Edward VII, called the Central Criminal Court, but the building retained the name "Old Bailey."

Privileged Statements

Certain conversations are assumed by the general public to have a privileged status in law in that they are absolutely confidential. Obvious examples are the confession of a killer to his priest, the conversation between patient and doctor or psychiatrist, the interview between a newspaperman and his source, and the interview between lawyer and client. With the exception of the last, such privileged statements have no special status in law, and at his discretion a judge can order a newspaperman to reveal his source or a priest to give details of a confession. However, the circumstances that would cause such a move on the part of the judge must be deeply significant to the outcome of a case.

If a witness refuses to reveal his source, he can be jailed for an indefinite period for contempt of court. Generally, such a witness is brought back to the court after spending several days in jail. He is questioned by the judge once again. If he refuses to answer then the procedure can be repeated, in theory, for as long as the judge lives.

American Lawyers' Jargon

Fishing Expeditions: counsel's attempt to wear down the opposition by requesting a seemingly unnecessary mass of documents at the pre-trial stage.

Bulletproof: a contract or other legal document with no loopholes.

Running up the Meter or Churning: research and activities which, although they have little relevance to the outcome of a case, are billed to the client.

Boilerplate: a standard language for lawyers in which routine legal documents are written which are incomprehensible to their clients.

Paper War: an attempt to submerge the opposition by legal motions, countersuits, cross claims, delays, and various rules of procedure.

Forum Shopping: seeking a friendly judge or a court that has the reputation for favourable decisions.

Cooling the Client: an attempt to lower the client's expectations regarding the outcome of his case. In this way, a client may be pleased with a lower settlement out of court.

Defenders, Right or Wrong

The counsel who fights tooth and nail to have an innocent man cleared of the charge of murder is one of the stock heroic characters of film and television. In such fictional accounts the accused is generally innocent. But what of the defender who fights for a corrupt politician, a habitual child-molester, or a homicidal maniac? Are his efforts diminished if "right" is not on his side?

It is often believed that the lawyer who has criminals for clients is "crooked" and that "good lawyers," by some magical process, have only innocent clients to fight for. For the legal profession, nothing could be further from the truth. The law, they insist, is concerned with matters of *proof* and not with that philosophical abstraction called *truth*. When it comes to ethics, a lawyer's first duty is to present the best possible defence for his client.

The Lawyer Rests His Defence

In 1973 Juan Corona was tried and convicted of the murder of twenty-five farmworkers in California. The prosecutor alleged that Corona had hacked and bludgeoned the workers to death and called 116 witnesses to support his case. The defence attorney confined himself to questioning a few of the witnesses, presented no testimony or witnesses for his client and confined his summing up to ten minutes. Five years later the California Court of Appeal ordered a new trial on the grounds that the defence had failed to raise all possible defences on behalf of his client. The Appeal Court learned that Corona's lawyer had been granted literary rights to his client's life story and had even negotiated a contract with a major publisher before the trial. This conflict of interest "rendered the trial a farce and a mockery" according to the Appeal Court. In addition, the court wondered why the defence had not brought out Corona's history of mental illness and raised the question of diminished capacity or insanity.

When a layman reads an account of a murder trial in a book or newspaper, it sometimes seems that the accused's guilt is obvious, and yet the lawyer has used every trick in the book to get his client acquitted. How does such a lawyer feel, the layman asks, if he is instrumental in allowing a hardened killer to go free? How can public morality be reconciled with the lawyer's ethics of presenting the best possible defence?

A lawyer would answer that in addition to defending his client, he also has the responsibility to uphold something even more important — the structure of the law. The words "due process of law" have deep significance to a lawyer; they dictate that a trial must be carried out so that rules of procedure that have evolved over generations of courtroom battles are obeyed. In every trial due process must be strictly observed and corners cannot be cut. Once this is eroded, the law itself stands in danger of corruption.

In certain cases the defence may object to the wording of the Bill of Indictment and attempt to have a charge of murder quashed on these grounds. Such technical objections may seem to be time wasting and superficial, yet they are a lawyer's only way of defending what he would call "due process of law." To a lawyer the correct rules of procedure, which extend even to the way a legal document is worded, are the keystone to the majesty of the law.

Provided that lawyers continue to fight to maintain "due process" and make their objections on the grounds of technical errors in procedures, society is safe. But once the law is "bent" and "interpreted" to suit private or political ends, then the ground has been prepared for an unscrupulous and corrupt legal system.

The Man They Couldn't Hang

In 1895, John Lee stood at the scaffold in Exeter, England. The hangman released the trap and, to his surprise, nothing happened. Hurried adjustments were made and the trap was successfully tested. Lee was again placed on the gallows and for a second time the mechanism failed.

Lee was led back to his cell while the hangman and workers worked on the gallows. Again the trap was tested and found to be in perfect working order. Lee was returned to the scaffold and for a third and fourth time the law attempted to hang Lee but to no avail.

In the end the sheriff stepped forward and stopped the proceedings. Lee was later reprieved and some time later released. With his hard-won freedom, Lee went on tour as "the man they couldn't hang."

Dilemmas for the Defence

A defence lawyer is bound by ethics to produce the best possible case in favor of his client. Although he offers advice on tactics and matters of law, he must to some extent honor his client's instructions.

There are occasions when ethical and moral conflicts arise between client and counsel. Some defence lawyers require the whole story behind a crime and demand complete truth from a client. They argue that a good defence is impossible unless the lawyer understands all aspects of a case. If the client is innocent then counsel will call witnesses and attack the prosecution's case by putting the accused person in the witness box.

When the accused admits his guilt in confidence to his lawyer he may still hope for an acquittal. In such a case the defence makes use of "due process" and forces the prosecution to prove each step of the argument against his client. Each witness will be subject to a stern cross-examination and holes made wherever possible in the prosecution's case. The defence counsel may suggest alternative interpretations to a particular witness's story or bring out evidence that tends to discredit a witness's power of observation or honesty.

In exceptional cases, a killer may insist that his counsel present a false alibi, making use of his close friends who will swear that he was with them on the night of a murder. If a client wishes to give false evidence, then the lawyer is placed in a difficult position. On the one hand, he must defend his client but on the other, he cannot risk the charge of being a party to false testimony. If the trial has only just begun he can ask the judge to relieve him of his responsibilities, but such a request is not always granted. In the end an honest lawyer can do only one thing — he can call his client to the witness box and put a question to him: "Do you have something to say to the court?" The accused will then give his fabricated evidence without any lead from the lawyer who, as far as the judge is concerned, has disassociated himself from the proceedings at that point.

Some lawyers do not insist upon a complete account from their client but act only on the facts given them and so avoid any moral and ethical quandaries that can arise. They are aware that an experienced criminal does not tell his lawyer the whole truth but only "what he needs to know." Rather than spend their time chasing after the "whole truth," they prefer to work with the facts given to them by their client.

The Cause of Crime

In an effort to understand why people commit crimes, psychologists have devised a number of different theories:

W.H. Allchin: it is a cry for help.

S. Hallech: a desire to make an impact against general feelings of insignificance and helplessness.

S. Freud: an attempt to rationalize inherent Oedipal guilt by performing a forbidden act that one can feel realistically guilty about.

T. Reik: a need for punishment is fulfilled by committing a crime and then getting caught.

G. Soloman: a need for attention is fulfilled through punishment.

K. Menninger: the desire to assert and obtain an identity.

Into the Witness Box

Not until the closing days of the last century was an accused person allowed into the witness box. Today it is generally accepted that the accused will have his "day in court."

If counsel believes that his client's claim to innocence is convincing he will want him to make a similar impression on the jury. If there are mitigating circumstances that could warrant a reduced sentence, he will, again, prefer his client to speak in court, and give the jury some insight into his mind and personality.

On infrequent occasions the accused never enters the witness box and is seen only in the dock. For example, if the murder occurred a long time ago an innocent person may be hazy and vague about his movements at the time and, under cross-examination, his story may be shaky and appear to lack credibility. With other clients, their guilt, or at least their shiftiness, is all too obvious. In the witness box they may be inclined to talk too much, attempt to cover up, or become aggressive. They may also be vulnerable to attempts by the prosecution to break behind their facade and get at a deeper account of what actually took place.

The defence may, on rare occasions, be faced with a client who is innocent of murder but wishes to hide something else. The accused may have been sleeping in someone else's bed on the night of the murder. There are cases when an accused person would even run the risk of a stretch in prison rather than chance being questioned about his shady past, particularly if he is a respectable person in the public eye. For some, a term in jail is preferable to the reactions of a jealous wife if a prostitute or girlfriend is their alibi.

If the defence decides against calling his client, he is in danger of prejudicing his case for, in the minds of the jury, the press and the public, the accused must have something to hide if he refuses to enter the witness box. The defence will do his best to restore balance by pointing out that an accused person is under no obligation to enter the witness box. Here he will be aided by the judge, who will be at pains to point out that no prejudice must attend the accused's decision not to appear in his own defence. In his final instruction to the jury the judge will also make it clear that the jury should not speculate upon what the accused might have said had he taken the stand. But, in refusing to enter the witness box, an innocent person's reputation may suffer for years to come.

The Judge

The final actor in the trial is the judge himself, who has remained silent throughout most of the trial. Until this point, he will have asked only the occasional question to clarify an ambiguity, or admonished counsel for leading on a witness. Now he commands the full attention of the court.

In his summing up and instruction to the jury, the judge will discuss evidence presented in the case and give his opinion about the credibility of witnesses; but he will emphasize that, in the end, it is their own opinion that matters. He will explain particular points of law that have emerged and may give his opinion on the legality of arguments presented by the prosecutor and defence.

The judge will make sure the jury members understand that they are to determine only matters of fact. The judge alone can rule on matters of law. He will instruct them on the various possible verdicts that can be returned and the questions they must ask themselves. The judge will also advise them on the important matter of "reasonable doubt." He will tell them that no case is 100 per cent certain and that any doubts they may have must be rational and supported by evidence presented in the case. They should not return a verdict of not guilty on the basis of, for example, intuition or because the prosecution made an error.

Regicide

Regicide, the murder of a king, is a crime for which dire consequences follow. Robert François Damiens did not so much murder Louis XV as prick him with a knife. His sentence, however, was cruel in the extreme.

> *...He shall be taken to the Grève and on a scaffold erected for the purpose his chest, arms, thighs, and calves be burned with pincers, his right hand holding the knife with which he committed the said parricide, burnt in sulphur; that boiling oil, melted lead, and rosin and wax mixed with sulphur be poured in his wounds, and after that his body be pulled and dismembered by four horses, and the members and body consumed by fire, and the ashes scattered to the winds...that before the said execution Damiens be subjected to the* question ordinaire et extraordinaire *to make him confess the names of his accomplices. Orders that the house in which he was borne be demolished, and that no other buildings be erected on the spot.*
>
> *Dated March 26, 1757.*

Within the same decade J.S. Bach composed "The Art of Fugue," Dr. Johnson edited "The Rambler" and David Hume worked on a revision of his "Enquiry Concerning Human Understanding."

The Verdict and Sentence

The jury then retires to consider their verdict. The judge at this point asks if the prosecution or defence objects to anything in his summing up. If necessary, he will recall the jury for further instruction.

The jury are placed under the authority of a bailiff, and under their elected foreman they retire, taking the exhibits in the case, to debate the facts. This must be done without contacting anyone outside the room in which they carry out their discussions. The jury may ask to visit the scene of the crime or have a piece of testimony read over to them. They may also request additional instruction from the judge on a particular verdict.

When the jury returns, the prisoner is put "into the dock" and the verdict is delivered verbally to the clerk of the court by the foreman of the jury.

If either counsel wishes, the jury can be polled one by one and each member asked to give his individual verdict. If the accused is found guilty, the judge can give his sentence immediately or adjourn for hours or even days to consider the sentence. He will listen to arguments by the defence and prosecution as to the prisoner's ability to contribute to society, and hear past convictions read from the police records. He can also request a doctor's or psychiatrist's report on the prisoner.

If the verdict is not guilty, the judge formally frees the prisoner, who can walk out of the courtroom to freedom — or to other charges arising from the crime.

Third Degree

The term "third degree" was applied to the torture and brutality used to extract information or a confession. It is believed to be a reference to the third degree in the ritual of the initiation of a Master Mason. The term may have been first used as a code word among Free Mason policemen for their practice of softening up suspects.

The third degree is not as common among contemporary police forces as it was in the United States during the first two decades of the twentieth century, although it is true that torture is still used by political police all over the world. At one time in the United States groups of suspects were rounded up and kept standing without food, water and sleep. Some were kept in the "sweat box" — a dark, heated cell — before being interrogated. One particularly gruesome incident took place in 1926 when a suspect was wounded during a hold-up. He was tracked down by the police and beaten, with particular attention being paid to the area around his bullet wound. In addition, lighted cigars were ground into his testicles.

In 1931 an investigation of police methods by the National Commission on Law Observance and Enforcement uncovered similar abuses. Its recommendations led to a tightening of control over the police, and today in the United States considerable emphasis is placed upon the rights of an accused person.

The Directed Verdict

In exceptional cases the police may turn up new evidence which tends to contradict their previous line of enquiry. A conversation is then held between the detectives in charge of the case and the prosecuting counsel. If the new evidence casts doubt upon the guilt of the accused, the prosecutor will announce in court that he does not wish to present further evidence in the case.

In other instances, the judge may feel that the prosecution's case is incomplete or that there is sufficient doubt that the accused could have committed the crime. In all these cases the judge will address the jury and instruct them to bring a verdict of not guilty.

"Guilty but Insane"

It is often thought that a killer found "guilty but insane" has avoided the penalty for his crime. This may be so in a formal sense, but in practice a defence counsel takes care to weigh the implications of an insanity plea against the prospect of prison on a lesser charge.

A person confined to a hospital for the insane faces an indefinite period of detention — compared with a prison sentence which is defined over a definite time period — and, in theory, need never be released. The defence counsel may feel that a plea of guilty to a manslaughter charge may serve his client better than a defence of insanity. The convicted killers, Thomas Staffen and Graham Young, who had previously been committed to mental institutions, both chose a life sentence in prison rather than return to their previous incarceration.

The Appeal

Following a verdict of "guilty" and sentencing by the judge, the defence lawyer and his client will discuss the possible grounds for appeal. There can be many reasons for launching an appeal; the defence may feel that the trial was not correctly conducted — for example, that the judge was in error over a matter of law or that a decision to omit evidence or testimony during a "voir dire" was incorrect. In other cases, additional evidence may turn up or an important witness may be found guilty of perjury. Even if the trial was well conducted, the defence may appeal for a reduction in sentence.

The Court of Criminal Appeal operates like a trial without a jury and may, for example, decide how new evidence or a different summing up would have affected the jury. The court can overturn a conviction, change the terms of a sentence or, in exceptional circumstances, rule that the original trial was invalid.

Double Jeopardy

It is a general principle of law in most countries that an accused person cannot be tried twice for the same crime. *Autrefois acquit* means that an accused person has been found "not guilty" and cannot later be charged on the same count. Since murder embraces several lesser charges, a person found not guilty of murder cannot later be faced with a trial for manslaughter. He can, however, be charged with illegal possession of a firearm or breaking and entering in connection with the crime.

There are situations, though, in which a person can find himself in court on the same charge without violating the principle of *autrefois acquit*. If it is decided on appeal that certain irregularities took place in the original trial, it might be ruled that legally this trial had not taken place. In such cases a second trial can be ordered and the accused put through the expense and worry for a second time. Most appeals are not, however, resolved in this way. The appeal judges usually decide amongst themselves what the jury's decision would have been, given a new piece of evidence or a different instruction from the judge.

Provided that the trial has been properly conducted and an accused has been found not guilty, the freed prisoner is not at liberty to sell his confession to the newspapers without fear of subsequent prosecution.

Hypnotism: Help or Hindrance?

Many psychologists believe that the human mind registers far more than it consciously recalls. This ability to filter things out may prevent our lives becoming cluttered up with unimportant details. But where the witness to a murder is concerned even the slightest detail may prove vital.

For this reason police forces across the world are using hypnosis on witnesses in the hope that they will recall significant events. In the hypnotic state a witness may "relive" an event so that his attention can be directed towards specific features such as articles of clothing, faces, automobile licence numbers and so on. Many police forces are happy with the results and in the U.S. over 1,000 police officers have been trained to use hypnosis. But some psychologists do not accept the premise of recall or are concerned that the technique may, on occasion, yield convincing but nevertheless incorrect results.

During the hypnotic state a witness may be particularly suggestible. For example, the witness may sense that a set of questions points towards a particular conclusion and, in the hypnotic trance, begin to fabricate evidence that supports this conclusion or pleases the questioner. In other cases the subject may be unable to make a clear distinction between what was actually witnessed and what was later overheard or read in a newspaper. When such errors of interpretation and later fabrications become entwined with an actual memory, the witness may be convinced of them even after hypnosis has ceased. Some experts feel that there is a danger in allowing previously hypnotized witnesses to give evidence in court. Several U.S. states have ruled that witnesses who have been previously hypnotized may not testify.

Hanging

Public hangings at London's Tyburn Hill were occasions for considerable festivity. Sweetmeats, trinkets and printed broadsheets were sold to the crowds. The killer's supposed "last confession" was specially composed for the occasion, along with a ballad which sang of the rewards of justice and the terrible deeds of the prisoner. Death was not instantaneous for the "drop" was generally not long enough to break the victim's neck. A slow death by suffocation usually resulted unless a humane, or bribed, hangman chose to leap on the dying man's back and break his neck.

It was the political agitation of Sir Bernard Spilsbury earlier this century which finally put hanging on a "scientific basis." The pathologist made a proper study of the technique and published a table of rope lengths related to body weight. He concluded that if the proportions were correct, the loss of consciousness would be rapid following breaking of the neck. The heart, however, would continue to beat for several minutes.

Madame Guillotine

Execution using a beheading machine was not unique to France. In the sixteenth century the "Maid of Halifax" was put to considerable use in Scotland. The "Maid" had the added attraction of a rope and peg attached to the weighted blade. The rope was pulled by a relative of the murdered person and the blade thereby released as a visible act of retribution.

On December 1, 1789, Dr. Guillotine put forward a motion to the French Assembly that a machine be produced to perform executions. After some discussion on the matter, a committee was appointed which, ironically, chose the rival design of Dr. Antoine Louis. The "Louisette" or "La Petite Louise" was field-tested on April 25, 1792, and subsequently performed with grisly success. Later its name was modified to "La Veuve" or "Guillotine."

Under the influence of the Enlightenment, natural philosophers showed a scientific interest in the heads that dropped, freshly severed, into the basket. Some philosophers wondered if a free head would support consciousness for seconds or minutes after death. None, however, appears to have put intellectual enquiry above direct personal discomfort and attempted to obtain experience of the phenomenon at first hand.

The Electric Chair

With the perfection of high-voltage current generation by Nikola Tesla and George Westinghouse, a modern all-American method of execution became possible. Experiments on cattle had shown that a sudden charge of high-voltage electricity would produce rapid death, and so the next step in the march of science was to try it on human beings.

The first electric chair was built at Auburn Penitentiary in New York State in 1890, but it was not the success its inventors had hoped it would be. Current was conducted through a condemned man, William Kemmler, by two electrodes; one was placed on a leg and a second, in a sponge soaked in saltwater, pressed onto his head. Contemporary accounts indicate that this first execution was a repulsive business and that several attempts were needed to kill the victim. Each charge of electricity produced burning flesh and severe convulsions in the condemned man.

Homicide

Homicide or murder is defined in most countries as a death that occurs not more than a year and a day after an unlawful assault. If a victim manages to survive longer than this time after a shooting or poisoning then the charge of murder cannot be laid. In some cases an accused person will try to argue that his victim would have survived if the ambulance had arrived more quickly or the doctor had given better medical care, but this is normally an insufficient defence in law.

A grey area, however, revolves around the possibility of negligence towards an assault victim. For example, if the victim of a beating dies in hospital after serious medical negligence then a court may decide that the cause of death was not the unlawful assault but subsequent medical abuse.

Autopsy on a Killer

All deaths that occur in prison must be investigated by the local coroner, including legal executions. Following the hanging of Ruth Ellis on July 13, 1955 for the murder of her lover, an autopsy was performed by the British pathologist Keith Simpson. His findings showed: "a fracture-dislocation of the spine at C.2 with a two-inch gap and transverse separation of the spinal cord at the same level."

"Fractures of both wings of the hyoid and the R. wing of the thyroid cartilage. Larynx also fractured." Simpson found the lungs free of engorgement and there were no changes to indicate asphyxia. There was terminal congestion in the liver and kidneys and the stomach had an odor of brandy.

The cause of death was listed as "injuries to the central nervous system consecuent (sic) upon judicial hanging." Simpson further remarked that death must have been instantaneous.

Execution

To some extent the degree of civilization a country attains is in inverse proportion to the number of executions it sanctions. At one time, execution in Europe was the penalty for crimes from the rape of a virgin to the theft of a loaf of bread. Towards the end of the last century, execution was the only penalty for such crimes as murder, treason and sabotage.

In those developed countries where execution is retained today, the emphasis seems to be moving towards sophisticated methods, such as injections of drugs and the use of poison gases, but at one time hanging or garotting was a widespread technique of execution.

The Garotte

As practised in Spain, the garotte replaced the more painful and primitive method of strangulation. The garotte consists of an iron collar and screw attached to a pillar. The condemned person's head is placed in the instrument and the apparatus is adjusted. In experienced hands the next move, a rapid rotation of the screw, causes instant dislocation of the vertebra of the neck and rapid loss of consciousness.

CASE HISTORIES

FROZEN TURKEY PIES FOR DINNER — OR A CORPSE?

Murder begins with a corpse, but that was something David Todd simply could not face. The killing was done in the heat of the moment. But Todd decided to keep the body "on ice."

Charles Cassidy and his friends began to wonder if reality ever imitates fiction as they sat watching television one January night in 1972. The play they were watching was about a dead body concealed in a trunk. A few feet away from them hummed a locked freezer which had been brought by their house guest, David Todd, at Christmas.

David was upstairs sleeping — and the freezer...? His curiosity inflamed by the events in the play, one friend brought out a screwdriver. Laughing, together they attacked the hinges on the freezer: "It's probably full of frozen turkey pies."

The freezer was opened and they had guessed correctly. Turkey pies there were, but among them lay the corpse of their guest's wife, Grace Todd.

David Wilfred Todd was born in Hamilton, in the province of Ontario, Canada, in 1934. After reaching grade six he dropped out of school and moved through a series of jobs until he met Grace Filmore in 1959. The couple married and moved to Toronto where David took a job in a rubber factory.

Marriage seems to have suited David, for he settled down until the factory closed in 1970. Suddenly out of work, David became depressed and consumed by feelings of worthlessness. Each morning Grace would head off to her office job, leaving David to sit around the house with a case of beer.

As the days dragged on he became obsessed with the idea that his wife was seeing another man. He began phoning Grace at work. In the end he could not bear to be apart from her, yet when they were together he would accuse her of being unfaithful. She in turn began to taunt him about being inadequate as a man.

By the summer of 1971 David's obsession had become intolerable. He was haunted by the image of other men touching his wife and taking her away. One day his accusations so exasperated Grace that she was driven to shout that she would go to bed with the first man she could find. Todd reached for his gun and shot his wife.

What happened next was the curious reaction of a warped and limited mind. With Grace laying dead at his feet, David began to apologize. He said that no matter what happened Grace must never leave him and he placed her body in the freezer. With that action his life seemed to become simpler and clearer to him. At night he would sleep beside the freezer, his unfaithful wife only inches away. "I felt my wife was with me. I dreamt good dreams, all the good times we had had in the past. I was going to look at her twice but somehow I couldn't," Todd later confessed.

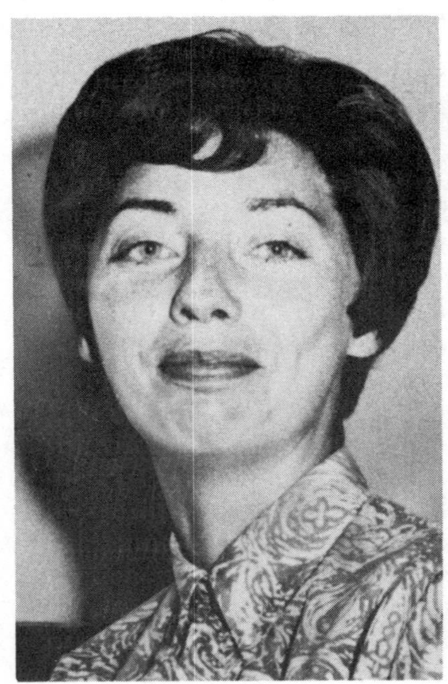

Grace Evelyn Todd whose deep-frozen body was discovered in a Toronto townhouse.
Toronto Star

David Todd, escorted by detectives, after being charged with non-capital murder.
Toronto Star

By Christmas of 1971, Todd was having difficulty paying the rent and so an old friend, Charles Cassidy, invited him to stay. To Cassidy's surprise David insisted on bringing the locked freezer with him. He also explained that his wife had left him.

It was on the night of January 12, 1972 that Cassidy discovered Grace Todd's resting place. At the trial a doctor gave his opinion that David Todd did not have the mental capacity to form the intent to murder. In the doctor's opinion, Todd could function only with a strong mother figure behind him and after his wife's death, he had begun to live in a fantasy world.

Todd changed his plea of not guilty to guilty of manslaughter. He was jailed for ten years.

JOHN GEORGE HAIGH

One murderer believed that without a corpse the police could not prove murder. But he was wrong. For even a bath of acid can tell tales.

A murder case usually begins with a body, but in the murders committed by John George Haigh no corpse was ever discovered. Haigh took the precaution of dissolving his victims in sulphuric acid, and, when arrested by the police, was quite confident that without the evidence of a corpse he would get away with murder.

Haigh, however, was to pay the ultimate penalty for his ignorance of an elementary piece of law.

Haigh was born in Stanford, in the English country of Lincolnshire in 1909, to a family that adhered to the strict puritanical code of the Plymouth Brethren. In his early years Haigh appears to have been a dutiful son. He studied organ and piano, sang in the choir of All Saints Cathedral, Wakefield, and even won a prize for his profiency in divinity.

At the age of eighteen he took his first job as a car salesman but this position, like so many others he drifted into, did not last long. Soon Haigh became involved in dealings that were on the fringe of the law, and in one instance his family was forced to part with their funds to avoid a prosecution.

In 1934 Haigh married Beatrice Hamer. After only a year of marriage, he was charged with fraud and imprisoned for fifteen months. On his release Haigh went from bad to worse. He abandoned his wife and son and obtained his income from petty fraud. As a result he was in and out of jail for the next ten years.

By 1945 Haigh had moved into the Onslow Court Hotel in South Kensington, London, the headquarters from which he plotted a series of killings.

One day, by chance, he bumped into an old friend, Donald McSwan, and invited him to visit a workshop he was using in the Gloucester Road. There Haigh hit his friend over the head with a metal pipe and dumped the body into a drum. He then filled the metal drum with two carboys of sulphuric acid, and set off for Scotland.

From Scotland Haigh mailed forged letters purporting to come from McSwan saying that he had slipped out of the country to avoid army service. When Haigh returned to London, all that remained of his old friend was unceremoniously dumped down the drain.

A year later Haigh was better prepared for his chemical exploits. He had bought a gas mask to protect himself against the acid fumes, a stirrup pump for transferring the acid, and two new drums — one for McSwan senior and the other for Donald's mother. The new killings proceeded without a hitch and, with the dissolution of the McSwan family, Haigh was free to liquidate the family assets in his favour.

Haigh's next foray into multiple murder was to cultivate a friendship with the wealthy Hendersons of Ladbrooke Square. Haigh, who had the charmed tongue of a confidence trickster, had no difficulty in persuading Dr. Henderson to visit his new "workshop" on Leopold Road. The doctor was shot in the back and placed in a bath of acid. Next it was Mrs. Henderson's turn. She was persuaded to visit the workshop because of an ironic message from Haigh that her husband had been taken ill.

As with the McSwans, Haigh kept up the pretence that his victims were still alive while he bled their financial assets. He even went so far as to write a fifteen-page letter to Mrs. Henderson's brother, asking him to pay off a debt to Haigh. Because of Haigh's skill in duplicating her style and hand-writing, Scotland Yard consider this letter to be one of the most brilliant forgeries they have ever encountered.

With the Hendersons and McSwans bled dry, Haigh turned his interests to his fellow lodgers at the Onslow Court Hotel. They were mostly elderly ladies with large incomes — easy prey for Haigh's old-world charm. But elderly ladies often have close friends who are jealous of intruders, and in picking Mrs. Durand-Deacon as his next victim, Haigh had made a mistake.

As with the other victims Mrs. Durand-Deacon was invited to view his workshop, where Haigh shot her in the head. Before dissolving the old lady, Haigh took a lunch-break, fortifying himself on poached eggs and toast at a nearby restaurant.

That evening, when Mrs. Durand-Deacon did not reappear, her special friend, Mrs. Lane, began to worry. In a moment of bravado, which he simply could not resist, Haigh offered to take the old lady to the police station himself and report the matter.

This move was Haigh's undoing, for Police Sergeant Lamborne, who took down the information, did not like the look of dapper George. Haigh seemed too much of a smooth talker and his story did not ring quite true. Over the next few days the police kept an eye on Haigh. On Saturday, February 26, 1949, eight days after the murder of Mrs. Durand-Deacon, they raided his workshop and found carboys of acid, a pump, rubber apron, gasmask, gloves, a .38 Enfield revolver, and a hat box containing papers relating to the Henderson and McSwan families.

Haigh was not arrested at first, but only "brought in for questioning." Eventually Inspector Symes administered the formal caution. To his surprise Haigh then asked if anyone had ever been released from Broadmoor — a prison for the criminally insane.

The inspector administered the caution for a second time and Haigh responded, "I will tell you all about it. Mrs. Durand-Deacon no longer exists. She has disappeared completely and no trace of her can be found again."

"What has happened to her?" the inspector then asked.

"I have destroyed her with acid," Haigh replied. "You will find the sludge which remains at Leopold Road. Every trace has gone. How can you prove murder if there is no body?"

Haigh soon got his answer. The techniques of modern forensic science were able to prove that the sludge contained the final remains of Mrs. Durand-Deacon.

At his arrest Haigh had asked the police about the Broadmoor prison for the insane. The reason for his question was revealed at the trial when Haigh attempted to plead insanity, claiming that he had murdered his victims so that he could drink their blood. Sensing a last-ditch attempt to avoid the gallows, and that Haigh was more con man than lunatic, the jury refused to swallow his story.

The jury retired for seventeen minutes and returned to find Haigh guilty of the murder of Mrs. Durand-Deacon. On August 10, 1949, Haigh was hanged. One of his last acts was to will his clothing to Madame Tussaud's Wax Musuem, with the stipulation that the pants should be pressed and the hair on the dummy kept well combed!

Still smiling, John George Haigh, arrives at Brixton Prison after being remanded in court.
BBC Hulton Picture Library

HELEN SMITH: ACCIDENT OR FOUL PLAY?

A coroner has the authority to investigate suspicious deaths. But how far does his jurisdiction extend and what happens when his judgment is questioned?

On May 19, 1979 nurse Helen Smith went to a party held by some friends at the Bakhsh hospital in Jeddah, Saudi Arabia. Next morning her body was found outside the flat block. Nearby was the trouserless body of Johannes Otten, another party guest. The verdict of the Jeddah police was that the young nurse had fallen seventy feet from a balcony while making love to the Dutchman.

A week later Helen's father, ex-Leeds policeman Ron Smith, arrived in Jeddah and, after viewing the body, refused to believe the official account of accidental death. In June Helen Smith's body was returned to her native Yorkshire where deputy coroner Coverdale ordered a post mortem. Michael Green, a Home Office pathologist, concluded that the injuries on the body were consistent with a fall. But in a later interview with the *Sunday People*, he drew attention to the injuries on her face and head and suggested that the death was not accidental.

Coverdale ordered Detective Superintendent Peter Smalley to investigate the case. Meanwhile, Ron Smith paid a Danish pathologist Prof. Jorgen Dalgoord to conduct a second autopsy. In December, 1980 Dalgoord, assisted by British pathologist Alan Usher, concluded that the nurse had been battered before death and that her injuries were inconsistent with a fall of more than twelve feet. The circumstances of Helen Smith's death appeared suspicious but on August 4th, 1981 Philip Gill, the coroner who had taken over the case, announced that an inquest would not be held. Gill argued that since Helen Smith's death had occurred in Saudi Arabia it lay outside his jurisdiction. However legal experts contacted by a number of newspapers pointed out that a coroner has the authority to investigate the death of a British subject anywhere in the world. Rumors began to circulate that, for political reasons, the case was being hushed up; and that there were connections between British Foreign Office staff in Jeddah and people who had attended the party on the night Smith died.

In March, 1981 Ron Smith applied to the High Court for an inquest to be held into his daughter's death. The West Yorkshire County Council also wrote to the attorney general, Sir Michael Havers, requesting an inquest. Smith lost his case, but in July the Court of Appeal overruled the verdict and an inquest was granted. Finally, in December, 1982 Philip Gill presided at the inquest on a death that had occurred three and a half years earlier.

During the inquest pathologist Dalgoord gave evidence of a "fairly extensive blow" to the head that probably caused unconsciousness or death. Dalgoord felt that such a blow could have been produced by an open hand but not as a result of a fall. Pathologist Green, who had performed the earlier autopsy, agreed that wounds on Helen Smith's head and face occurred before death and could have been caused by a fist.

The jury rejected the coroner's suggestion of accidental death and returned an open verdict.

THE TRIAL OF JOHN BODKIN ADAMS

After the prosecution's first address, the public may be convinced of a killer's guilt. But through the skilful work of defence counsel, an element of doubt may creep into a "cast-iron" case.

Dr. John Bodkin Adams stood charged with the murder of his patient, eighty-one-year-old Mrs. Morell, who lived in Eastbourne, England. She had suffered a stroke some years earlier and was being treated by Dr. Adams, who used heroin and morphia for her condition. In November, 1960 the old lady fell into a coma, after which Adams prescribed two syringes of paraldehyde. Mrs. Morell passed away during the night and Adams subsequently benefitted from her estate.

It was not until six years later that the doctor came under police investigation, at first in regard to possible abuses under the Dangerous Drugs Act. It ended in the charge of murder. On the day Adams was arrested, he uttered two particularly damning verbals: "Murder...can you prove it?" and "I do not think you could prove it was murder...she was dying in any event."

At first, the Crown seemed to have possession of an open and shut case. The prosecutor told the jury that he intended to show how the doctor had introduced Mrs. Morrell to larger and larger doses of addictive drugs until she was dependent upon his injections. In a virtually comatose state she was made to change her will in favour of Adams, who then dispatched her with a dose of paraldehyde. The Crown indicated it would call the nurses who had attended the old lady and expert medical witnesses to support their case.

But Dr. Adam's defence counsel, Geoffery Lawrence, had done his homework in an exceptionally thorough fashion — even to the extent of tracking down notebooks used by the nurses six years previously. Armed with an excellent brief, he was able to punch holes in the prosecution's argument and even suggested that the whole case should be dismissed. He began his attack on the nurses by encouraging them to stress how methodical they were and how all their observations were recorded in special notebooks. Then, with a flourish, Lawrence produced the books under their very noses. Each nurse was forced to read from her own notebook. It soon became apparent that the evidence they had given during the Examination-in-Chief did not agree with the records they had kept. In place of the rambling addict they had described, stood an elderly lady who had responded so well to Dr. Adams' treatment that she had lived long beyond her allotted span. The nurses were shaken by Lawrence's cross-examination. One of them admitted, "It is a long time to remember these things."

Lawrence was not above having these witnesses followed. On the third day of the trial, he announced in court that the three nurses had discussed the case and one of them had said, "Don't you say that or you will get me into trouble."

Having disposed of the Crown's three star witnesses the defence then went on to dispose of the motive. In the cross-examination, he had Mrs. Morell's solicitor agree that the nurses themselves benefitted from the will and even the chauffeur had inherited 1,000 pounds. As for Dr. Adams? A chest of silver and an old Rolls Royce were hardly motives for a man of his background.

Several years after his acquittal on a murder charge, Dr. Bodkin Adams (right) at the Savoy Hotel, "Men of the Year" luncheon.
Syndication International

JOHN THOMAS STRAFFEN: MENTALLY DEFICIENT OR INSANE?

Every client is given the best possible defence by his counsel. Even when he is a multiple child-murderer, "due process of law" must be observed.

In the summer of 1951 three little girls were murdered in the South of England. A mentally defective labourer was arrested for the killings and committed to Broadmoor Hospital for life. But within six months, he was to escape and kill yet again.

John Thomas Straffen was the third of six children, born to the wife of a regular soldier in the British Army. The boy was slow to learn and became a problem child. Certified as a mental defective, with an I.Q. of 58 (100 is the average), he was sent to a special school. There he adopted a solitary life, appearing timid and docile, yet reacting badly to any form of correction. During this period some geese were found strangled, and Straffen was suspected but no proof of his involvement materialized.

Straffen left the school at sixteen but soon found himself back in an institution after assaulting a thirteen-year-old girl. At the age of twenty-one, he found employment with a market gardener in Bath but was unable to settle down. Again his uncontrollable violence dominated him, this time ending in the murder of small girls.

His first victim, five-year-old Brenda Goddard, was persuaded by Straffen to go to a special place where they could pick flowers. As Straffen lifted her over the fence his hands closed around her throat. Afterwards he went to a movie. Three weeks later Straffen met Cicely Batsone at the cinema. He took the child for a bus ride and at the end of their journey, walked her into a field and strangled her. There is no doubt that Straffen was feeble-minded, for he took little trouble to cover his tracks. People saw him enter the field, and a couple were close by when he killed the second girl (after which he bought some fish and chips and went home).

The police eventually tracked Straffen down and accused him of killing the children. He replied in his own simple-minded way that he had left a little girl asleep in a field. He also believed that he could not hang because no one had actually *seen* him kill the children. Straffen was charged with murder but on being found "insane on arraignment," was committed to Broadmoor Hospital. Broadmoor, once a prison for the criminally insane under Home Office jurisdiction, had by the time of Straffen's commitment become classified as a hospital. The institution contained violent patients, the criminally insane and regular patients suffering from various mental disorders. The inmates were no longer referred to as prisoners but as patients, since not all had been sent by the courts and the hospital was administered by the Ministry of Health.

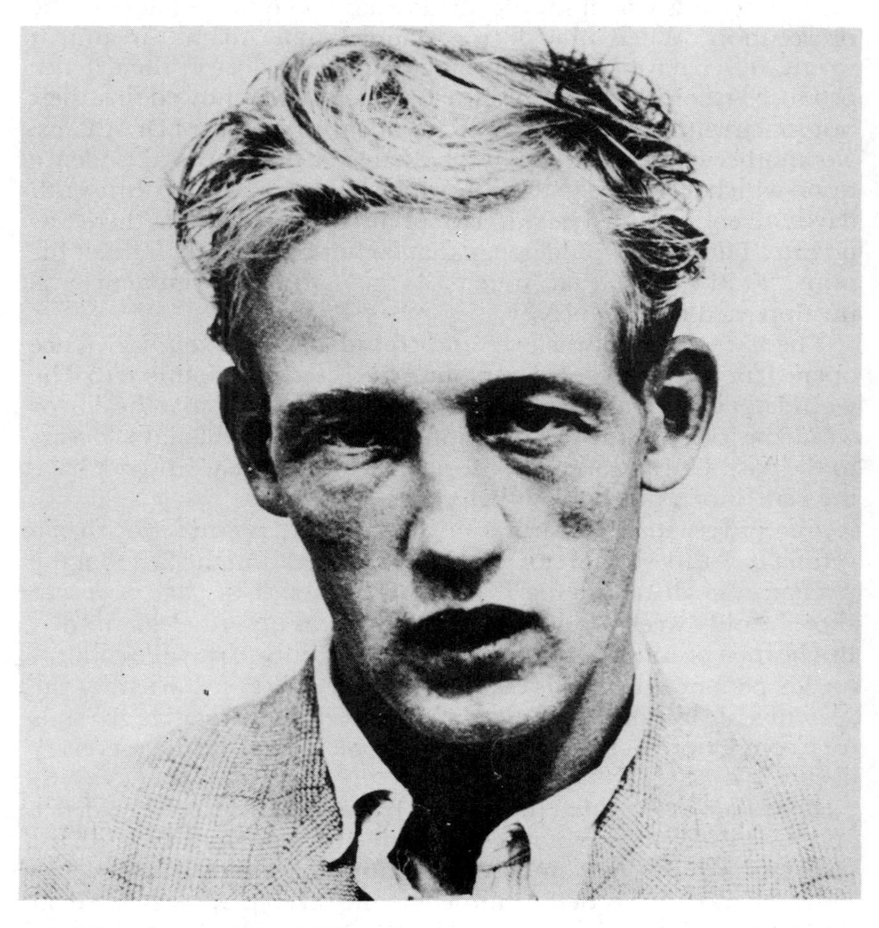

John Thomas Straffen — child murderer.
Syndication International

Lawrence was a master of the cross-examination even with the strongest witnesses. When he noticed that two of the detectives in the case had consulted the same notebook in the witness box, he burst with incredulity: "Am I really hearing what you are saying?" he exclaimed. "Has the whole of your evidence as to what the doctor said been given from some notes which were made by another officer?"

The defence also pointed out that the officer who had been named in the search warrant had not been present in the doctor's surgery during questioning and suggested that the police had harrassed their suspect.

Lawrence's attack on the Crown's expert medical witnesses stemmed from hard work and his skill in obtaining copies of medical records which should already have been in the hands of the prosecution. When one doctor claimed that Adams' treatment would never have been given by a competent doctor, the defence produced records from a Cheshire hospital which showed that their original treatment of Mrs. Morell was identical to that of Dr. Adams. To another witness's theory he challenged, "The medical evidence upon which it is based is absolute rubbish, isn't it?" By the thirteenth day Lawrence was in a position to submit to the judge that there was no case. The judge would not go that far but Lawrence had made his point to the jury that much of the Crown's argument was unsupported by evidence.

The Crown's case was over and considerably shaken. Lawrence opened for the defence. To everyone's surprise, he announced that he would not call his client to the stand. He pointed out that the doctor would be forced to answer questions about matters that lay six years in the past. Unlike several of the other witnesses he would not have the benefit of a notebook to help him.

The judge, in his instructions to the jury, pointed out that a verdict of guilty should not take into consideration the fact that the woman was already dying from other causes; if life had been cut short by only weeks or months, the crime was nevertheless murder. But he then pointed out that it was a doctor's duty to provide comfort for his patient even if this comfort had the effect of shortening the patient's life by hours or longer. Such action could not give grounds for a conviction for it was the type of problem faced by doctors every day.

The judge stressed that the accused had a right not to give evidence and instructed the jury not to speculate on what Dr. Adams might have said. Finally, he pointed out a unique aspect of the case — that the actual possibility of the murder having taken place was based on the testimony of expert witnesses and their assessment of the effects of Adam's treatment.

After retiring for less than an hour, the jury found Adams not guilty of murder. At once the judge referred to a second indictment of murder, this time of a Mrs. Hullett. The attorney general indicated that the case was largely based upon the administration of drugs and was unsupported by other evidence. He murmured, "Nolle prosequi," and mentioned that it would be difficult for the doctor to obtain a fair trial on the charge.

The judge then informed Adams, "All further proceedings on this indictment are stayed in this court. You are now discharged."

THE CLICKING ALIBI

A clock with a click helped to free a convicted killer from a life sentence.

In October, 1973 the sexually assaulted body of fifteen-year-old Jacqueline Seston was found at her home in Peterborough, England. Suspicion fell on twenty-nine-year-old Albert Taylor, the man Jacqueline's sister intended to marry. In court, however, Taylor claimed that he was at the Peterborough train station at the time of the murder. He was sure of the time — 1:15 p.m. — because the station clock had made a distinct click. He arrived at Mountsevern Avenue at 2 p.m. to find Jacqueline lying in a pool of blood. As Taylor had been in trouble with the law before, he panicked and ran.

The police refuted Taylor's statement about the clock's clicking, and the judge suggested that Taylor may have lied. The accused was found guilty of murder and sentenced to life imprisonment.

On appeal, Taylor professed his innocence and made allegations about the police's handling of the case. The subsequent investigation, carried out by Detective Chief Superintendent Peter Crust, did not substantiate the allegations. However, Crust became intrigued by the mystery of the clicking clock. It turned out that the station had acquired a new clock but Crust was able to trace the original one to examine it. Sure enough, in cold weather the hands of the electric clock stuck at 1:15 and then would race to catch up. The day of the murder had been extremely cold and the clock could indeed have jammed, making the click that Taylor had heard.

In March, 1979 the Appeal Court judges found that if the jury had known about the clock, it would have introduced doubt into their minds. The conviction was quashed and Taylor was released after spending five years in jail.

Six months after his arrival, Straffen climbed onto a roof, jumped over a wall and walked away to freedom. His brain may have been child-like but he possessed enough cunning to hide civilian clothing beneath his hospital uniform. Unlike a normal escapee, Straffen did not try to run or hitch a ride but simply wandered around the area. By mid-afternoon he had walked seven miles and stopped at a house to ask for a drink of water. Because Broadmoor maintained a "low profile" which extended to its escaped prisoners, and feared adverse public reaction, no warning siren sounded in the district, and police did not call from house to house.

Straffen hung around the local village. At 5:30, he was seen in the area of the local school, standing near a little girl named Linda Bowyer. A few minutes later the girl was dead. Straffen knocked at yet another door and asked for water; this time he was invited in for a cup of tea. After drinking it, he walked down the road and thumbed a lift to the bus stop where Broadmoor nurses were waiting for him.

Straffen was escorted back to the hospital where none of the staff realized the enormity of what had happened. Later that evening Linda was reported missing and by 5:25 a.m. her body had been found. As with Straffen's other victims, the girl had been strangled. There was no evidence of sexual interference nor any attempt to hide the body.

The police were faced with a difficult legal problem. Could they arrest a man who was already technically in custody? Could they question him or even enter the institution? They decided to do so. When approached, Straffen uttered a damning verbal: "I didn't kill the little girl on the bicycle." He then gave a detailed statement about his movements which avoided mention of Linda Bowyer.

Straffen was committed to Winchester Assizes. At the same time the British public erupted with an outburst of angry questions. Why had this murder happened, the papers asked? Why was no warning given when Straffen escaped? Why was the hospital not properly guarded? Why should killers get off lightly by pleading insanity?

When it came to Straffen's trial, several important points of law were debated. For example, although Straffen was defective in intelligence, was this the same, for defence purposes, as being insane? Henry Elan, for the defence, advised Straffen to plead not guilty and opened with an interesting legal argument. Straffen stood charged with the murder of Linda Bowyer. To emphasize its case against the accused, the Crown needed to refer to Straffen's killings which had taken place before he had been committed to Broadmoor. Elan argued that this evidence of earlier killings should not be allowed in court for it would prejudice the jury. If this plan was allowed, the case against Straffen would become extremely weak since there were no witnesses to the killing of Linda Bowyer. The most damning argument against Straffen was that the killing was a continuation of what had taken place before Straffen had been committed to Broadmoor. Elan claimed that this argument could not be used. The judge, however, ruled against the defence claim and evidence of earlier crimes was admitted.

Elan made a further objection that none of Straffen's replies to the police could be used in court since Straffen had been technically in Broadmoor custody at the time and had not been cautioned. Again the judge overruled the motion by pointing out that "custody" did not include detention in hospital. The defence then faced the tricky problem of Straffen's state of mind. In the first trial Straffen's low intelligence had been sufficient to rule him "unfit to plead." Elan did not use the tactic at the present trial; instead Straffen entered a plea of not guilty. But was his state of mind serious enough to classify as insanity under the M'Naghten Rules?

A number of experts were called and testified that the killer's mind was feeble but that he understood he had taken life and that it was wrong to do so. There were not therefore sufficient grounds for a plea of insanity. (Since the Straffen case England has introduced the Scottish plea of "diminished responsibility" for the feeble-minded.) Straffen was found guilty and sentenced to death. However, against considerable public outrage, a reprieve was granted to a life sentence in a normal jail. A detailed evaluation of Straffen's mind has not been published, for a Broadmoor patient's anonymity is respected. It is known, however, that his *EEG* ("brain waves") exhibited gross abnormalities, suggesting some brain damage, possibly caused by encephalitis as a child.

Straffen's motives have never been explained. Some commentators suggest a compulsive desire to do wrong or a need to spite the police, whom Straffen disliked. To others, the killings suggested a sexual outlet, not so much a desire for rape but a need to violate the fragile and innocent.

SPLIT-SECOND MURDER AND A BROKEN WATCH

The exact time of death is usually difficult to determine. But police were able to pinpoint the precise moment at which the corpse of Mrs. Hepplewhite was dumped into the River Tyne.

Britain's Tyneside lies at the eastern end of Hadrian's Wall, built by the Romans to provide a defence against the primitive tribes to the north. The area is bleak and cold; its industries are mining, shipbuilding and fishing. One morning, in the spring of 1966, a local Tynesider spotted what looked like a quilt floating in the murky waters of the River Tyne as it flowed between Gateshead and Newcastle.

The workman looked again and realized the "bedspread" was in fact a nightgown wrapped around the body of a dead woman. The river police were called and the corpse was pulled out of the water.

The autopsy showed that the body was that of a woman aged between forty and fifty who had been murdered by strangulation. The state of decomposition of the body indicated that it had been floating in the river for about a month. There would have been no way of determining the exact time of death except for one curious fact — the dead woman was wearing a watch that had stopped at 2:53.

The police examined the watch carefully and found it to be partially wound and in good condition. They obtained similar watches from the manufacturer and subjected them to a variety of tests to see if they would stop when immersed in water. At first the results were discouraging. The watches ticked on undisturbed at the bottom of glasses of water and appeared to be quite watertight.

One of the detectives suggested that water pressure could have something to do with the watch's stopping and so, using a fishing line, the detectives dangled a watch at the bottom of the River Tyne. It stopped within seconds.

The conclusion was obvious; the dead woman's watch stopped as soon as her body had sunk deep under water. The police deduced that the body had been dumped in the river at 2:53 a.m. some time after the end of January or in early February of that year. They assumed that the body must have been dumped at night and not at 2:53 p.m., in full daylight.

These deductions did not take them very far. Missing person files had been searched but no one could put a name to the body. As a next step the police appealed for information on radio, television and in the newspaper.

As usual there was a spate of crank calls. There was also a call from a Mr. Armitage of Sheffield, who wondered whether the dead woman could have been his neighbour, Mrs. Hepplewhite, who had been missing from her home for about a month.

Sheffield was over 200 miles from Gateshead but since the dates were about right, the Tyneside police got in touch with Mr. Hepplewhite. To their surprise they discovered he was a sergeant in

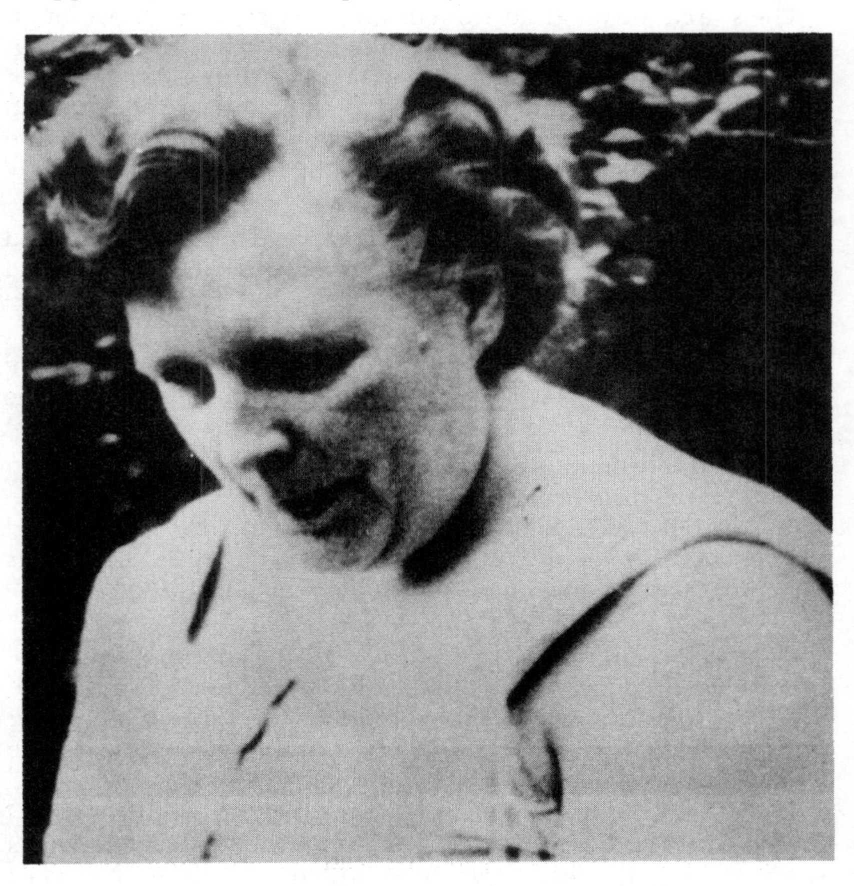

Winifred Jessica Hepplewhite whose body was dragged from the River Tyne in March 1966.
Syndication International

the Sheffield Police. He said he was quite willing to go to Tyneside to identify the missing body.

Hepplewhite saw the body and the jewellery found on it and said he could not help the police. The corpse was not his wife. As far as he was concerned his wife was missing and since she had left him before he did not bother to report the matter.

Hepplewhite did not leave Tyneside at once but stayed on to talk to the officers in charge of the case. He was interested in detective work and had taken the trouble to read some books on forensic science. In particular, he was interested in the watch and speculated whether it had simply run down or if it could have indicated the time of death.

The search for the dead woman's identity continued. Although decomposition had set in, the pathologist was able to remove skin from the fingertips and obtain a readable set of prints. As a matter of routine, Sergeant Hepplewhite's home was checked and found to contain identical prints. Faced with such evidence, Hepplewhite agreed that he had been mistaken when he had first seen the body and that it was indeed his wife's.

As a double check, the pathologist compared an x-ray of the dead woman's leg with one taken of Mrs. Hepplewhite's leg when she had been in hospital following a bus accident. Finally, Mrs. Hepplewhite's grown son was called in to identify the body.

The police went over Hepplewhite's story again and again. According to him, his wife had walked out of their Sheffield home on February 1 and he had not heard from her since.

Who had killed her? And how had her body come to be found in a river 200 miles from her home? The police combed every mile of the main road between Sheffield and Gateshead: they interviewed service station attendants; they asked questions at hotels, restaurants and every possible stopping place on the way. No one had seen the dead woman.

As a last resort the police requested an examination of the Occurrence Books at every police station in the north of England. One entry stood out. On the night of January 31, 1966, a car heading north from Sheffield had been involved in a minor accident. The driver's name was Kenneth Hepplewhite.

At about midnight on January 31, two officers in a police car had noticed a car driving north on the main highway along England's eastern spine. The weather was foggy and the car was going so fast they were not surprised to find that it had crashed into a wooden barrier near Wetherby, several miles further on.

The driver identified himself and told the police his front tire had blown out and he needed a tow to the nearest service station. One of the officers saw a bulky sack in the back of the car but, knowing the driver was a policeman, did not bother to question him. The police also noticed that Hepplewhite's face was cut. Hepplewhite explained that he had been in a hurry shaving because he'd just received a phone call that his wife had been injured in a crash, and he was on his way to see her.

At the local garage the mechanic remembered Hepplewhite. He changed the wheel on the car but the door had been kept locked, and when the mechanic tried to check the steering Hepplewhite had driven away. The car had left Wetherby at 1 a.m.

The net began to close around Hepplewhite. Why had he not mentioned his wife's "accident" before? The police made enquiries in the neighbourhood and heard how Alice Hepplewhite had constantly nagged her husband and taken a perverse delight in humiliating him in public. They also learned that she had left home without taking the canes she needed to help her walk.

Suppose Hepplewhite had indeed murdered his wife on the night of January 31, put her body in a sack and driven north to dump the

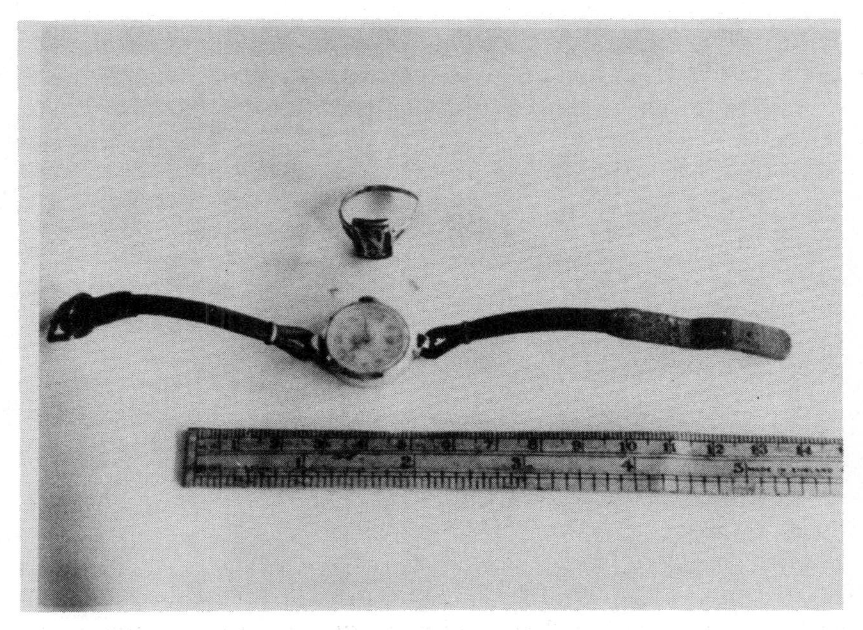

Mrs. Hepplewhite's watch — stopped at 2:53 — and a ring taken from her body.
Syndication International

corpse in the River Tyne. Could he have reached Gateshead before 2:53 a.m. — the time shown on her watch — if he had left Wetherby at 1 a.m. in heavy fog. At first the police were inclined to believe that such a drive would have been impossible because of the fog that night.

Help was solicited from the Automobile Association, the Royal Automobile Association, the RAF, the Meterological Office, and the Tyne river police. Between them they produced a detailed map on weather conditions during the early hours of February 1. Using this map of road conditions, the police calculated that Hepplewhite would have reached the River Tyne shortly before 3 a.m. on the morning in question.

Hepplewhite was arrested and charged with murder. During his trial he stuck to the story of the telephone call about his wife's accident that had caused him to go out that night. As for the sack in the back of the car — well, the police should have looked; it had contained vegetables.

The jury did not believe Hepplewhite and he was sentenced to life imprisonment. The hands on his wife's watch had pointed the way to his guilt.

THE GREASY FINGERPRINT

Fingerprints are generally found at the scene of a crime but in the case of the Newbery murder, the killer's print turned up days later in a post office — still perfectly visible.

In October 1964, the body of a murdered man was discovered near a farm track in Southampton, England, its head bashed in. A search of the victim's pockets showed him to be George Newbery, a local taxi driver. No other clues were found.

The man in charge of the case was Walter Jones, head of the Hampshire CID, who had the distinction of possessing the "Sherlock Holmes Pipe," awarded to him by the Crime Writer's Association. The award was made in recognition of the fact that never in his long career had Jones failed to make an arrest in a case. This time, however, it seemed his winning streak was over.

The police soon found Newbery's taxi, licence plate R0R 721, abandoned in a tough area known as Six Dials. The cab was covered in blood, yet a close examination revealed no clues. There were no fingerprints, hairs, fibres, or particles of dust.

The pathologist deduced that the man had been battered to death with a blunt instrument, possibly a tire iron, by someone sitting in the offside passenger seat. The exact time of death was difficult to establish, and the police had nothing to go on beyond the dead man's identity.

A house-to-house search was made in the Six Dials area, and residents were questioned. In addition, the area around Southampton docks was searched and crews of ships in the harbour questioned.

Just when the case was at its bleakest, the police got a lead. The Post Office told them a withdrawal had been made from Mr. Newbery's savings account in Southampton the day after he had been killed.

By the time the withdrawal slip reached the police forensic laboratories, it had passed through a great many hands, from clerks at the local post office to officials in central administration. Nevertheless, the slip bore a distinct greasy fingerprint and, unless George Newbery's post office book had been picked up by a tramp, the chances were that the killer himself had left the telltale print when he withdrew the pitifully small sum of three pounds.

For the first time the police had a definite lead. But could they be sure that this was the killer's print and not that of some official who had touched the book? Fingerprint experts took elimination prints of over four hundred postal workers who might have touched the slip. Then a search was made through the Central Criminal Office fingerprints records. None of these prints corresponded with that on the withdrawal slip. Acting on another possibility, handwriting experts began to plough through the mass of forms the Southampton public had filled out. Labour exchange cards, driver's licences — anything that might reveal handwriting similar to that on the post office slip was examined.

Months passed and it looked as though Walter Jones' string of successful cases had come to an end, for no one was able to trace the fingerprint or the handwriting on the post office form. Then, one day, a Mr. John Stoneley was arrested on a charge of breaking and entering. He was released on bail but, as a matter of routine, his fingerprints were taken and later sent to Walter Jones for comparison. One was identical to the greasy fingerprint. John Stoneley must have handled George Newbery's post office book the day after the murder.

At first Stoneley denied everything and made an attempt to cover his tracks by claiming he had gone into the post office to fill out a telegram form. His next step was to invent an alibi involving a man with the improbable name of Bill Sykes. Sykes actually existed but denied knowing anything about the affair.

George Newbery with his wife, alongside the taxi found abandoned after the murder.
Syndication International

The police continued to press Stoneley until he broke down and wrote a rambling confession. He claimed that Sykes had been his accomplice but that they had not in fact committed murder because the taxi driver was still breathing when he was dumped. "His death was caused by him not getting help," Stoneley claimed.

The jury did not think much of Stoneley's excuse and found him guilty of capital murder. Sykes, his accomplice, was found guilty of non-capital murder.

John Stoneley, one of the two men accused of the murder of George Newbery.
Syndication International

THE GOLF COURSE MURDER AND THE BLOODY PALM

A palm print can be just as damning as a fingerprint if found at the scene of a murder.

Potter's Bar is a commuter suburb ten miles north of London, past Barnet on the northern underground line; here Mr. and Mrs. Alfred Currell lived in their house on Cranborne Road. After his evening meal, on April 30, 1955, Alfred changed into his slippers and sat down in front of the television to relax. Elizabeth, an attractive woman in her mid-forties, decided to take the dog for a walk and about eight o'clock set off along Cranborne Road towards the golf course. As she had done so many times before, Elizabeth Currell followed the path under the railway tracks and set out across the course. Unlike the other evenings, she did not return.

About 9:30 p.m., Alfred began to wonder where his wife had got to. At the back door, he discovered that Tina, their Corgi, had returned. Alfred walked to the golf course and began to shout Elizabeth's name. After some time, his feelings of panic mounted and he called the police.

The next morning a police search team spotted a woman's body in a clump of long grass close to the seventeenth tee. The corpse was almost naked and the head had been battered.

The area was roped off and the forensic experts began their search under Chief Inspector Leonard Crawford and Detective Inspector Dennis Hawkins of Scotland Yard's CID.

A reconstruction of the crime indicated that the killer had knocked Mrs. Currell out and then attempted to strip off her clothing. She must have regained consciousness for he first tried to strangle her with one of her stockings and then battered her head with an iron tee marker. The marker was found close by and carried the bloody impression of a human palm.

The police guessed that the killer was a local man and asked permission from the commissioner of Scotland Yard to take the palm print of every male in the area over sixteen years of age.

A squad of thirty detectives went from house to house in Potter's Bar and asked each adult male to volunteer his palm print. To their surprise they discovered that about eight hundred potential suspects, men who had been in Potter's Bar on the night of the murder, were now missing. Many of them were on holiday, and some had moved to new jobs or had been transferred by their firms. Police enquiries went out to Canada, Chile, Malaya, and the Gold Coast.

In the end the killer was found close to home — he worked as a clerk at the Potter's Bar Town Hall. On the morning of the murder, eighteen-year-old Michael Queripel had bloodstains on his clothing. He told his mother he had cut himself fixing his motorcycle and she burned the clothes in the back garden when the stains would not come out.

In making their routine enquiries the police had called at the Queripel home and asked for Michael's palm print. At first he refused, saying it was a matter of principle, but in the end he agreed.

By mid-August a team of fingerprint experts were hard at work examining each card. When they came to number 4,605, they realized that the killer had been found. The pattern was double-checked and the police visited Queripel again.

At first he claimed he had discovered the body but was too frightened to tell the police. Then he admitted to the murder and made a statement. He said he had hit Mrs. Currell on the jaw and then tried to remove her underwear. She began to come around and he tried to strangle her with her stocking but it broke. He grabbed the tee marker and hit her on the head until she was silent.

Queripel was tried at the Old Bailey and found guilty. He was detained at Her Majesty's pleasure.

THE GREAT BLACKBURN FINGERPRINT HUNT

Police will go to any lengths to trap a killer — even as far as fingerprinting a whole town.

At midnight on Friday, May 14, 1948, Nurse Gwendolyn Humphries was on duty in the children's ward of Blackburn Hospital in England. She had put her charges to sleep and was working in a kitchen just off the ward when she thought she heard a child's voice.

Nurse Humphries went back to the ward to check her charges, but since everything seemed peaceful she returned to the kitchen. A little later she felt a draft of cold air around her legs and realized that the porch door to the ward must be ajar. She walked to the door and closed it. Looking around the ward again, she saw that one of the cots was empty — a four-year-old child was missing. Being particularly observant, the nurse noticed that a large bottle of distilled water had been moved and that there seemed to be a trail of footprints on the highly polished floor leading to the crib.

The police were called and the hunt began. Three hours later, the body of the little girl was found beside the hospital wall. Even the experienced officer who was called in to head the case, Ernest Millen of Scotland Yard, was shocked. The child had been sexually assaulted, her body bruised and bitten. Then she had been picked up by her feet and her head smashed against the hospital wall.

The killing was obviously the work of a sex maniac and Millen was determined to track down the killer before the scent grew cold. In the end, however, it was to be a combination of brilliant forensic deduction and routine foot-slogging that led to the arrest of the Blackburn killer.

Experts concentrated on the bottle of distilled water. It contained a perfect set of prints that told a detailed story about the killer. Careful examination convinced the police that the man was tall, worked as a manual labourer and was young. His height (deduced from the size of his prints) was confirmed when the police examined the hospital cot; only a tall man could have lifted a child without first letting down the side.

Next the floor was examined. Using a carefully angled light, the footprints were illuminated to their best advantage and photographed. They showed that the killer had walked in stockinged feet from the opened porch door to the crib. Piece by piece the floor was scraped and the fresh scrapings placed in sample bags and sent for analysis. Under the microscope, tiny fibres of red wool were found; these were assumed to have come from the killer's socks.

The next step in the murder hunt was to fingerprint all hospital staff and visitors. When all 2,017 prints had been eliminated from the enquiry, it was the turn of all patients and ex-patients in the area with a history of mental disorder. This check yielded an additional 3,600 prints, but no killer. An attempt was also made to fingerprint vagrants and tramps in the area.

The bites on the child's body caused some forensic experts to assert that the killer could not be British. Biting was a more common characteristic of continental rape, they claimed. But enquiries on the continent drew a blank.

While the fingerprint investigation was being pursued, the police were making routine enquiries among the hospital staff and several other groups of people. One of their leads was provided by a taxi driver who had dropped a man near the hospital on the night of the murder. The driver could remember little about his fare except that he spoke with a local accent. If the passenger had been the killer, then their prime suspect was probably still in Blackburn.

But six days had passed and Millen was worried that the trail was getting cold. Forensic experts, meanwhile, came up with a new suggestion; since the prints had been made by a young man accustomed to manual labour, it was possible he was still serving in the British Army (for the year was 1948). A call went out for fingerprints to those cities all over the world where British troops were stationed. Possibly the killer had struck before and a record might exist of his activities. But like the others, this lead drew a blank.

On May 20, the chief constable of Blackburn made a bold decision. He gave permission for fingerprints to be taken of every male over the age of sixteen who lived in the city or who had visited the area on the night of the murder. Two teams were organized, one to visit each house in the city and the other to classify the fingerprint cards and set up an index system. A month later every home had been checked and 100,000 people interviewed. But the killer was still at large.

As June drifted into July the atmosphere of the town began to change. At first people had been cheerful in their cooperation with the police but now they began to grumble. What use were all the questions and fingerprints, they asked, when the police seemed no closer to finding the killer? To make matters worse, many of the police teams were forced to visit the same homes again to ask a new question: "Did you have an out-of-town visitor on the night of the murder?"

Then, towards the end of the month, someone discovered a simple clerical mistake. Each fingerprint had been checked off against the electoral role, but now it was discovered that 900 ration books that had been issued (in 1948 ration books were still in use in Britain) bore names that were not on this electoral role. Several service men — the owners of the ration books who were now living in the city — had not been fingerprinted.

The police team was alerted and the 900 prints were taken. On August 12, card 46,253 was classified and found to match the print taken from the distilled water bottle in the hospital. The killer was found. His name was Peter Griffiths and he had recently been dismissed from the Welsh Guards. An ominous note was struck when the police checked into his army record. On several occasions while abroad, he had gone missing and refused to say where he had been.

Griffiths was arrested on his way to work and taken in for questioning. At first he denied everything, but faced with evidence of his own fingerprints, he made a statement. Griffiths said that on the night of the murder he had been on a pub crawl. It began with five pints of beer at the Dun Horse, then on to Yates Wine Lodge for two rums and a couple of Guinness, and back again to the Dun Horse for six more pints.

At closing time, Griffiths decided to walk around to clear his head and claimed that a man had given him a lift as far as the hospital. As a child Griffiths had been a patient in the children's block and he began to wander around. He took off his shoes, entered the children's ward and picked a little girl out of her crib. The child trustingly put her arms around his neck and he took her outside and laid her on the grass. The child began to cry and to stop her he picked her up and banged her head against the wall. Then he went back to the verandah, put on his shoes and walked home. The next day he went about his normal business.

In addition to the fingerprint evidence the police discovered a pair of woollen socks in Griffiths' possession whose red fibres exactly matched those on the hospital floor. Their case against the killer was closed.

Griffiths was found guilty of murder and hanged at Walton Jail, Liverpool on November 19, 1948. In the process of filling in the murderer's background the police heard a rumour that Griffiths had VD. While in Egypt with the army, he had been told that the only cure lay in having intercourse with a virgin. They also discovered the following poem beside his bed, signed "The Terror":

> Warning
> For lo and behold
> When the beast
> Looked down upon the face of beauty
> It staid its hand from killing
> And from that day on
> It was as one dead.

Peter Griffiths, brutal killer of a four-year-old child.
Syndication International

THE CASE OF THE FINGERPRINT FORGERY

Fingerprints are taken as positive identification throughout the world. When a fingerprint spells guilt, the accused has little chance of convincing the jury of his innocence.

William De Palma felt that his world had collapsed about him when he faced fifteen years in a federal prison for a crime he claimed he had not committed. He was convicted of the armed robbery of a bank in Buena Park, California in 1969. Although De Palma had been identified by thirteen witnesses as working at a coffee stall seventeen miles away when the crime occurred, the prosecution's evidence carried the court. Two bank tellers identified De Palma as the robber, but the most damning evidence came from a fingerprint discovered at the scene of the crime. It belonged to De Palma.

Appeal followed appeal but to no avail and, in August 1971, De Palma began his sentence. Not everyone, however, was convinced he was guilty. A private investigator, John Bond, began by looking into details of similar cases investigated by the Buena Park police.

One lead took him to a detective who had since moved from the area and had an interesting story to tell. Some years ago, the officer had investigated a hold-up and dusted a gun for possible prints. The gun was clean of prints, and so the detective wiped it and passed it on to the identification officer who, much to the detective's surprise, later claimed to have found prints on the gun that exactly matched those of the prime suspect. But Bond's informant was certain the gun had been perfectly clean when it left his possession. Bond was interested to learn that the identification officer in question, James Bakken, was the same officer who had dealt with the prints in De Palma's case.

Bond next checked into Bakken's background and discovered that his training and references were not all that he had claimed. The private eye took his evidence to the police department and persuaded them to take another look at the evidence in the De Palma case. It was then that the experts discovered something very curious about the print; it was too similar to the one on police files. Each time a finger touches an object, a different pressure is used or the finger is pressed onto the surface at a slightly different angle. Yet the print left at the hold-up and that in the police records was identical.

Using a microscope, forensic experts examined the powder that formed the print and found the grains to be larger in composition than the powder normally used to lift prints at a crime scene. Tests showed it to be toner powder, used in Xerox machines.

It appeared that Bakken had xeroxed prints from the police file, then "lifted" them and transferred them to an exhibit fingerprint card. The print used in court was a forgery lifted from a file at the police station.

In December 1973, after completing two-and-a-half years of his sentence, De Palma was released from prison and two months later the charges against him were quashed. The fingerprint officer, meanwhile, was serving a year in jail for falsifying evidence.

The De Palma case gained considerable publicity because of the fingerprint forgery. It showed, above all, the importance of continuity of evidence between the print at the crime scene and the comparison chart presented in court. When one of the links in the chain of latent print/dusted print/transferred print/blow up/comparison chart is broken by a corrupt officer, the door is open to all manner of forgeries.

BELLE PAULSEN

Statistics show that most killers are men but, as if to set the sexual balance right, Belle Paulsen butchered her way to infamy with a remarkable number of victims.

Born in 1859 to a Norwegian magician, Belle emigrated to the United States, and at the age of twenty-four married Mads Sorensen. Their marriage produced two children but was cut short when Mads succumbed to a heart attack. The more uncharitable whispered "poison."

Belle collected the insurance money and moved to Austin, Illinois, where, shortly afterwards, her new home burned down. Armed with yet another insurance settlement, Belle opened a candy store in Chicago. "Arson" struck again and this time Belle made enough profit to buy a forty-eight-acre farm in Indiana. At a hearty 230 pounds, Belle was every ounce a farmer and did not shrink from the work around her, even butchering her own hogs.

After a few years of this bucolic life she decided to remarry. Her new husband, Peter Guiness, was no stayer and passed away after only seven months of marriage when a sausage grinder fell on his head. Belle's insurance company paid up yet again.

With two marriages and several possible arsons behind her, Belle began to advertise for husbands. Several prospects replied and visited her farm, only to disappear. John Moo and Bud Bedsbergs were never seen again and neither was the money they brought with them. George Anderson had better luck and ran away into the night, crying for his life.

As the suitors poured in, Belle erected a high fence around the property and continued to "slaughter hogs." At the height of her activities Belle fell out with one of her farmhands, Ray Lamphere, who began to gossip to the locals about the strange goings-on at the farm. Deciding that attack was the best form of defence, Belle made a counterclaim that Lamphere had tried to murder her and burn down her farm.

Events proceeded quickly when a relative of one of Belle's suitors began to make enquiries about her. Within a matter of days, the Paulsen farm burned down, and in the ashes of the building the bodies of three children and that of a headless woman were found.

The police decided the body was that of Belle and charged Lamphere with her murder. He, in turn, claimed that she had despatched twenty-eight men, butchered the bodies and fed the best pieces to the hogs. The remains were buried in quicklime. Excavation around the farm revealed the truth of Lamphere's story but the charge of murder remained. But for years to come there were some who claimed that Belle had not died but was living under a new name — and, who knows, she may even have married again!

The prosecution, faced with the problem of identifying a headless body, had a particularly weak case until a dentist came forward and said he would be able to identify Belle if the gold caps worn on her teeth could be found. An enterprising miner offered his services. He built a sluice and panned for gold in the wreckage and ashes of the Paulsen farm. After four days the miner came up with gold caps, which were then identified as coming from Belle's mouth.

The State felt its case was complete but neither the locals nor the jury believed Belle was dead. Lamphere was found guilty, not of murder but of arson. He was sent to prison, where he maintained his innocence of the murder of Belle Paulsen until he died there in 1909.

As for Belle, did she die in the fire or did she survive to trap yet another husband into marriage? Only her insurance company knows for sure.

BRIAN DONALD HUME

The absence of defence wounds in a stabbing is an indication of either suicide or an attack by more than one assailant. On this basis Donald Hume's lawyer argued that his client could not have committed murder alone.

Brian Donald Hume was born in England in 1919, the illegitimate child of a woman he knew as Aunt Dodie. His first years were spent in an institution, where he was profoundly unhappy and where on one occasion he launched a violent attack on a member of the staff who was tormenting him.

At the age of eight, Hume went to live first with his grandmother and then with Aunt Dodie, who had married by that time. The child heard rumours that this woman who had taken him in was, in fact, his mother and, as he grew older, he developed a hatred towards her. In the end, obsessed with the ambiguity of his origins, he ran away to London and looked up his birth certificate at Somerset House.

In 1939 Hume joined the Royal Air Force, but was been badly injured during training, and was discharged. There is medical evidence to indicate that Hume received a brain injury at the time of the accident. Possibly this affected his personality and led to the development of his psychopathic tendencies. For the next few years Hume led the life of a "spiv" or "wide boy." He posed as a Royal Air Force officer in order to cash dud cheques and became involved in a number of shady deals.

As the war drew to a close, Hume began a small electrical business, which quickly prospered. Before long he had a staff working for him, he drove a luxury car and had an attractive wife. But in the post-war depression Hume's business suffered a setback. Just as he was about to sell his assets he bumped into Stanley Setty, who was to be his future partner in crime.

Born Sulman Seti in Baghdad in 1903, he had become a master of the darker side of the used-car business. Setty had the habit of carrying large amounts of cash on his person, for he also cashed cheques for a large commission. The two men became partners but there was no love lost between them and on the fatal day that Setty kicked Hume's dog his fate was sealed.

Setty was last seen on October 4, 1949 at 5:50 p.m. by his cousin, who told the police that the used-car dealer had one thousand pounds in bank notes on him and was on his way to Watford to do some business. The next morning his car was discovered but Setty himself was nowhere to be found.

On October 21, a farm labourer, who was wild-fowling on the marshes north of the Thames estuary, saw a parcel in the water. It contained the headless and legless trunk of a man.

The post mortem showed that death had been caused by stabbing but considerable violence had been done to the body after death — damage consistent with being dropped from a great height. There was little hope of a visual identification but Superintendent Cherrill, the Scotland Yard fingerprint expert, was able to peel skin from the fingers and obtain a usable print. The fingerprints from the body matched those of Stanley Setty.

The police assumed that the corpse had been dropped from a plane and enquired at local airports. They discovered that Hume had hired a plane the day after the murder. Staff at the airport also remembered he had had two very heavy parcels with him.

Carpet and floorboards from Hume's home are taken into the Old Bailey.
BBC Hulton Picture Library

Brian Donald Hume was arrested on October 27. He told the police a curious story to account for his actions. Three men, he said, "Greenie," "the Boy" and "Mac," had asked him to drop three parcels containing forged printing plates for bank notes into the English Channel. He said he had been paid in bank notes. The bank notes found on Hume were traced to Setty, and Hume said he supposed that the three men who gave him the money must have had something to do with Setty's murder.

The police did not think much of Hume's story and he was sent to trial. In the hands of the defence, however, the Crown's cast-iron case began to show some cracks. Could Hume, the defence asked, have cut up and parcelled a man's body while his wife was still in the flat? How was it possible to attack a healthy man with a knife without producing defence wounds on the dead man's arms and hands?

The defence argued that Hume's account was the only story that would fit the facts. Setty had been stabbed by one of the missing trio while the others held his arms. The three men then cut up Setty's body, took the parcels to Hume and paid him to get rid of the body with bank notes taken from the dead man's pocket.

The Crown countered by pointing out that no bruises had been found on Setty's arms. How would it have been possible to restrain him against a murder attack without gripping his arms tight? They also pointed out the fact that Hume had run across the road on the day of the murder to have a carving knife sharpened. And as for the hypothetical trio of Greenie, the Boy and Mac, the Crown asked if they existed anywhere but in the mind of the accused? Indeed, the description of the trio given by Hume was strikingly similar to the three police officers who sat opposite him in the interview room!

The jury retired for two-and-a-quarter hours but they could not agree. A new jury was sworn in, and this time the prosecution offered no evidence on the count of murder. The judge directed the jury to return a verdict of not guilty. Hume was then charged with being an accessory to murder and this time pleaded guilty. He was sentenced to twelve years in prison and released on February 1, 1958.

The story of Brian Donald Hume does not end at this point. Out of prison and acquitted by a jury on the charge of murder, he sold his confessions to the British newspaper, the Sunday Pictorial. *He claimed he had murdered Setty, cut up the body and dropped it at sea from a hired airplane. Some commentators believed, however, that the confession was fabricated by Hume. It contained inconsistencies and did not agree with evidence presented at the trial.*

Hume took a new name and moved to the continent where he continued his criminal profession. On one occasion he returned to his native country to pull a bank robbery.

Hume's life of crime finally ended when he was arrested and convicted of murder in Switzerland. Deported on August 20, 1976 he was met at Heathrow by the police and two doctors. After the doctors examined him, Hume was removed to Broadmoor hospital for an indefinite period of detention.

THE BRIDES IN THE BATH

Every year people drown accidentally in their baths. In the case of Joseph Smith, three of his wives died this way. The coincidence was too great and the eminent pathologist, Bernard Spilsbury, deduced they were victims of a new murder technique — dry drowning.

Behind Joseph Smith's dapper exterior, as he walked along the promenade at Herne Bay, England, the astute observer would have discerned the swagger of a blackguard adventurer. For George Joseph Smith made his living in English seaside towns by preying on the frailty of women. His technique was unerring. Within an hour or two of meeting his victim he would propose marriage and a flight to distant parts. Just as quickly he would extract the blushing maiden's savings, then disappear into the seaside crowd.

Smith began his "rake's progress" with petty thievery. In addition to spending two terms in Queen Victoria's prisons, he boasted a variety of professions: baker; song writer; gym instructor; and antique dealer. But it was not until he discovered his true calling — playing upon the not-so-deeply hidden dreams of faded spinsters — that Smith achieved the fortune he longed for.

His first wife, Caroline Beatrice Thornhill, knew him as George Love, a baker. They married in 1898 and soon Mrs. Love was out at work while her devoted spouse strolled around Herne Bay or dropped in at a tea shop to plan his fortune. He decided that Caroline would steal from her employers and take the loot to a pawnbroker. Things worked out well at first, but one day as George stood outside the pawnshop after their latest foray he realized suspicions had been aroused. Ever the realist, he left his wife to the mercy of the police, rushed back to their lodgings, sold her belongings, and took the next train for London.

George had a terrible power over women. They said it was "something in his eyes." Respectable women in their thirties were hypnotized by his charm. They would agree to his proposal of marriage at the drop of a hat and draw out their life savings so that they could "run away to Canada" or "set up in business together." Smith would pocket the money, then "just nip into the Gents." Alas, for his brides-to-be, he never returned.

Some later said that Smith used mesmerism or occult magnetic powers to entrap his victims into parting from their savings. The true reason is probably more prosaic. Smith picked ladies who had come face-to-face with the lonely prospect of being "left on the shelf." They may have had some inclination of the risk they took when they handed their savings to Smith, but after all, Smith's may well have been the last offer they would ever receive.

Occasionally Smith went so far as to marry his conquests in order to separate them from their money. In the case of Bessie Mundie, he deserted her after marriage on the grounds that he had contracted a "bad disorder" from her. In a letter, he told her that he must leave to take a cure and he was deeply shocked that she "had not kept herself clean." Bessie was heartbroken and went to live with a friend in Western-super-Mare.

Two years later, by pure chance, Bessie bumped into George — or Henry Williams as he then called himself. One glance into his flashing eyes was enough to make her forgive him. As for Smith, he was particularly magnanimous and took her back into his bosom, for she had a 2,000-pound legacy that was being held in trust. Not long after, Smith took Bessie to a local doctor and complained that she had suffered a fit. The doctor examined her and found nothing particularly wrong. Two days later he received a note from Smith saying, "Do come at once. I am afraid my wife is dead."

The doctor rushed over and found Bessie's body submerged in water, one hand clutching a piece of soap. A verdict of misadventure was recorded at the inquest. The woman had apparently suffered an epileptic seizure "causing her to fall back into the water and be drowned."

Smith invested his wife's estate, changed his name and moved on to his next victim. This time he married a young girl he had found praying in a chapel in Southsea. Smith had arranged for a 500-pound insurance policy, and the couple took rooms in Blackpool. It was not long before the landlady noticed water dripping through the ceiling — another young bride had died in her bath. Although grief-stricken, Smith acted like a gentleman under the strain. He even suggested that a plain coffin would suffice for "when they are dead, they are done with."

George Smith poses with his first murder victim, Beatrice Mundy, who died in June 1912.
BBC Hulton Picture Library

His next stop was London where, a year later, he married a clergyman's daughter. The day after the marriage a great deal of splashing was heard in the bathroom, followed by the strains of "Nearer My God to Thee" played on the harmonium by Smith.

At the inquest Smith exhibited such a wealth of emotion that the popular press had a field day. The *News of the World* carried the headline, "Bride's Tragic Fate on Day after Wedding." Over their breakfast of kippers the following Sunday, the British public read the sad story of a romance submerged almost as soon as it had started. One of the readers was a landlady who had recently turned Smith away. She recalled how Smith had been preoccupied with the size of the bath, and she took her suspicions to the police.

Smith was kept under observation, then arrested and charged with the murder of Bessie Mundie. His trial at the Old Bailey in 1915 proved to be one of the high points of the season. Every day, scores of women would clamour for admittance to the court. The great advocate, Marshall Hall, sensing publicity in the case, took the defence for the nominal fee of three pounds, five shillings and sixpence, paid by the Poor Prisoner's Defence Act. To support the prosecution, Mr. Archibald Bodking produced pathologist Dr. Bernard Spilsbury who would unveil an amazing story of forensic deduction.

One drowned wife appeared as an accident, two were a coincidence but three looked like the start of a bad habit. But how could the prosecution convince the jury that healthy women could be drowned without any sign of a struggle? It was left to Spilsbury to demonstrate that it was possible. If a person's feet were taken hold of and tugged upward so that the head was suddenly and completely submerged, water would rush into the back of the mouth and cause a nervous spasm that would stop the heart. In the course of these forensic experiments a police inspector duplicated Smith's method on a woman swimmer. As soon as her face went under water, she lost consciousness and it was only with considerable difficulty that she was revived. Spilsbury showed that a fall or an epileptic fit would not leave the body in the same position. His conclusion was murder — death by deliberate drowning.

For his part, Marshall Hall did not call any witnesses but confined his case to a skilful examination of the expert witnesses and an address to the jury. From Spilsbury he was able to obtain the qualified admission that the soap found clutched in the dead woman's hand was some indication of a fit. To the jury he stressed the difficulty of drowning a healthy woman without leaving signs of violence on both the victim and the attacker.

The Crown and defence case over, the Judge began his summing up, at which point Smith cried out, "I am not a murderer, though I may be a bit peculiar."

The jury found him guilty and sentenced him to hang at Maidstone Prison. Yet up to the time of his execution, Smith maintained his innocence, and the prison chaplain later said that although he believed that Smith had committed many crimes, he was not a murderer. And even as the hangman adjusted the noose, Smith declared, "I'm innocent."

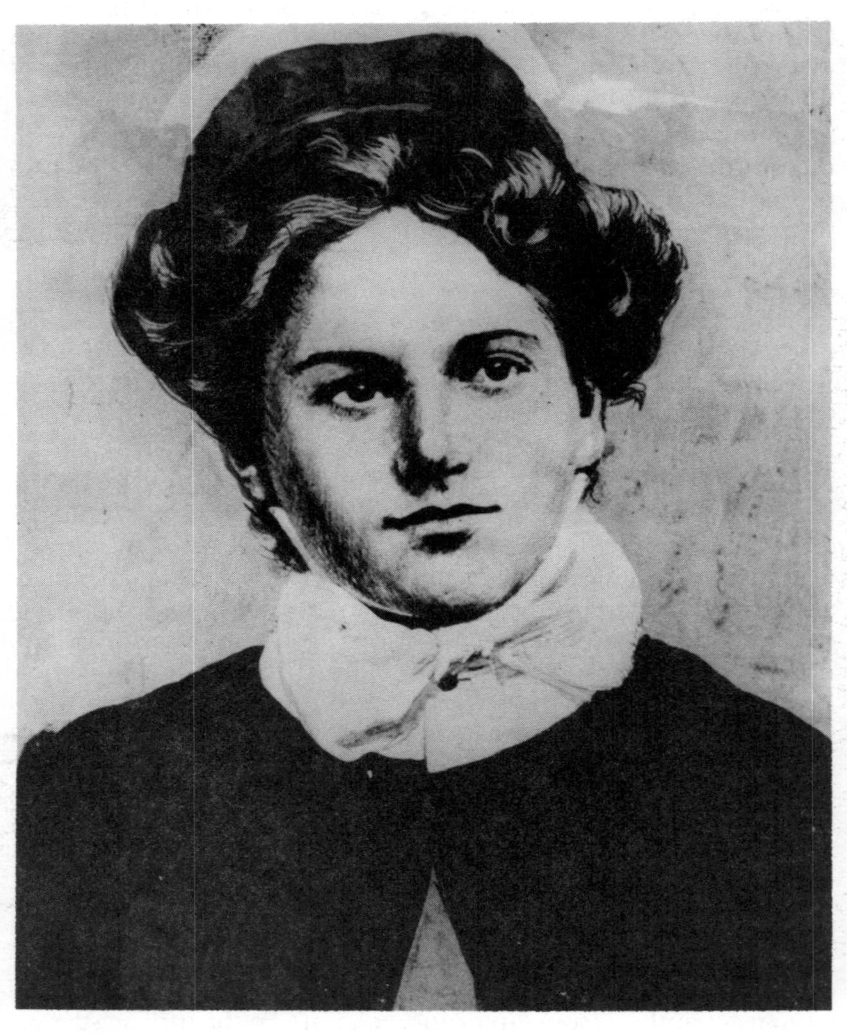

Alice Burnham, Smith's second "Bride in the Bath."
BBC Hulton Picture Library

MRS. MAYBRICK — DEADLY SOUTHERN BELLE

Arsenic is a cumulative poison easy to detect. In the death of James Maybrick, forensic evidence was complicated by the fact that Maybrick took arsenic in a patent medicine.

But for the suspicions of her children's nurse, Mrs. Florence Maybrick may well have been able to escape arrest on the charge of murdering her husband. For the ideal poison is not so much one that is undetectable as one that produces a seemingly natural death. The doctors were perfectly satisfied with their diagnosis, and the matter would never have reached the ears of the police; for the victim's health tonic was arsenic!

James Maybrick, a wealthy Liverpool cotton broker, met and courted American-born Florence Chandler while returning from one of his visits to the United States. The couple married in London in 1881, settled in Virginia and then moved back to Liverpool in 1884.

Maybrick was something of a hypochondriac and regularly dosed himself with an arsenical preparation. His other weakness was for ladies and, after the birth of his two children, he decided to return to his old practice of keeping several mistresses. Florence, in distress at her husband's infidelity, turned to the comforting arms of another man, Alfred Brierly. She committed the then-unforgivable sin of spending two nights with him at a London hotel.

What was sauce for the gander was certainly not sauce for the goose. Angered by his wife's behaviour, Maybrick blackened her eye and made her sleep in the dressing room. It was about a month after this incident that James Maybrick first fell ill. His doctors, accustomed to a patient who dosed himself with patent medicines, were not particularly concerned when he complained of stomach pains. The first diagnosis was "liver" or indigestion, for which a mixture of arsenic and potassium carbonate was prescribed. When a second opinion was sought the expert diagnosis of "upset stomach" was given.

Maybrick's illness began on April 19, 1889 and when after several days he showed no sign of improvement, the children's nurse became suspicious of Mrs. Maybrick. She noticed that Florence had purchased a large number of fly papers which she found soaking in a bowl of water. Victorian fly papers contained arsenic.

By May 8, Maybrick was vomiting constantly and his brother, Edwin, began to listen to the servants' gossip. Edwin was slipped a letter addressed to Mr. Brierly from Mrs. Maybrick that was couched in the most affectionate terms. A second brother was summoned from London. After a brief conference the brothers searched the house, where they discovered a package marked "arsenic for cats."

James Maybrick died on May 11, and his brothers were convinced he had been murdered. The doctors, however, were less emphatic, for Maybrick had been taking arsenic for years and it had even been prescribed for his recent illness. In the end the police were called in. They arrested Florence Maybrick on a charge of murder and she was put on trial at St. George's Hall, Liverpool. The forensic evidence presented in the case was far from strong. (Yet it should be remembered that only six months earlier attempts to catch Jack the Ripper had been hampered by constant botching of forensic evidence.)

Possibly the most damning evidence against Mrs. Maybrick lay in the letter she wrote to her lover. It indicated to the Victorian middle class that even if she were not guilty of murder she was certainly a very wicked woman.

Although it was not until 1898 that an accused was allowed to give evidence at his trial, Mrs. Maybrick was permitted to make a statement to the court. She told how, two days before her husband's death, he had pleaded with her to add a certain powder to his food. Mrs. Maybrick agreed and took the powder, together with some beef juice, into his room. An analysis of the juice later showed it to contain half a grain of arsenic.

The jury retired for thirty-eight minutes and returned to find Mrs. Maybrick guilty of murder. She was sentenced to hang. But on August 23, 1889, three days before the date set for her execution, the Home Secretary issued a curiously worded statement which commuted her sentence to life imprisonment. The statement pointed out that although there was evidence that Florence Maybrick had "attempted" to murder her husband, there was reasonable doubt that he had actually died of arsenic poisoning.

To some legal observers it appeared that Mrs. Maybrick had been cleared of the charge of murder; yet she was to serve a life sentence on a charge of attempted murder for which she had never been tried. It was rumoured that Queen Victoria had been so shocked by the case that she refused to have the woman set free.

With the accession of Edward VII to the throne, Florence Maybrick was released. She had spent fifteen years in jail. After leaving prison in 1904, at the age of forty-one, Florence Maybrick wrote a book entitled *My Fifteen Lost Years.* She moved to the United States where on October 23, 1941 she died in the village of South Kent, Connecticut.

The exact circumstances of James Maybrick's death will always be in doubt and the case has a serious moral for forensic scientists and potential prisoners. The "ideal poison" is not so much one that is undetectable but one that does not arouse suspicion. If a death appears natural and consistent with a patient's general condition then a doctor will sign a death certificate and burial or cremation will follow without the need for an autopsy. But for the suspicions of the children's nurse, Florence Maybrick would never have ended up on trial for murder.

Florence Maybrick — murderess or victim of suspicion?
Syndication International

Mrs. Maybrick, forty years after her trial for murder.
Syndication International

DR. CRIPPEN

Being a doctor, Crippen was above using such mundane poisons as arsenic or strychnine. He chose hyocine. It was not the poison that trapped him but a chemical error in disposing of the body — in place of quicklime Crippen used slaked lime which preserved the flesh!

Hawley Harvey Crippen is a thoroughbred among killers. His figure occupies pride of place in the "Chamber of Horrors" in Madame Tussaud's and he has spawned a host of fictional imitations. But Crippen was not a particularly sinister person. His lust was not for rape or blood; he did not murder little children or defenceless old women; his victims did not number in the tens of hundreds. He simply murdered his wife who nagged him.

Dr. Crippen was the worm who turned.

Crippen's early years show a man whose talent for enterprise was a far cry from the later henpecked husband of 39 Hilldrop Crescent, Holloway, London. Born in Coldwater, Michigan, in 1862 of prosperous and religious parents, Crippen as a young man specialized in homeopathic medicine and, as befitted a man of respectable means, he took a wife.

His first wife, the moody Charlotte Jane, died in childbirth. Crippen's second wife, Belle, was to become the sexual anvil of his life. She was all passion and mystery, if somewhat overweight. Born Kunigunde Mackamotski, and nicknamed Belle, she fancied herself the daughter of a count with a romantic career as an opera singer before her.

Some have said that Crippen's passion for this energetic and overpowering woman bordered on the masochistic for he was entrapped in sexual bondage by her overblown charms. As the years passed this thrill of bondage changed into the shackles of humiliation and Crippen became a beaten man who no longer possessed the will to escape.

The doctor was able to pay for his wife's singing lessons by working for "Professor" Munyon of "Munyon's Pile Cure." Crippen had a talent for such work and became manager of the Toronto office. Belle, for her part, wallowed in the fragments of her dreams and in the arms of other women's husbands.

In 1897 the "Professor" opened an English branch of his company and made Crippen head of the London office. As Crippen's star rose, Belle's vision declined and dreams of La Scala were replaced by the reality of second-rate music halls and corner pubs.

Then, one day, Crippen's name appeared on a theatre bill as Belle's manager. The "Professor" was offended that mere entertainment should walk hand in hand with pile cures and Crippen was sent in search of a new job. While Belle sat drinking with her theatre friends or flirting with her latest beau, Crippen tramped the streets selling nerve tonic.

Belle's habit of humiliating her spouse extended not only to constant nagging but to blatant activity with other men. Men friends would call at the house to take her out while the poor doctor waited at home. On some of these occasions, Crippen would go with her to the pub and sit silent at the table neither drinking nor smoking. On weekends the neighbours saw him pottering about in the garden, never far from the huge frame of his nagging wife.

As a new century dawned, things changed again for Hawley Harvey Crippen. By now he was working as a quack doctor for the even more quackish Deaf Institute. It was there he set eyes upon Ethel Clara le Neve, who became his secretary. Ethel was puckish, almost to the point of being a tomboy, yet troubled by a sickly constitution.

Crippen offered her the kindness and understanding of an older man and, not surprisingly, she fell head over heels in love with him. It has been said that the relationship lasted some seven years before it was consummated. It began as a fantasy marriage and it was time before Ethel realized that her knight in shining armour was burdened with a real-life wife. On the day Belle walked into the office the doctor fainted clean away.

In 1904 Crippen had changed his profession yet again, this time to a dentist specializing in crown work for actresses. Ethel was now pressing him to leave his wife but the doctor appeared paralyzed by the situation and their relationship was confined to hand holding and occasional dinners together.

By 1906 the Crippens were taking in lodgers. At 6 a.m. the doctor would rise, make the fires, clean the lodgers' shoes, do the housework and then carry up a cup of tea to Belle. One afternoon he discovered his wife in bed with one of the lodgers but quietly shut the door and let them carry on.

At the start of 1907 Ethel and Crippen spoke of the "sacred marriage" they had contracted. On afternoons they would go to a hotel together and ask for a room, pretending that they had lost their luggage. Each night Crippen would return home. Inevitably Ethel became pregnant and Belle determined to get rid of her rival. But Ethel had a miscarriage and with this misfortune Crippen acquired the necessary determination to murder.

On January 17, 1910 he placed an order for five grams of hyocine — a drug that, in large doses, is poisonous. On the evening of January 31, the Crippens held a dinner party and, after the guests had departed, Belle Crippen vanished. The doctor claimed she had gone to America and showed farewell letters to prove it. Unfortunately the letters were not particularly convincing for they were in Crippen's handwriting and had been "dictated" by Belle.

Her friends in the Music Hall Ladies Guild were concerned that Belle should have left without even telling them. Their suspicions were increased when Ethel turned up at a ball in Belle's place wearing her jewellery. And when the local newspapers listed "Mrs. Crippen" as a guest at a local function, Belle's friends read "murder."

Crippen moved Ethel in with him and decided to "kill Belle off" for the benefit of the Music Hall Ladies Guild. First he claimed he had received a cable saying Belle was ill. She then became worse — and at last, died.

Belle's friends were not satisfied and after making enquiries in the United States took their suspicions to Scotland Yard.

On June 8, 1910 Inspector Drew paid Crippen a visit. The doctor made a "clean breast" of his wife's death. She had not died in America, he said; she had run away with another man and was probably living in Chicago — the whole business was very embarrassing.

Dr. Crippen and Ethel le Neve being arraigned in court.
Toronto Star

The victim — Belle Crippen who dreamed of an operatic career.
Toronto Star

The inspector was satisfied and the pair went out to lunch together. There the matter may well have rested but Crippen panicked and the next day he and his mistress disappeared.

Drew returned to find Crippen missing and began a search of the house and garden. The investigation was extensive but fruitless. But as Drew was about to leave he decided to take one last look at the coal cellar. He pulled up a few floor boards and began to probe beneath. He was met by a terrible stench.

Underneath the coal cellar was buried a human torso, without head, arms or legs. An autopsy showed the body had been poisoned with hyocine but there was little to indicate identity beyond a hair curler and a scar on a piece of rotting skin.

Crippen had made a stupid chemical mistake. Instead of covering the body with quicklime, which would have destroyed it, he had used slaked lime, which only preserved the remains.

The problem of identity proved the biggest stumbling block in making a case against Crippen. But Inspector Drew happened to overhear two of Belle's friends talking about an operation. He learned that her abdomen carried a large operation scar that could very well match that found on the skin beneath the Crippen's coal cellar.

Meanwhile, Crippen seemed to have disappeared from the face of the earth. Enquiries in North America and Europe brought little in the way of results. In fact the doctor and Ethel stayed in Brussels first and then in Rotterdam before taking a ship for Canada.

The captain of Crippen's ship fancied himself an amateur detective and his curiosity was aroused at the sight of two men holding hands as the S.S. Montrose left port. Captain Kendall invited the man and his son to eat with him and engaged in conversation. The elder man was a spirited talker; his son's voice tended to oscillate between a very high and low pitch.

Back in his cabin the captain made what may have been the first Identikit. He drew glasses over a newspaper photograph of Crippen and placed a cut-out toque over the image of Miss La Neve. Both pictures matched the passengers on his ship and Kendall telegraphed the ship's owners in Liverpool.

Inspector Drew followed the pair in the faster SS Laurentic and the world was able to follow the chase thanks to the cables sent by Captain Kendall. Kendall's dispatches described the unsuspecting Crippen's condition and even mentioned that the killer was reading Edgar Wallace's *Four Just Men*.

At Farther Point, Quebec, Inspector Drew boarded the S.S. Montrose, went up to his suspect and said "Good Morning, Dr.

Crippen." The actual arrest, however, was made by Chief Constable McCarthy of the Quebec Provincial Police.

The murder trial began on October 18, under Lord Chief Justice Alverstone in the Old Bailey. The costs of the defence were partly borne by Horatio Bottomley, editor of *John Bull,* who hoped to increase his circulation with some exclusive interviews. Crippen's solicitor was a disastrous choice. Alfred Tobin had previously represented Lord Arthur Somerset in the Cleveland Street Male Brothel affair and had been jailed for smuggling witnesses out of the country. After Crippen's trial he was suspended by the Law Society for twelve months.

The defence hoped to obtain a reduced sentence by having Crippen plead guilty to manslaughter and invoking Belle's foul temper, infidelity and heavy drinking. Ethel would then be called as a witness. Crippen, however, demanded to take the case on his own shoulders and insisted that Ethel should not be involved. He pleaded not guilty and repeated his story that Belle had run away and that the body found under the coal shed floor was a complete surprise to him.

The trial was conducted in a blaze of publicity with celebrities and theatrical folk filling the vistors' area. Crippen was found guilty and sentenced to death. His last request before being hanged was to have Ethel's photograph and letters buried with him.

On the same morning of Crippen's execution, Ethel set sail for New York under the name of Miss Allen. She lived for a time in Toronto, working as a typist, then returned to England and married Stanley Smith, who bore a marked resemblance to Crippen. Ethel died in 1967.

At the time many people believed in Crippen's innocence. Marshall Hall, the noted barrister, made a special study of poison and believed he had the key to the Crippen murder. In his opinion Belle was a nymphomaniac whose sexual demands had become an embarrassment to the doctor. Encouraged with a new love life, Crippen had given his wife hyocin hydrobromide as a sexual depressant. It was possible, Hall theorized, that Belle Crippen's death was not murder but the result of an accidental overdose.

GRAHAM YOUNG: THE "ST. ALBAN'S POISONER"

Graham Young, despite his youth, saw himself as a master amongst poisoners. For his campaign of death he turned to a rare poison — thallium.

Murder often arouses our interest because we have a secret desire to know what it is that motivates a fellow human being to commit this cold-blooded act in full knowledge of what he or she does. Graham Young, the "St. Alban's Poisoner," provides a particularly good subject for the student of murder, for although his childhood was by no means harsh or corrupting, his youthful development was a training ground for multiple murder.

Graham was a smart child from a middle-class background. Most schoolteachers have had a child like Graham in their class. Often nicknamed the "mad professor" or "the brain," it is through book-learning or an eccentric love of facts that they gain the recognition and power they crave.

Graham was a sensitive, poorly adjusted boy who lived in a world of books. When he was only three months' old his mother died, and his father cracked under the strain of bereavement. While his father and older sister stayed together, Graham was sent to live with his aunt's family.

The boy grew so attached to Aunt Winnie that his father's eventual remarriage came as a great shock to him. Rather than move Graham back into his home, Mr. Young bought the house where Graham was living. At the age of three, Graham suddenly found himself living with a new mother and a father he hardly remembered.

The boy became withdrawn and in company would behave in a stupid way, refusing to reply to questions. He hated to fail or feel inferior. As he grew older, Graham learned to retreat into his books. He spent all his spare time at the local library while his life at home was punctuated by outbursts of anger against his stepmother.

About the time Graham moved into secondary school he began to take an interest in chemistry and earned the nickname of "mad professor." He delighted in building up the image of a mysterious and mad scientist who carried secret weapons within his brain. Graham wore a swastika and read books about Hitler, black magic, war crimes, and poisons. His school books contained drawings of his mother and father in coffins — a portent of what was to come.

Graham began to ingratiate himself with a local chemist and was soon able to get his hands on antimony, which he could display at school as "one of his poisons."

The first evidence that Graham was prepared to put his fantasies to the test came when he was bettered in a fight by one of his friends. Within a week the victor became ill. Heated by success, Graham turned his attention to his mother and father. He intended to overcome them with the power of his chemical allies. In a long, drawn-out experiment, Graham administered poison to both his parents and, at Easter, 1962 Molly Young died in Wilsden Hospital. Graham did not appear to be distressed at his stepmother's death; indeed he was eager that the body be cremated with all speed. Two weeks later it was the turn of his father to enter hospital. Graham spent most of his visits discussing symptoms with the doctor and telling them how to distinguish between antimony and arsenic poisoning.

Frederick Charles Young at the time of his son's first trial for poisoning.
Syndication International

By then Graham's chemistry master had begun to suspect poisoning and decided to examine the contents of his pupil's desk. To his horror he discovered notebooks that betrayed a complete obsession with poison. To the "mad professor," each poison had a character of its own and his experiments, he believed, transcended the "vulgarity" of mere murder.

On being questioned by his teacher, Graham boasted of his "control experiments" with poison. The boy was arrested but on medical examination was found to be a psychopath. He was committed to Broadmoor hospital for the insane.

Graham's career as a poisoner should have come to an end then, at the age of fourteen, because the hospital had been instructed not to release him for fifteen years. With skilful therapy it is possible that Graham could have been cured. At least an accurate diagnosis of his condition would have prevented a killer being let loose on the public. But Graham was determined to fool the authorities.

Like the character from a Ken Russell film, he moved about the hospital with his Hitler mustache; his room was filled with photographs of Nazi heroes and bottles labelled with the names of various poisons. Around him the music of Wagner blared at full level.

He spent his spare time reading forensic medicine in the hospital library. Just as he had become the mad professor at school, Graham was determined to impose his fantasy life on the patients and staff around him. Recognition and the power it brought were food and drink to Graham's ego.

A month after his admission a patient died of cyanide poisoning. The authorities wondered how such a chemical could have found its way into a hospital. One rumour had it that a toxological expert had extracted the cyanide from laurel leaves that grew outside the hospital and fingers pointed to Graham. This story of a secret poison laboratory seems far fetched but it suited Graham's character. No doubt he was instrumental in encouraging the rumour.

Despite his eccentric behaviour, Graham managed to get around the hospital psychiatrists and nine years after his first murder, he was released on their recommendation.

Within a month Graham travelled to London to buy some antimony. The chemist was suspicious, so Graham was forced to try again several days later. This time he used a faked letter of reference and was able to purchase twenty-five grams of tartar emetic and twenty-five grams of thallium.

The ball was set rolling and Graham was back at his "experiments." He found a job with John Hadland Ltd., a company that made precision photographic equipment, and a new laboratory of "subjects" for his experiments.

In a little over a year his investigations into the power of thallium as a poison had resulted in six people falling seriously ill; two of them died. What is most surprising is that none of Graham's colleagues suspected they were being poisoned. They would fall ill with cramps and vomiting after the tea trolley had passed, whereupon, with forensic delight, young Graham would enquire about their exact symptoms.

When discussing the illnesses at Hadlands, Graham gave accurate medical opinions. He even attended the funerals and discussed the doctors' diagnoses. Yet no one suspected him. It has been estimated that a total of forty different doctors examined Graham's victims but none of them raised the question of metal poisoning.

On the right, Aunt Winnie who gave Graham Young his first home. On the left, Graham's sister Winnifred who survived an earlier poisoning attempt.
Syndication International

Towards the end of Graham's first year at Hadland's, workers became concerned about their safety and rumours began to circulate. Some thought they were being attacked by radioactivity from a nearby factory, others that the water supply was poisoned. A local medical officer of health visited the factory and ordered a complete investigation but nothing was discovered. Next it was the turn of the firm's doctor to give the staff a pep talk.

On November 19, 1971 a doctor addressed the assembled workers and suggested three possible explanations for the illnesses: radiation sickness, heavy metal poisoning or an elusive virus. He ruled out the first two and began to concentrate upon the possibility of a virus. After his talk the doctor asked for questions and, to his surprise, found himself attacked on specific medical points by a young man from the factory stores. Graham Young began a defense of the theory

Bob Egle who took eight days to die in agony.
Syndication International

of metal poisoning and attempted to overcome the doctor's objections by suggesting subtle differences in the symptoms that would support his own diagnosis.

After the meeting the doctor spoke to Graham in private. Although the young man was no medical genius he certainly possessed a knowledge of toxicology and forensic science that was far beyond anything expected of a layman.

Without delay the management called in the police, who ran a spot check on Graham's record. Through a piece of bureaucratic

The apprentice poisoner, Graham Young, at the age of fourteen.
Syndication International

stupidity, the reply was that Graham had no criminal record. It was only later that the police learned Graham had been released from Broadmoor on a charge of poisoning. Reacting quickly to this information, they picked him up for questioning. In his room they found Nazi insignia, books on war crimes and a notebook containing detailed information about the factory poisonings. Faced with this evidence Graham calmly told police he was writing a novel and had been keeping notes.

Throughout police questioning Graham refused to confess, and his only concession was to write out a prescription for one of the victims still in hospital. As the interview dragged on Graham said to one of the officers, "You've treated me better than I deserve." He was asked if he were beginning to feel remorse. He replied, "No, that would be hypocritical. What I feel is the emptiness of my soul."

Graham pleaded not guilty to murder and released photographs to the press depicting himself as a brooding mass murderer. In the witness box he behaved in a brilliant fashion and at times ran rings around the prosecutor.

As a boy John Williams once beat his friend Graham Young in a fight. Young retaliated by attempting to poison him.
Syndication International

At the end of the trial he was found guilty of the murder of two of his workmates and guilty of the attempted murder of two others. The judge committed him to life imprisonment and his counsel suggested the sentence be spent in a regular prison. Speaking about his release from Broadmoor his counsel said, "That release appears to have been a serious error of judgement, but the authorities now have a duty to protect Young from himself as well as a duty to protect the public."

Frederick Biggs whose death agonies were so great that he tried to throw himself from a hospital window.
Syndication International

Graham Young — mass poisoner. This is the carefully posed photograph the killer circulated to the press.
Syndication International

AGATHA CHRISTIE AND THE THALLIUM POISONER

By coincidence two great poisoners struck in 1961 — one the real-life killer, Graham Young, the other a fictional character of Agatha Christie's. Did life imitate fiction?

The trial of Graham Young, the St. Alban's poisoner, for the murder of his workmates aroused considerable interest in Britain. Possibly the most bizarre factor in the blaze of publicity that attended the case was the theory that Graham's actions had been inspired by Agatha Christie's detective story, *The Pale Horse*.

The Pale Horse is an ingenious story of murder by contract. Behind the facade of black magic and psychic killings, a dowdy little pharmacist, Zachariah Osborne, carries out a series of murders by contaminating foodstuffs and toothpaste with thallium.

Dame Agatha's insight into the mind of the psychopathic killer is faultless, even down to his obsession with "helping" the authorities. What she wrote about Osborne could just as well have been written about the St. Alban's poisoner. "The actual mechanics of the thing was child's play to a pharmacist. As I say, if only Mr. Osborne had had the sense to keep quiet...I think his sense of power was exhilarated by the actual performance of the murder. To get away with murder again and again intoxicated him, and what's more, he'll enjoy himself in the dock. You see if he doesn't. The central figure with all eyes upon him."

As to the truth of the theory that Graham Young modelled himself on Zachariah Osborne and discovered the secret of thallium poisoning from *The Pale Horse* it seems nonsense, based as it is upon the assumption that thallium is a rare poison known only to a handful of experts. While the symptoms of thallium poisoning did fool a number of doctors, the poison itself is hardly exotic. The fourth edition of Keith Simpson's *Forensic Medicine*, published in the same year as *The Pale Horse*, contains a discussion of poisoning by the heavy metal group with specific reference to antimony and thallium, both of which metals were used by Graham. Forensic books such as Simpson's, with their gruesome illustrations, were no doubt read by Graham Young in the early stages of his career.

A boy who immersed himself in the "dank miasmas of putrefaction" of Dennis Wheatley's black magic books would hardly have found the cool, controlled prose of Agatha Christie very exciting. And it is hardly likely he would have bought the book for its black magic element, since the advertising for the book made no mention of witchcraft.

It is the date of publication of *The Pale Horse* that gives the lie to the "copycat murder" theory. The book did not appear in the bookshops until November 1961, by which time Graham was well advanced in his experiments on his family and needed no help from fiction. Dame Agatha was in no way to blame for Graham Young's activities as a poisoner. The plan was his alone and the motivation hidden in his childhood. His knowledge about the use of poisons came from textbooks on chemistry, medicine and forensic science rather than a work of fiction.

DR. WILLIAM PALMER

Strychnine induces the most painful of deaths, and yet William Palmer was not above using it on his family and friends.

Dr. William Palmer was a master poisoner. When he was arrested in November, 1955 for the murder of John Parsons Cook, the police were to uncover a total of fourteen victims who had met their deaths from the doctor's administrations. Their deaths were particularly gruesome for Palmer's choice of poison was strychnine, which drags the victim to his grave by means of the most terrible convulsions.

Palmer did not have the best possible start in life. His mother possessed an unconcealed appetite for men and his father was far from honest. As a young man Palmer was apprenticed to a firm of chemists in his home town of Rugeley in Staffordshire, England. After getting a young girl pregnant he had to leave Rugeley, and he moved to London and St. Bart's Hospital where he qualified as a surgeon. During his student days Palmer was the subject of a nasty rumour involving the death of a man whose wife had taken Palmer's fancy.

Returning to Rugeley as a doctor, Palmer married and settled down to a respectable practice. This period of calm did not last long for soon the high life exerted its attractions. Dr. Palmer bought a string of race horses and took several mistresses. Then, at the height of his playboy activities, disaster struck in the shape of his mother-in-law. The old woman was alcoholic and could barely look after herself. Mrs. Palmer put her foot down and insisted that her mother should live with the family.

Palmer's unwelcome relative went to meet her maker after only two weeks and the house was quiet again. But this was only the beginning. An uncle died the day after one of the doctor's visits. Next it was the turn of Palmer's children; four of his legitimate and two of his illegitimate children died of "convulsions." The doctor began to get an unfortunate reputation.

But Palmer was made of too stern a stuff to bother about the neighbours' gossip and when a Mr. Blandon came to collect a gambling debt he sent him quickly on his way — via the undertaker. Mr. Blandon was followed by Mr. Bly, who came to collect eight hundred pounds.

Encouraged by his success Palmer turned to his wife, who caught the "English chlorea" and died, leaving him an insurance policy of 1,300 pounds. But Palmer had increasing debts and his love for gambling soon ate up this latest windfall.

His next plan was to invite his brother-in-law, Walter, to his home. Walter was a heavy drinker and short of money so Palmer generously offered to stand him all the drink he could swallow if he would take out an 82,000 pound insurance policy. This time the insurance company was less enthusiastic about the prospects and would only agree to a policy of 13,000 pounds.

With a generous supply of gin (or was it strychnine?) at his elbow, Walter soon joined his various relatives and Palmer looked forward to collecting the insurance money. But by now the company had begun to investigate Palmer, who, at the same time, found himself in the grip of a money-lender who charged a staggering sixty per cent interest.

Taking a last chance on the horses Palmer went to the races where, to his very good luck, he bumped into an old friend, John Parsons Cook, whose pockets were stuffed with bank notes. Palmer helped Cook celebrate and within a few hours his friend became violently ill.

Palmer took him back to Rugeley, where he could treat him. Over the next few days, as Cook lay ill in bed Palmer rushed about town paying off debts. Even Cook's healthy body could not long survive Palmer's ministrations and soon the doctor was forced to forge signatures on the dying man's cheques.

Within days of Cook's death, his father arrived in Rugeley, and was surprised to learn that his son had died with only five pounds in his pocket and owing four thousand pounds to Dr. Palmer. Cook, senior, consulted a solicitor and a post mortem was ordered. The doctor's certificate of death indicated "apoplectic seizure" but the medical evidence suggested tetanus poisoning. There was a strong suspicion of poisoning by strychnine, but the autopsy did not support this deduction.

Despite the autopsy findings, a verdict of "willful murder" was recorded at the inquest and an order made to examine the bodies of Palmer's wife and brother-in-law.

Palmer went to trial for murder and, despite conflicting forensic evidence, was found guilty. He was hanged in public before a crowd who jeered "poisoner."

It is said that after all the publicity of the trial the citizens of Rugeley petitioned the prime minister to have the name of their town changed. The prime minister agreed, provided they renamed the town after himself — Palmerston. Not surprisingly, mid-way between Stafford and Lichfield, the birthplace of William Palmer still bears its original name.

Dr. William Palmer, the Rugeley Poisoner.
(Engraving by Holywell after J.T. Wood)
BBC Hulton Picture Library

RASPUTIN: THE STOMACH THAT CHEATED DEATH

Cyanide is not always fatal. A serious stomach disorder may enable the victim to survive a poisoning attempt.

During the reign of Emperor Nicholas II, Grigory Yefimovich Rasputin was to become the most powerful and influential man in Russia. To some he was a saint and healer, to others a lecher and drunk. The truth of the man lies not between these two extremes but embraces both of them, for Rasputin reconciled within his own person the paradox of holy man and sensualist.

For a variety of motives, influential parties in Russia agreed that Rasputin must be removed and on the night of December 16, 1916 (Old Calendar) he was invited to the house of Prince Feliks Yusopov. The cakes and tea he consumed were heavily dosed with salts of cyanide and the conspirators expected Rasputin to fall dead at their feet.

The monk would not die. Maddened with fear that Rasputin may truly have possessed supernatural powers, Yusopov pulled out a gun and shot the holy man. Rasputin fell but regained his strength and ran from the house, only to be shot again.

The conspirators then tied Rasputin and carried him to the Neva River where his body was placed under the ice. Legend has it that he revived again and attempted to claw his way through the ice to freedom.

Did the monk possess amazing healing powers that were able to counteract the action of cyanide in his system? Could mental energies alone reverse the chemical reactions taking place in his stomach?

The answer is more prosaic. Rasputin had an upset stomach. For cyanide salts to work on the blood supply they must be first broken down to release free cyanide ions. In severe cases of upset stomach, brought on by overeating or drinking, there may be little acid secreted in the stomach and, under such adverse conditions, the cyanide salts remain in a chemically inert form.

This is probably what happened to Rasputin, who had spent the months before his death in indulgent eating and drinking. The poison he consumed lay dormant in his stomach, his gluttony enabling him to survive and enjoy life for a few more minutes until he was cut down by a bullet.

GEORGI MARKOV: MURDER BY RICIN

Poisoning is rarely used for murder today. The case of Georgi Markov shows that the use of exotic poisons may have been adopted by political assassins.

Consider the irony — that the everyday accessory of the city businessman, the rolled umbrella, was used as a device for murder by a foreign agent in the heart of London. It was a man with a tightly rolled umbrella who bumped into Georgi Markov as he walked across Waterloo Bridge one morning in September, 1978. The man melted into the crowd and Markov walked on, apparently none the worse for his encounter. Four days later he died in hospital, and forensic experts were faced with a puzzling form of assassination.

Markov was a broadcaster and writer who worked for the overseas service of the BBC at Bush House. He had gained considerable fame in his native Bulgaria as a playwright and novelist but after the Czech uprising Markov found himself in disgrace and was forced to flee to the West.

In 1971 he joined the overseas service of the BBC and became responsible for news programs to Bulgaria. But Markov had additional fish to fry and, to the BBC's embarrassment, he joined Radio Free Europe, then funded by the *CIA*. His satirical broadcasts on the United States funded network caused embarrassment to the Bulgarian government and, according to Markov's friends, eventually led to his death at the hands of a political assassin.

When he got home, Markov mentioned the incident on Waterloo Bridge to his wife. In the hours that followed, his temperature rose and his condition worsened. On September 11, he died of unknown causes and Scotland Yard's Special Branch and the Anti-Terrorist Squad were called in to investigate. They learned of a similar attack on Vladimir Kostov in the Paris metro. Kostov, too, was a Bulgarian and worked for Radio Free Europe.

The autopsy on Markov showed an abnormally high white blood count and collapse of his cardio-vascular system. Careful examination of his body showed no wounds or injuries and the x-rays that were taken showed no abnormalities. Doctors examined Markov's body again, this time using a scanning electron microscope. It was then that they discovered a minute "bullet" embedded in Markov's thigh. Comparison with x-ray films taken at the first autopsy showed that what had been taken for a tiny flaw in the film was, in fact, the bullet.

British police requested the Paris police send them the portion of Kostov's back that contained a similar bullet. It was made of a platinum-iridium alloy and contained four holes. Tests made at Porton Down, Britain's Chemical Warfare Station, revealed that the bullets contained a substance known as ricin.

Ricin is a toxalbumin that acts to destroy vital enzyme systems in the body. The poison can be chemically extracted from castor beans, physic nuts or prayer beads. Doses as low as 100 millionths of a gram can be fatal. It is even more lethal if injected directly into a muscle as was done with Markov.

As far as Scotland Yard was concerned, it seemed unlikely that the killing could have been done by one individual working on his own. The preparation of the drug and the delivery system required considerable toxological and technical expertise. Political assassination seemed a reasonable deduction. The coroner's verdict on Markov was "unlawfully killed by ricin poisoning when a metallic pellet was inserted into the back of the thigh." To many observers the culprit was the Bulgarian government.

The ricin-filled bullet, smaller than a pinhead, used to kill Georgi Markov.
BBC Photo

Some time before the assassination, warnings had been sent to Markov's brother, Nikola, that if the propaganda broadcasts did not stop, Georgi would die. Months before the incident on Waterloo Bridge, a Bulgarian had visited Georgi Markov's home and warned him that he was under sentence of death, and that the killing would be carried out by the Dazjavna Sigurnost — the Bulgarian State Security. The informant indicated that poison had been passed to a Bulgarian consulate in the West. The reaction of the Bulgarian government to questions asked by the media was that the whole story was propaganda and the killing had probably been carried out by a *CIA* agent.

MURDER BY INSULIN

Kenneth Barlow believed he had found the ideal poison in insulin, which is undetectable in the body. But forensic science proved him wrong. Through a process of brilliant laboratory deductions, his technique for murder was uncovered.

The Barlows of Thornbury Crescent, Bradford, England appeared to be a happily married couple. So when the local doctor received an emergency call at midnight on May 3, 1957 the scene he encountered had all the appearance of a domestic tragedy. Elizabeth Barlow was lying dead in her bath. There were no signs of violence on her body and no evidence of a struggle in the bathroom or bedroom.

According to her husband, Elizabeth had been feeling unwell all evening. She had been in bed since 6:30, feeling very hot and nauseous. At ten o'clock she had taken a bath, during which time Kenneth must have dozed off. He woke a little later and went into the bathroom to see if his wife was feeling better, only to discover her lying under the water. Kenneth Barlow struggled to lift her out but she was too heavy. He then pulled out the bath plug and tried to give her artificial respiration. At last, realizing she was dead, he called the doctor.

As he examined Mrs. Barlow, the doctor became suspicious of the husband's story. After all, why should a healthy woman collapse and drown in her bath without any signs of a struggle to get out? He also wondered what had caused Mrs. Barlow's eyes to dilate.

The Bradford *CID* were called and Detective Sergeant Naylor realized that elements of Barlow's story did not ring true. If Barlow had attempted to lift his wife from the bath, why were his pyjamas and the bathroom floor perfectly dry? In addition, close examination of the body showed water still trapped in a fold of her arm. If Barlow had tried to give his wife artificial respiration, the detective speculated, surely that bit of water would have been dislodged.

The body was removed for a post mortem but no signs of foul play showed up. There was no unusual bruising of the body, no poisons or drugs in the body organs — nothing, in fact, to indicate that Mrs. Barlow had been murdered. However, the pathologist, Dr. David Price, discovered that she was two months pregnant. This fact, together with the evidence of the dilated pupils, led him to suspect that somehow she had been murdered. A second post mortem, during which the body was examined with a magnifying lens, disclosed four tiny puncture marks on the buttocks. Price believed these were the marks of a hypodermic needle and that one of the marks had been made within hours of Mrs. Barlow's death.

No common drugs or poisons could be found in the blood samples or body organs, and the pathologist was faced with the problem of determining what substance had been injected into the victim's body. Since normal analytical methods had failed, he attempted to reverse the accepted procedure and work backwards from symptoms to cause. The pathologist called a meeting of doctors and toxicologists to diagnose Mrs. Barlow's fatal illness on the basis of the symptoms described by Barlow, assuming that even a murderer would keep close to the facts in order to make his story more credible. Mrs. Barlow had perspired so heavily that her pyjamas were soaked. This symptom, together with malaise, nausea, coma, and death caused the doctors to suspect acute hypoglycemia or "insulin shock."

Insulin is regularly taken by diabetics to enable them to metabolize the sugars formed from the food they eat. If too large a dose is taken — or if a person not suffering from diabetes takes a dose of insulin — then the level of sugar in the blood can drop to a dangerously low level, resulting in a condition known as acute hypoglycemia. If the condition is not treated at once, death can result.

The doctors guessed that Elizabeth Barlow had been injected with insulin and died shortly after. The problem with such a diagnosis was to demonstrate that the abnormally high level of insulin in her body was due to an injection, for insulin is produced and metabolized by the body's normal processes. Somehow the doctors had to devise a lab test to prove their theory.

While the doctors were at work, the police searched Kenneth Barlow's home and found two hypodermic needles. Barlow worked as a male nurse so this find was not unusual. However, when pressured into answering further questions, Barlow changed his story. This time he confessed that the couple were worried about the pregnancy and he had given his wife an injection of ergot shortly before she died to abort the baby.

The police went to the hospital where Barlow worked and found several ampoules of ergometrine missing from the store of supplies. They also learned that his duties included giving insulin injections to diabetics. Inquiries at other hospitals where Barlow had worked revealed that he had once talked about insulin as being the perfect murder weapon, since it would be undetectable after death.

Forensic scientists working on the case were determined to prove Barlow wrong. First they made an extract from the tissue around the hypodermic puncture marks. The solution was injected into groups of mice which then showed exactly the same symptoms — excitability, coma and death — as those of a control group injected with insulin. Next, the forensic scientists had to demonstrate that none of the drugs or household chemicals found in the Barlow home would have a similar effect. By the end of the experiments over a thousand mice had been sacrificed to demonstrate the Barlow murder.

To some extent Barlow had been correct when he said insulin was undetectable in the body; however, the chemical processes that take place after death prevent the normal breakdown of insulin so that the contents of the injection were preserved in her corpse. Although science could not prove that insulin had been injected into Elizabeth Barlow before her death, it was able to show that a substance extracted from the area of the puncture marks on her buttocks produced similar effects to those of insulin on laboratory mice. Armed with this information the police felt that their case was complete. At the trial, however, some ingenious arguments were presented by the defence.

First, Barlow's counsel pointed out that blood from Mrs. Barlow's heart was abnormally high in sugar. How was a high level of blood sugar compatible with insulin shock? Experts for the Crown countered by claiming that during panic or violent struggle, the liver would send an emergency charge of sugar directly to the heart. The defence argued that panic would also release a high level of adrenalin and insulin into the body. The prosecution attempted to discredit this suggestion by asking why this naturally produced insulin happened to concentrate in Mrs. Barlow's buttocks.

The forensic arguments were subtle and difficult for laymen to follow but the jury agreed that Kenneth Barlow was guilty of murder. He was sentenced to life imprisonment.

GASSING: ACCIDENT OR SUICIDE

A running car in a closed garage is a death trap. In the case of Major Dunning the courts had to decide whether his death was suicide or accident.

In February, 1931 Major James Dunning was discovered dead in his garage, with a number of tools laid out beside his car, the ignition switched on and the doors to the garage closed. He had died from carbon monoxide poisoning.

A verdict of death by misadventure was recorded at the inquest when it was learned that the major often worked on his 1913 Rolls. Since the evening on which he died was cool, the jury did not find the fact of the closed garage doors surprising. However, the major's insurance company was more skeptical, particularly in light of the fact that he carried 10,000 pound's worth of life insurance and had been having income tax problems.

The dispute over the insurance was taken to court, where it was scientifically shown that after the car's engine had run for about thirty minutes, an atmosphere of two per cent carbon monoxide would have formed. With the garage doors closed it was possible that the major was overcome while tuning the engine of his Rolls. The engine continued to run until oxygen in the garage became low, at which point the engine would stall, leaving the ignition switched on. The servants recalled that Major Dunning went out to work on his car at 10:35 p.m. and at 11:15 p.m. they still heard the engine running. It stopped about thirty minutes later.

The judge upheld the coroner's verdict and ruled that Major Dunning died by misadventure.

BLOOD ON THE CABIN FLOOR

Blood groups and antibodies can trap a killer. But what can forensic science do when faced with a stain nine years old?

Arthur Kendall, his wife, Helen, and their five children, ran a farm in Elma Township, Ontario, Canada. In the spring of 1952, Arthur planted a crop of flax before going off to a fishing trip. It was on that trip he was offered a summer job fixing up an old sawmill on Lake Huron.

Arthur returned home and explained to his wife that the family could spend the summer in a small cabin across from the mill. It would be something of a holiday and when the job was finished they would be back in time for the flax harvest.

Despite the cramped conditions in the small cabin the family enjoyed the summer. While Arthur went to work, Helen kept the cabin tidy and cooked for the three temporary workers Arthur had hired.

That bright summer there was only one cloud on the horizon — Beatrice Hogue, a waitress with six children who had caught Arthur's fancy. The days passed and on July 16 the work was finished and Arthur drove the hired hands into town, on the way picking up Beatrice and her children.

By the start of August Arthur Kendall was back in Elma Township working on his farm. But instead of Helen, his wife, he had Beatrice and her children as guests. Arthur explained to curious neighbours that his wife had left him for another man but refused to go into details.

The Ontario Provincial Police made a routine investigation. There seemed little that was suspicious about the case except the children's distressed reaction when they were questioned. Then, on September 3, a box containing women's clothing was found near the Kendall farm. The police searched the whole area and even looked around the sawmill on the Bruce Peninsula but nothing more was found.

The case of the runaway wife seemed closed. From time to time in the years that followed there were complaints that Kendall had been violent towards his children and on one occasion they were placed in the care of the Children's Aid Society. Then, in 1959, a motion was made to have Helen Kendall declared legally dead. Freed from his wife, Arthur married Beatrice Hogue.

One day, nine years after their mother had disappeared, several children decided to talk. Seventeen-year-old Anne Kendall contacted the police and told them that on the night of July 26, 1952 her mother had been killed. Anne had awakened early and heard her mother cry out, "No, Art, please don't." Moments later, she saw her father lay a bloody butcher's knife on the table and drag her mother to the door and out towards the sawmill. When Art Kendall returned a while later, he took the sheets off the bed, used them to wrap up his wife's clothing and the knife and carried the bundle outside. He returned to scrub away the blood stains that had dripped from the corpse onto the cabin floor.

The police questioned the oldest sister who substantiated the story and on January 27, 1961 Arthur Kendall was arrested on a charge of murder.

But the crime was nine year's old and there was no body or murder weapon. And even though Kendall was found guilty at the trial, during his subsequent imprisonment he protested his innocence, claiming that his wife had left him years ago, and asked a significant question: Why had the children waited so long to tell their story if he had, in fact, murdered their mother in front of them? (Possibly the children were frightened to come forward, having received numerous violent beatings from their father while growing up.) And why was the body never found?

As far as the body was concerned, the police believed it to be hidden in a swamp close to the sawmill mentioned by the children. A dense mass of underwater weeds and roots would have been strong enough to keep the body submerged (it had proved impervious to police divers). As for incriminating evidence, the police case hung on a blood stain. They discovered a dark mark on the cabin floor and a trail of spots leading to the door. Temperature changes, dampness, sunlight, and putrefaction had turned the stain a dark brown. But was the mark, in fact, human blood? Serologists were able to identify it as blood but not specifically as human or animal blood.

To find out how a blood stain would age, forensic scientists built a replica of the floor of the Kendall cabin and stained it with blood. The floor was then scrubbed and placed in a well-walked area for several weeks. The scientists estimated that during this time the stain would have received something like nine years' normal wear. At the end of the experiment the floor was washed again and the stain examined. Its remnants were similar to those found on the cabin floor. Yet, despite this interesting piece of forensic deduction, the police were never able to prove that the blood was human and not from a deer or rabbit that had been shot and taken to the cabin for butchering.

The force of circumstantial evidence and the testimony of his own children, however, told against Kendall. He was found guilty of capital murder and sentenced to hang. One week prior to the execution of the death sentence, his penalty was commuted to life imprisonment.

TOM PONZI — PRIVATE EYE

Not all detectives work for a police force. Tom Ponzi decided that his independence was too important to sacrifice.

If most private eyes follow in the footsteps of Sam Spade then Tom Ponzi swaggers like James Bond. His lifestyle and client list lie closer to the world of Ian Fleming than that of Dashiel Hammet.

Ponzi is founder of the Italian Mercurius Agency centred in Milan, which has numbered Aristotle Onassis, Pablo Picasso, Gina Lollobrigida, and the Vatican among its clients. For adversaries, Ponzi has tackled everyone from last-ditch gunmen to the Mafia itself. The Mercurius Agency keeps international crime dossiers, numbering in the millions, and hires squads of detectives, forensic scientists, electronics experts, and lawyers. At Ponzi's disposal is a fleet of fast cars, high-speed boats, underwater diving equipment, planes, helicopters, and some of the most sophisticated electronic equipment yet designed.

Ponzi is not content merely to administer his agency. More often than not, he is out on the street taking charge of a more interesting case. Like James Bond, Ponzi is a parachutist, scuba diver, an expert shot with a gun, as well as bow and arrow, and trained in boxing, karate and savate — obviously, a dangerous man to come up against.

What was probably the detective's greatest triumph occurred during the siege of Terrazzano di Rho, a small town outside Milan. On the morning of October 10, 1956 two men arrived in the town with a carload of ammunition, gelignite and sulphuric acid, intent on taking over the local school and holding the children hostage. Arturo Santato and his brother Flavio, had just been released from a prison for the criminally insane, and were bent on revenge.

At first they demanded a hundred million lire, but as police, infantry and tanks surrounded the school the demand went up to a billion; unless the money was paid, the brothers would pour acid over the children, then blow up the school.

By early afternoon, television and radio crews from all over Europe almost outnumbered the soldiers, and programs were interrupted to show the two madmen at the school window. It was to this scene of an apparently impotent military force that Ponzi and a colleague arrived by fast car from Milan.

The detective observed that the brothers were playing to the world's news media, shouting and screaming insults at the police. He pinned his strategy on the hope that the men were so absorbed with their audience that they would not see him as he crept up to the school. Using a ladder found by a young labourer named Sante Zenare, Ponzi and his colleague climbed into a window adjacent to the one occupied by the madmen. Zenare joined them.

Relying on his skill in unarmed combat Ponzi rushed the siege room. Zenare received a bullet wound in the skirmish, while Ponzi and his colleague beat the two brothers into submission.

The day should have ended in triumph. Ponzi held onto the Santatos while Zenare cleared away the barrier at the front door and stepped into the square. He was cut down in a hail of bullets. Thinking that Zenare was one of the gunmen trying to escape, the police killed Ponzi's plucky volunteer.

Overnight the man who had broken the Terrazzano di Rho siege became a hero. Other pages from Ponzi's casebook show just as much bravery and excitement. Once, on the occasion of an American Army PX fraud, Ponzi declared war on the Mafia; on another occasion, he created a "Gorilla Squadron" to ride shotgun on airlines to discourage terrorists. (It was named gorilla because the squadron was picked from the worst-looking applicants — those with facial scars, broken noses, and so on.) The English *Sunday Times* hired Ponzi to prove that the "Mussolini Diaries" had been forged. And once Ponzi broke up a faked drug ring whose ineffective chemicals were being marketed as antibiotics and tranquilizers.

For Ponzi, King of the Private Eyes, crime in all its variations certainly pays well.

THE QUÉBEC AIRLINE MURDER

Most killers stick to the family. Despite the wonders of forensic science cases are still cracked by routine interviews and patient leg work.

Today's airlines have learned to anticipate bomb-ings and hijackings. X-ray machines and magnetometers detect guns and ammunition, and trained dogs or electronic detectors give warning if an explosive device has been smuggled aboard an aircraft.

But aircraft bombings are by no means new. On September 9, 1949 a Québec Airways flight, approaching Cap Tourmente, exploded and went into a power dive. The *DC-3* crashed vertically into heavy bush, killing all the crew and passengers. Within hours airline officials were faced with determining the cause of the crash. Since the aircraft had not caught fire after the crash, the wreckage was more or less intact and experts deduced that an explosion in the forward hatch had destroyed the plane's control systems, causing it to go into a dive.

On September 12 the case was handed over to the Royal Canadian Mounted Police, assisted by the Québec Provincial Police and the Québec City Police. Two lines of enquiry were followed: one was to investigate the background of all the passengers; the other was to trace all the baggage and freight that had been loaded onto the aircraft.

While one team of officers questioned relatives of the victims and investigated insurance claims, the other examined the company's freight records. It turned out that one of the parcels carried onto the plane bore a fictitious forwarding address. Upon questioning the freight clerk, the police learned only that a fat woman had brought the parcel into the terminal and that it had been carried for her by a taxi driver.

The police then questioned taxi drivers in the city and were in luck, for one remembered the fare. He had picked up the fat woman at the train station in Québec City and dropped her outside a downtown hotel. This promising first lead began to fizzle out when the mystery woman could not be traced.

In the meantime, the other police team was looking into the background of Albert Guay, husband of one of the crash victims. Several months earlier Guay had caused a scene in a restaurant involving a waitress named Marie-Ange Robitaille. While being questioned by the police, Marie-Ange mentioned a fat woman nicknamed "The Raven." On September 20 "The Raven" was identified by the cab driver as the woman he had picked up. Unfortunately the same woman was now in the Infant Jesus Hospital suffering from an overdose of sleeping pills. While they waited for The Raven to recover, the police discovered that Guay had been having an affair with Marie-Ange and using The Raven's home for their meetings.

When The Raven recovered, police detectives questioned her, and on September 23, just two weeks after the crash, Albert Guay was arrested for murder.

Twenty-eight-year-old Mrs. Albert Guay who left a $10,000 insurance policy behind her.
CP Photo

It turned out that The Raven had been in Guay's power for years, ever since she accumulated large financial debts. At first he had asked her to provide a room for his meetings with Marie-Ange. Then, as his wife became more of a problem, he asked The Raven to get hold of some dynamite. The Raven's crippled brother, a watchmaker, had used his workshop to make a timing mechanism for the bomb. The Raven was then forced to deliver the device to the airport on the day Madame Guay took her flight.

A clinching piece of evidence was discovered in the watchmaker's workshop in the form of some powder burns made during a test of the device. The pattern of these burns matched those found inside the plane's baggage compartment. The principals in the bombing were brought to trial. Albert Guay made a statement which implicated The Raven and her brother and all three were later hanged in a Québec jail.

DR. BRUSSEL AND THE MAD BOMBER

Psychiatry is the latest force to be brought to the aid of the police. In the case of the New York Mad Bomber a psychiatrist was able to deduce the suspect's appearance and background.

When all else fails the police will turn to unorthodox methods to track down a killer. For instance, detectives have been known to consult clairvoyants whose dreams and special insights could provide clues not normally available through forensic means. Psychiatry is another resource which is increasingly being used by some police forces.

To understand the power of forensic psychiatry one need look no further than in the notebooks of Dr. James Brussel who, after reading through the file on New York's "Mad Bomber," gave an accurate description of the maniac. He even predicted that the man the police should look for would be wearing a double-breasted suit.

Brussel began his psychiatry career at the Pilgrim State Hospital in New York in the early 1930s, not long after he began specializing in the criminally sick mind. During World War II he worked with army offenders and afterwards resumed his treatment of the criminally insane. His contributions to the apprehension of such criminals as the "Mad Bomber," the "New York Christmas Eve Killer" and the

"Boston Strangler" have earned him the title "Sherlock Holmes of the Couch." Dr. Brussel's method was to apply psychiatric experience to the circumstances of a case and, combined with a dash of intuition and a good measure of deduction, form a detailed history of the criminal's behavior, appearance and habits. Knowing his man, Brussels could then give the police sufficient details to help in tracking down their suspect.

Dr. James A. Brussel, the psychiatrist who helped the police solve the "Mad Bomber" and "Boston Strangler" cases.

One of his most outstanding series of deductions was made in the case of a man who had been planting bombs all over New York City. On November 16, 1940 the first bomb made its appearance on the window ledge of the Consolidated Edison Company. It had been designed not to explode, and bore the inscription "Con Edison crooks, this is for you." The Bomber's reign lasted sixteen years, during which time over thirty bombs had been planted, some of which caused serious injuries. In addition, he sent a storm of letters to newspapers, theatres, department stores, and hotels about the need for justice and the "dastardly deeds" and "ghoulish acts" which had been carried out by the Con Edison company.

The Bomber's activity continued with regularity until the United States entered the war against Germany. At this point he mailed the following note to the Manhattan police:

> I WILL MAKE NO MORE BOMBS FOR THE DURATION OF THE WAR — MY PATRIOTIC FEELINGS HAVE MADE ME DECIDE THIS — LATER I WILL BRING THE CON EDISON TO JUSTICE — THEY WILL PAY FOR THEIR DASTARDLY DEEDS. *F.P.*

The Mad Bomber kept his word and in place of bombs, letters were planted. With the declaration of peace, bombs exploded in the New York Public Library, Grand Central Station, Radio City Music Hall, Macy's Department Store, and several other locations.

By 1956, the Bomber's letters had become more incoherent. To the *Herald Tribune* he wrote:

> WHILE VICTIMS GET BLASTED — THE YELLOW PRESS MAKES NO MENTION OF THESE GHOULISH ACTS. THESE SAME GHOULS CALL ME A PSYCHOPATH — ANY FURTHER REFERENCE TO ME AS SUCH — OR THE LIKE — WILL BE DEALT WITH — WHERE EVER A WIRE RUNS — GAS OR STEAM FLOWS — FROM OR TO THE CON EDISON CO. — IS NOW A BOMB TARGET — SO FAR 54 BOMBS PLACED — $ TELEPHONE CALLS MADE. THESE BOMBINGS WILL CONTINUE UNTIL CON EDISON IS BROUGHT TO JUSTICE — MY LIFE IS DEDICATED TO THIS TASK — EXCEPT NO CALLS ABOUT BOMBS IN THEATRES AS YOUR ACTIONS — NO LONGER WARRANT THE EFFORT OR DIME — ALL MY SUFFERINGS — ALL MY FINANCIAL LOSS — WILL HAVE TO BE PAID IN FULL — IT MUST ALARM — ANGER AND ANNOY THE N.Y.

YELLOW PRESS AND AUTHORITIES TO FIND ANY ADDITIONAL CAN BE JUST AS MEAN — DIRTY AND ROTTEN AS THEY ARE. I MERELY SEEK JUSTICE. F.P.

At the end of the same year, Inspector Howard E. Finney of the New York Police Department's crime lab consulted Dr. Brussel and showed him the letters and file on the Bomber. The psychiatrist's deductions were surprising and far-reaching. Firstly the act of constructing the bombs indicated that an intelligent, highly skilled man who prided himself on his work was involved. Although he wrote of justice and the terrible deeds done by Con Edison, the bombs themselves were directed at general targets. Brussels therefore diagnosed him as suffering from paranoia: a persistent, unalterable and logically constructed delusion.

Paranoia is a self-centred disorder in which the sufferer attempts to protect himself against the reality of his own failures and weaknesses by attributing them to external powerful agencies and hostile forces. Authorities are seen to be plotting against him, and no amount of logical argument can convince him that his basic assumption is wrong.

The paranoiac is controlled, neat and respectable. He is flawless in everything he does; indeed, it is vital to what sanity he has left that he preserve a perfect image of himself. Brussel knew that paranoia develops around the age of thirty-five and since the bombings began in 1940, he guessed that the bomber must be older than fifty — but not too much older — for something in the Bomber's handwriting told Brussel that his sexual drive had not yet cooled. Each note was neat and the letters were perfectly printed, with the exception of the letter W. This letter dramatically stood out from the others, for it was formed by combining two curved *U*'s which, to the psychi-atrist's eyes, had the form of a pair of breasts.

This observation may have seemed a little far-fetched until Brussel noted the actual location of the bombs. Each had been carefully planted so that they could not be seen, except for those concealed in cinemas. In these cases the Bomber had slashed a *W* into the seat next to him and inserted the bomb into the fabric. Brussel guessed that the breast-like *W* indicated some unresolved conflict with the Mad Bomber's mother.

Finally, there were clues in the letters themselves. The "un-American" wording and choice of phrases pointed to a particular ethnic background.

By the end of the file Brussel was ready to make his prediction. The Mad Bomber was just over fifty years old and of good physical build. He was Slavic in origin, neat and precise in his habits. He had been a good worker but inclined to flare-up under criticism. The Bomber lived in a better part of New York with an elderly female relative, and was a regular attendant at Mass. He had once worked for Consolidated Edison, or one of its subsidiaries, but was presently suffering from some chronic disease. As a final touch, Brussel told police that the Bomber would be wearing a double-breasted suit.

Inspector Finney was impressed and asked Brussel for a suggestion on how to catch their suspect. The doctor said that an appeal to his sense of superiority and need for attention would work. Issuing a challenge in the press would probably inspire the Bomber to reveal himself.

Sure enough, as soon as the newspapers published details of the diagnosis, Brussels received a call from a man calling himself "F.P." He warned Brussel off the case. The *Journal-American* had issued a challenge and received two letters from the Bomber.

George Metesky, an elated bomber on his arrival at N.Y. Police Headquarters.
World Wide Photo

At the same time, police investigated the files held by Con Edison subsidiaries for anyone who might fit Brussel's description. One of them concerned a George Metsky and an almost endless flow of letters concerning a minor injury he had received at the Hell Gate Plant on September 5, 1931. Metsky demanded a considerable sum in compensation, and in one of his letters referred to the company's "dastardly deeds." This phrase — which featured in many of the Bomber's letters — stuck out like a sore thumb. Metsky became suspect No. 1.

At the same time the *Journal-American* received a third letter in which the Bomber mentioned an incident at Hell Gate on September 5, 1931. A police check on Metsky revealed a man surprisingly close to the description deduced by Brussel. He was 5'10" tall, well proportioned, aged fifty-four, and living with two older sisters. Born George Milauskas, he appeared aloof but inoffensive to neighbours and was believed to have been a chronic invalid since leaving work in 1931. His file at the company indicated that before the accident, he had been a well-behaved model employee.

The police went round to Metsky's house late at night. He seemed pleased at the sudden attention and told the officers that "*F.P.*" stood for fair play. He then asked if he could change his clothes before being taken to the station. He reappeared after several minutes, his hair well combed, his shoes polished and wearing a double-breasted suit!

THE HUNTER AND THE HUNTED

The police usually maintain their objectivity. But on occasion an officer will devote his career to pulling in a wanted man.

Some murderers kill for gain, others out of jealousy or revenge. But for Emile Buisson murder was simply part of the job of a master criminal.

Born at the turn of this century, Buisson graduated from boyhood crime to a series of robberies and frauds which confounded the Paris police force. The arrest of Buisson became such an obsession of Charles Chenevier that he predicted the exact hour when he would face his prisoner: June 10, 1950, 1:45 p.m.

The story began as World War II peace treaties were being signed in Paris. Emile Buisson angrily paced his prison cell after being convicted of a robbery worth Fr. 800,000. He decided that his best chance of escape was to be transferred to an asylum for the insane. Over the next weeks, Buisson screamed, moaned and pleaded with the guards to be transferred to a hospital. By the fall of 1947 Buisson was a patient at the Villejuif Asylum, busy plotting his escape.

On the night of September 3, 1947 an armed gang robbed the customers in a Montmartre bar. Their leader was identified as Buisson. When the police checked the asylum they discovered that a few hours earlier Buisson had climbed over the wall.

Buisson quickly made up for lost time and within a week he raided a restaurant and, after crashing through a road block, sprayed the police with a machine gun. The raid had tragic consequences for one of the gang members, Henri Russac. In the heat of the robbery he had called to one of his partners, using his correct name. As punishment for the mistake, Buisson put a bullet in his head.

After going into hiding for several months, Buisson emerged and organized a new gang. In February, 1948 they began a new series of robberies that succeeded under the noses of the police until May of the following year when Buisson executed another member of the gang.

This time the victim lived long enough to identify Buisson and a murder hunt began. Under the leadership of Charles Chenevier of the Sûreté Nationale, the police put all their energy into tracking down Buisson. Instead of hunting the killer in the manner of a pack of hounds after a fox, Chenevier favoured a more cunning approach. He knew that Buisson would be a difficult man to trap, and so rather than hunting him in the underworld, the detective lay low, waiting for Buisson to show himself.

Chenevier reasoned that when his funds ran low, Buisson would be forced to plan another robbery. Chenevier kept his ear to the ground and, sure enough, by May of the following year, the killer, under the illusion that the "heat" was off, approached an ex-convict for a gun and car. The detective allowed the deal to go through, and early in June, he announced to his colleagues that he would make an arrest in seven days' time at 1:45 p.m.

Chenevier knew that his quarry was hiding in a small inn on the outskirts of Paris. He arranged, on the morning of June 10, for his men to go to the inn in plain clothes, accompanied by their wives. As an added touch, he suggested that they drive up in flashy cars to make the appearance of holiday-makers. Chenevier himself was known to Buisson by sight and so he walked through the woods until he was hidden in the trees across from the inn.

Just as Buisson was finishing his lunch, Chenevier burst into the room and made his arrest. The time was 1:47 p.m. — he was two minutes late. Then sitting down at the same table the hunter and hunted drank coffee and ate strawberries which had been freshly picked that morning. Buisson was returned to Paris, tried and executed for his crimes.

THE DUSSELDORF KILLER

The sex killer has little connection with his victim and offers few leads to the police. Peter Kurten seemed free to wage his campaign of murder and rape through pre-war Dusseldorf.

Peter Kurten was born in 1883 in Koln-Mulheim, Germany and executed in 1931 after committing innumerable murders and assaults in a lifetime, over half of which was spent in prison.

One of a family of thirteen, Kurten lived in sordid and cramped conditions. His father was a violent drunk — as keen to take his sexual satisfaction with his daughters as with his wife. In this atmosphere of sexual brutality, the young Kurten was seduced by his own sisters.

At the age of eight, the boy struck up a friendship with a sadistic dog catcher who amused himself with acts of sexual torture on his animals. Kurten claimed that a year later he had drowned two boys who were playing on a raft. As the boy grew older, his perverted sexual drives became insatiable; not only would he experiment on his sisters and their friends but he had taken to stabbing animals while having intercourse with them.

Over the following years Kurten enjoyed an orgy of petty crimes and violent assaults on women. It was during this same period that he realized he could also obtain sexual release by starting fires. At the age of thirty, he murdered a thirteen-year-old girl and gained considerable delight in recalling the enormity of his crime. He claimed that simply overhearing a conversation about another of his murders — an axe killing of an old couple — produced such intense pleasure that he experienced an orgasm.

Kurten spent the First World War in prison and, on his release, moved to the town of Altenberg where he posed as a prisoner-of-war released from the Russian front. During this latter period Kurten met the woman who was to become his wife. She was a gentle and submissive woman and, for a time, Kurten settled down to a period of relative peace. He held a steady job, and with the exception of mistreating his servants, was to all intents a well-behaved citizen.

In 1925 Kurten, at age forty-two, began his final reign of terror. In that year he moved to Dusseldorf, where he experienced elation from his vision of a blood-red burning sunset over the town — a vision strikingly similiar to that of the murderer in Buchner's "Woyzeck." It symbolized the insane lust for blood which he would spread across the city. While Kurten's wife worked at night as a waitress, the killer roamed the city, a nocturnal predator in search of victims. At first his attacks were confined to rape and attempted strangulation, but they only served to feed the fires of his increasing sadism. (Later, he confessed to experiencing sexual ecstasy while watching a street accident, and on another occasion to cutting the head from a swan and drinking its blood.) In 1929, he began to use knives, scissors and an axe in a series of multiple murders. His thirst for victims seemed insatiable; on one occasion after murdering two children, he rested briefly, then went out and stabbed a servant.

Kurten's obsession even overcame concern for his own safety. He would collect with the crowd at the scene of his killings and revel in their comments. He even went as far as to masturbate on the graves of his victims and, in one case, dug up the corpse to satisfy his lusts.

Then, just as suddenly as his insanity started, it stopped. Like the Boston Strangler, Kurten seemed to have exhausted his desire for murder. He confined himself to attempted strangulations and, on one occasion, after an attack he calmed his victim and walked her home.

In the quiescent period which followed his last killing, Kurten began to take an interest in his own "case." He read widely and was particularly interested in the psychoanalysts and their writings on the origins of sadism and violence.

By May of 1930 Kurten believed that the police were closing in on him. He took his wife to a restaurant and explained that he was the Dusseldorf killer. She was deeply shocked, particularly since he had always conducted himself in a respectable manner during their marriage. Kurten calmly finished his own and his wife's meal — he appeared to have destroyed her appetite if not his own!

Kurten's wife went to the police and on the afternoon of May 24, armed policemen surrounded the church where Kurten had arranged to meet her. Seeing the crowd which had come to arrest him Kurten smiled and said, "There is no need to be afraid."

The killer proved to be one of the more fascinating of mass murderers for he was both intelligent and deeply interested in his unique condition. During his time in prison he cooperated fully with psychiatrist Professor Karl Berg, who later wrote a book on the case.

Kurten appeared to enjoy his trial and the horror expressed at his crimes. In particular, he spoke of reading accounts of Jack the Ripper as a child and boasted that one day he would occupy a place of honour in the Chamber of Horrors. Overwhelmed by his client's testimony the defence counsel, Dr. Wehner said, "This is a dreadful thing. The man Kurten is a riddle to me. I cannot solve it. The criminal Haarman only killed men, Landru only women, Grossman only women but Kurten killed men, women, children and animals, killed anything he found."

Kurten was sentenced to death on nine counts and his execution took place on July 2, 1932. The condemned man enjoyed his last meal of wiener-schnitzel and white wine so much that he requested it over again. Facing the guillotine, he asked, "Tell me, after my head has been chopped off, will I still be able to hear, at least for a moment, the sound of my blood gushing from the stump of my neck? This would be the pleasure to end all pleasures."

WOYZECK: FACT BECOMES FICTION

An understanding of the killer's mind may help society to combat crime. One of the earliest studies in forensic psychiatry was made in 1824 on Johann Christian Woyzeck.

It is a curious accident of fate that a sordid murder, committed early in the nineteenth century by a simple-minded soldier should have proved the catalyst for a literary revolution.

Johann Christian Woyzeck was born in Leipzig in 1780. Despite a conventional middle-class upbringing, Woyzeck did not adjust to the challenge of adult life and drifted from job to job in a state of near poverty, until he found some relief in the ordered life of an army mercenary. At the age of thirty, Woyzeck fell in love with a young woman who bore him a child. Woyzeck's happiness was shortlived, however, for he found that she was sleeping with other men. Ten years later he found himself back in Leipzig, this time attracted to Frau Woost, the widow of a surgeon. As with the previous affair, Woyzeck was not the only recipient of her love and he periodically fell into rages of jealousy. One day in 1821, he waited for Frau Woost who had gone walking with another soldier and, when she appeared, stabbed her several times with his home-made knife.

Woyzeck was arrested and sent for trial. The case against him was clear and he was convicted. After an unsuccessful appeal, he was condemned to death. Woyzeck's execution took place on August 27, 1824 and there, but for the intervention of Dr. Clarus, the story would have ended.

George Büchner, revolutionary and dramatist, became interested in the case of J.C. Woyzeck.
Deutsche Presse-Agentur Gmbh.

Dr. Johann Christian August Clarus was a physician to the Saxony Court and he took a considerable interest in the murder. He interviewed witnesses, talked to the prisoner and then published a report with the imposing title: "The Soundness of Mind of the Murderer Johann Christian Woyzeck, Proven on the Basis of Documents According to the Principles of State Pharmaceutics."

This paper was hotly debated in the pages of the *Journal for State Pharmaceutics*, and a decade later aroused the attention of a medical student and writer named Georg Buchner. Dr. Clarus had discovered that Woyzeck could converse clearly and discuss the events leading up to the murder. But Woyzeck's conversation also included accounts of faces in the sky, voices which whispered through the walls and the visitation of Freemasons during sleep. These same voices commanded Woyzeck to kill Frau Woost but they were absent on the day of the murder. Clarus argued that the voices were a projection of Woyzeck's fears and apprehensions, but that the man was not insane. His conclusion was that the murder had been premeditated and performed in a rational state of mind.

Clarus's story of Woyzeck's visions and the murder itself haunted Buchner, who believed the soldier to be a victim of the society around him. Using the figures of Woyzeck, the doctor, a flirtacious captain and the unfaithful mistress, Buchner began to write a powerful play of revolutionary structure.

Buchner died of typhus in 1837 with the manuscript incomplete and the order of its scenes ambiguous. It was not until forty years later that the tattered and faded manuscript again came to light. By that time the writing was virtually indecipherable and the title mistakenly read as "Wozzeck." Its rediscovery acted as an inspiration for the new German school of expressionist writing. The play was first performed in 1902, and its text was made the basis of Alban Berg's opera "Wozzeck." Today, its themes and images are still to be found in a number of films, plays and novels; for the image of the haunted and tormented soldier strikes a chord in our own regimented times.

THE BOSTON STRANGLER

"When will the Boston Strangler strike again?" asked the police. "Never," replied the psychiatrist who had been able to psychoanalyse the killer on the basis of the nature of his crimes.

Major criminals are often distinguished by their title: "Jack the Ripper," "The Moors Murderers," "The Yorkshire Ripper," "The Mad Bomber." Albert de Salvo had the unusual distinction of being known by three names: "Measuring Man," "The Boston Strangler" and "The Green Man." His story has a curious element to it since a noted psychiatrist claimed that a mental progression could be traced in his journey through murder and rape. Like Peter Kurten, the Dusseldorf Murderer, de Salvo may have exorcised his demons through murder to a point where lesser crimes provided the release for his perverted mind.

The Boston Strangler was not an unintelligent man; he took an interest in his condition and the motivation for his crimes but, in the last analysis, he was an incomplete human being, detached from the pain and suffering he caused.

Like Kurten, de Salvo's childhood was excessively brutal and sexually sadistic. He grew up near Boston in a family of three boys and two girls with a father given to violence. On one occasion a brother was so badly beaten with a rubber hose that he was forced to hide the scars on his back for several months before they healed. During another outburst, de Salvo's father systematically broke his wife's fingers.

De Salvo's mother did nothing to stop the abuse to her children and spent as much time away from home as possible. As a child de Salvo would slip away and sleep beside a stray dog in a local junk yard. Yet this attachment to the dog had little to do with a love of animals, for he could also amuse himself by torturing cats and dogs.

As the boy grew older his father began to bring home prostitutes and have sex with them in front of the children. Albert himself was introduced to sex at the age of five or six by his sisters, and as the boy matured, the ideas of sex and cruelty became entwined in his mind and powered by a virtually insatiable drive. From incest de Salvo graduated to sex with his schoolmates, although to his teachers he appeared to be a well-behaved boy willing to go on errands and cooperate in class.

After a minor adventure into crime de Salvo joined the army in 1948 where its strict discipline and regimented structure provided the environment de Salvo needed. He rose to the rank of sergeant and orderly to the colonel. His free time was spent not in the normal outlets of drinking with the other men but in excesses of sensuality. At first he used prostitutes but soon discovered that frustrated wives of absent officers would serve as well. At times his sex was violent and he delighted in tying his partners before serving them brutally.

Up to this point in his life de Salvo does not appear to have been involved in anything like a close relationship or to have known moments of love and romance. But in occupied Germany he met Irmgard, fell in love and married in 1954.

Irmgard insisted that de Salvo leave the army and the couple settled down in Boston, where a daughter was born in 1955 and a son in 1959. His daughter had been born with a deformity of the legs and was forced to wear a cast which splayed out her legs in a frog-like position — a fact which was to haunt de Salvo's mind, with horrific implications.

De Salvo was an affectionate father who would massage his daughter's legs several times a day and decorate her cast with pretty bows. But from his wife he made unbearable demands for sexual satisfaction. The more difficult she found it to respond, the more he demanded reassurance until Mrs. de Salvo could stand no more. Feeling rejected by his wife, de Salvo struck back as "Measuring Man."

The creature who plagued the women of Boston in 1960 was more of a schoolboy than a serious threat. Measuring Man posed as a talent scout, and using his considerable power of persuasion, he gained entrance to the women's apartments, where he measured their busts, thighs and waists in a particularly lingering fashion. After a short spell of measuring activity, he was arrested and imprisoned. Within the hostile prison environment, the school-boy prankster died and the killer was born.

The Boston Strangler's first four victims were women whose ages ranged from fifty-five to seventy-five, and the killings all followed the same pattern. Although he had strangled each one, all the women had died with a calm expression on their face, which fact suggested to the police that the killer had gained entrance into each apartment without force. He must have chatted calmly with the women until at some point, they turned away from him — literally "turned their backs on him" — at which point de Salvo reached out and strangled them with great force and speed. After the murder he placed their legs in a frog-like position, adding a decoration of scarves and hand-kerchiefs tied in bows around the victim. The

Strangler did not attempt to have intercourse with the women but in some perverted way the crime was connected in his mind with the condition of his crippled daughter.

The first of the murders took place on June 14, 1962 and the last in mid-August of the same year. Although the killer had searched the houses, nothing of value was ever taken. The motive for each murder appeared to be sexual, for although intercourse was never attempted, semen was found near the bodies.

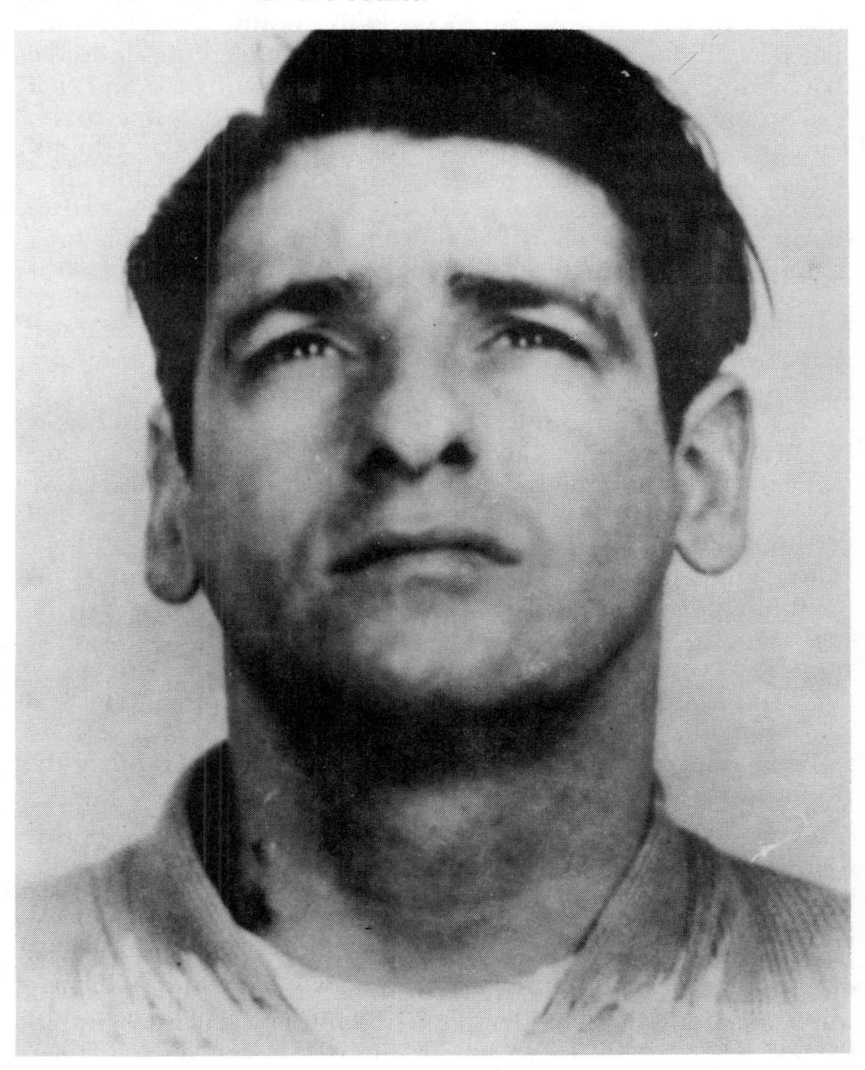

Albert De Salvo, the Boston Strangler.
Wide World Photo

For several months the killings stopped until, early in December, a second set of murders began. Several members of the Boston police force believed that this new wave of killings was the work of another man called "The Second Strangler." Although there were similarities between the killings, the difference between the two sets of crimes seemed too striking. In the first killings the victims were older women but this wave of stranglings involved attractive young girls. In the first of the second series of murders, a twenty-year-old girl was found strangled and arranged in a frog-like position, but this time semen was discovered near her vagina. Two more killings followed that month. As before, the bodies were decorated with bows and their legs arranged in an unusual position. The killer had intercourse with his victims and had even bitten them on the breasts and thighs. There were two killings in 1963 and one in 1964. In this final murder, the victim was arranged sitting up in bed with bows tied all over her body and evidence of a different form of sexual violation.

Forensic psychiatrist Dr. James Brussel argued against the two-strangler hypothesis. He came up with his own theory which explained the different nature of the killer's crimes. Brussel suggested that through murder the Strangler was actually *progressing* to a more mature psychological stage of development. The first killings, he believed, were infantile acts of violence against a surrogate mother. The Strangler's real mother, Brussel felt, must have in some way failed him and the killer carried a terrible anger within him. After he had killed these substitute mothers, the child-like mind of the murderer led him to masturbate in a furtive way. But, after the fourth murder, a maturation took place and the man turned his attention towards attractive young women. In a perverted way he had sexually "come of age." His victims were no longer mother figures but women he could regard as potential sexual partners.

Brussel suggested that the Boston Strangler was a paranoid schizophrenic, whose disorder was actually improving and after looking at the bizarrely repulsive violations of the last murder, the doctor predicted that the Strangler would never kill again.

A year passed and no further killings were reported. To the police it appeared that the Boston Strangler, like Jack the Ripper before him, would never be caught. In fact de Salvo had gone into the final phase of his metamorphosis — as "The Green Man."

Dressing himself in green, de Salvo used an excuse to get invited into a home and chatted to the woman occupant. When the mood was relaxed, de Salvo would pull out his knife and lead his victim to the bedroom where she was forced to undress. De Salvo would then tie the naked woman to her bed and begin a curious ritual which was strikingly different from the animal violence of the Boston Strangler.

Taking all the time in the world, the Green Man would caress and fondle his victim, sometimes in an apologetic fashion. After an hour or so of this treatment he would attempt intercourse, provided that the victim was not too distressed. Finally, muttering an apology, he would leave. The Green Man boasted of two hundred such conquests until in November, 1964 de Salvo's luck ran out when he was identified by one of his victims and committed to the Bridgewater State Mental Hospital. It was not until 1966 that the authorities began to wonder if the Green Man had also been the Boston Strangler. In 1967, de Salvo was placed on trial in Cambridge, Massachusetts and was defended by the famous attorney, F. Lee Bailey. The specific charge arose from his activities as the Green Man and the question of murder was not formally introduced in the trial. Despite a defence plea that de Salvo was insane, he was committed to life imprisonment.

A month later, de Salvo escaped from prison and gave himself up to F. Lee Bailey on the following day with the plea that he should receive psychiatric help because he needed to understand what had motivated his criminal activities.

In discussing one of his killings with the police, de Salvo once said, "I don't know whether I did this for the sex act or out of hate for her...not her particularly, but a woman. After seeing her body, naturally the sex act came in. But I did not enjoy it. There was no thrill at all...she did me no harm, and yet I did it. Why to her?"

De Salvo was never to achieve the understanding he desired. He was returned to Walpole State Prison where, on November 29, 1973 he was found murdered in his cell, the victim of sixteen stab wounds.

Five of the Boston Strangler's victims. Left to right are Sophie Clark, 21, Jane Sullivan, 67, Helen E. Blake, 65, Ida Irga, 75, Patricia Bissette, 23.
Wide World Photo

THE BLACK DOG OF LOWER QUINTON

The motive for a murder is often instrumental in trapping a killer. But when the motive was witchcraft, the crime proved insoluble.

The village of Lower Quinton stands close to Shakespeare's birthplace in a part of England steeped in mystery and legend. Standing stones, ancient man-made hills, stepping stones, and fairy glades pre-date the Roman occupation and speak of the time when a more primitive religion gripped the land, a religion attuned to the movement of the seasons, the waxing and waning of the moon and the secret germination of the seed in the dark earth.

Ash Wednesday fell on February 14 in the year 1945 and on that day a rheumatic old man named Charles Walton set out to work in a field on Potter's Farm. When Walton did not return for his tea his niece called on a neighbour for advice. Together with Farmer Potter they walked to the field where Walton had last been seen working. Dusk was thickening when the trio discovered Walton's body under an elm tree. His corpse had been pinned to the ground with a hay fork, a cross carved on his chest with his own hedging tool.

By the time the detectives arrived, most of the existing forensic evidence had become useless. Potter had pulled the murder weapon from Walton's body and the ground had been trampled by well-meaning helpers. After a preliminary reading of the police reports, the chief constable of the area called "Fabian of the Yard." Robert Fabian was a Scotland Yard detective whose successes would one day make his name a household word in Britain, but the Lower Quinton murder was to prove beyond even his considerable powers of detection.

At first the police followed the routine practice of questioning friends and relatives of the victim. Their investigation then extended to the village itself and beyond as strangers seen in the area were tracked down and eliminated from the enquiry. Elimination, however, required innumerable interviews as a prisoner-of-war camp was situated nearby.

As Fabian talked to the locals he built up a picture of Walton as a man isolated from the flow of life around him. The old man did all his drinking alone and seldom entered "The Gay Dog," as the local pub was called. There were rumours that he possessed the power to talk to birds and understood the wisdom which dictated the fruitfulness of the earth and the lives of animals.

Did Walton possess the evil eye? Had he practiced witchcraft, dispensed love potions and curses? Fabian began to wonder if there was substance in such stories or was it simply a mixture of half-remembered superstition and village gossip trotted out for the detective from the big city?

The case progressed slowly and the trail appeared to be going cold when one day a curious incident took place. Fabian was examining the scene of the crime when a large black dog ran past him. A few minutes later a boy appeared and when Fabian asked him about the dog the boy became confused.

Fabian mentioned the incident that evening in the village pub. The atmosphere became electric and from that day a wall of silence descended around Lower Quinton. Faced with this unexpected hostility Fabian looked into the legends of the surrounding area. After some research he came across a book written by Reverend Harvey Bloom entitled *Folk Lore, Old Customs and Superstitions in Shakespeareland.* One of the incidents described a black dog which appeared in the village of Lower Quinton in 1885. On successive evenings the dog was seen by a young plough boy and on its last appearance it changed into a headless woman. The next day the boy's sister died.

The story by itself was curious enough but the name of the plough boy set Fabian back on his heels — Charles Walton. The dates and ages matched. Without doubt the murdered man had been the subject of an eerie legend set in the previous century. Walton may not have been a real-life witch but in the mind of many of the locals he had the power to summon up dark forces.

Fabian set his team to comb libraries and interview local historians in an attempt to piece together the magical history of the area. They uncovered a case in 1875, similar to the Walton murder. An old woman had been stabbed with a pitchfork and a cross carved on her throat. Several years later, in the same area, a police constable was found with his throat cut. In both cases the records showed there had been talk of the supernatural in connection with the murders.

The police uncovered legend after legend and even found that the local blacksmith possessed nails which supposedly had the power to pin down witches. Fabian also heard complaints that the crops had failed the previous year and a heifer on a nearby farm had died in a mysterious fashion. Black dogs were a common feature and during Fabian's investigation a police car ran over and killed a black dog.

The case naturally attracted a considerable amount of attention in the press and there was no end of suggestions as explanations were sent in by the public and "Black Magic" experts. Even the noted anthropologist, Dr. Margaret Murray, author of *The Witch-Cult in Western Europe*, spent some time in the area posing as an artist and trying to help the police by talking to locals.

In the end the murder remained unsolved and the police were forced to direct their energies to other post-war crimes. But the idea of a ritual murder or killing which resulted from black magical practices had caught the public's imagination. One woman confessed to being a member of a witch's coven and claimed that the Lower Quinton killing — which took place on a day significant in the calendar of the Black Art — was a ritual act carried out by a cult which operated in the area. In general the police were skeptical about such information, for they knew that the organized practice of magic in Britain was confined more to executives from the middle class than simple country folk and farm labourers. Magical societies had evolved from a Victorian interest in the occult and tended to attract the bored, the moneyed, and seekers of sexual excitement — as well as the occasional genuine student of ritual magic. Such organizations would hardly welcome a farm hand such as Walton.

But what could have been the motive behind the Lower Quinton murder if a ritual killing by a coven was ruled out? The most probable explanation still involves witchcraft but in a more subtle sense. The village had experienced a particularly bad year, and rumour had it that Walton possessed the power to talk to animals and could put curses on the land. Possibly his curses had extended to members of the village itself. Had he perhaps brought down the threat of impotence and infertility on those who crossed him?

It is possible that one of the locals, a simple and superstitious person, may have feared and hated Walton. On that fateful day, did he perhaps summon up the courage to act? The weapons were close at hand, a pitchfork and a hedging hook. At the very moment of violence, the old stories may have come back, heard in childhood, of protection against the "evil eye"; hence the cross carved on Walton's chest.

One of the detectives on the case, Alex Spooner, returned each year on St. Valentine's Day to the spot where the murder had taken place. He believed that one day the killer would come up to him and confess. But in the end Spooner retired and the killing became one more unsolved crime.

Did anyone know the identity of the killer? It is probable that the man's name was whispered among the locals and he may even have been shielded from the police. And did the police ever guess? In retrospect it seems reasonable to assume that they must have had some idea as to the murderer's identity, but because of the lack of cooperation in the village and the destruction of the forensic evidence, they had little to go on in the way of hard evidence. Walton had taken the final mystery of the Black Dog of Lower Quinton with him to the grave.

The thatched cottage where murder victim Walton lived.
Syndication International

THE CAMEO CINEMA MURDER

The double killing at the Cameo Cinema proved a hard case to crack until someone grassed on the gang.

At around 9:30 on the evening of March 19, 1949 the cashier at the Cameo Cinema in the Wavetree district of Liverpool, England heard shots coming from the manager's office. She called the supervisor and the building's fireman and together they ran to investigate. The door appeared to be jammed when suddenly a man ran out waving a gun and then disappeared down the stairs. Inside the room the manager lay dead, his assistant badly bleeding and the night's taking, about fifty pounds, gone.

By 10 p.m., the police had arrived and the assistant manager was rushed to Sefton General Hospital, where he died without making a statement.

Chief Inspector Balmer of the Liverpool CID decided at once to start questioning his contacts in the area. One man who received an early morning call the next day was George Kelly, a local gang leader who often sold information to Balmer. Kelly did not seem surprised to see the detective and was able to account for his movements the night before with great precision. But Balmer felt there was something suspicious in Kelly's alibi — his story seemed too facile, the account of his movements from pub to pub too well rehearsed.

Balmer checked into Kelly's alibi and discovered that he had, indeed, been drinking at the pubs named. In fact, he had drawn attention to himself by buying a round of drinks and arguing with the publican of the Leigh Arms — an ex-policeman — about the time (9:50 p.m.) shown on the pub clock. But when Balmer made a detailed calculation of Kelly's movements he found that there was just enough time to leave one pub, commit the robbery, and arrive at the next before 10 p.m.

But if Kelly's alibi had a short gap in time, so did the alibis of thousands of other Liverpudlians who had gone about their business of drinking, talking and arguing on the night of March 19.

The case showed little progress until April 4, when an anonymous letter arrived at police headquarters. The writer claimed to know details of the crime but he felt in danger of his life. He asked the police to contact him through the personal column of the *Liverpool Echo*, if immunity from prosecution could be arranged. Balmer replied through the pages of the evening paper but no one responded. The envelope had been smeared with lipstick so Balmer and his men decided to call on all prostitutes and women with criminal records in the area and ask for handwriting samples. Balmer was next approached by an informant who claimed he had spoken to the killer but had taken an oath to the Holy Eucharist never to reveal his name — not a particularly promising contact.

Then on May 14, Jackie Dickson and Stutty Norman, the writers of the anonymous letter, turned up. They told Balmer that Kelly had planned the crime in the Beehive Inn on the night of the murder. Norman, Jackie Dickson, Norwegian Marjorie, and a man named Charles Connolly had talked about the robbery and Kelly had shown them his gun. Norman and the two women refused to get involved, and so Connolly and Kelly set off for the Cameo Cinema after borrowing an overcoat and scarf. Two days later Kelly returned the coat and told Norman to burn it because it could be used as identification.

Balmer listened to the story and felt he had enough evidence to arrest Kelly and his partner. Connolly was brought in for questioning but the detective was worried about arresting Kelly because he was known to be a particularly violent man. By coincidence Kelly turned up at the station that very morning asking for Balmer. But instead of selling information, Kelly was arrested and charged with murder.

On the morning of January 16, 1950 ten male and two female jurors began to hear the story of the Cameo case. They learned of the frightening power the Kelly gang held over the witnesses. It was almost as if gang members were holding a "watching brief" in the courtroom. Balmer had received death threats and Jackie Dickson had been placed under the protection of the police and moved to another city. Despite these precautions, Jackie was badly beaten on Christmas Day — two weeks before the trial began — by three women in a busy Manchester street. Another witness present when the murder had been plotted, Norwegian Marjorie, did not appear in court and her corpse was found on a Manchester bomb site some time later.

The case proved a difficult one for the jury. Much of the evidence came from the mouths of experienced criminals from Liverpool's underground gangs. At one point in the trial, the jury began to have doubts that a robbery could be planned in secret within the confines of a small public house. The foreman asked permission to visit The Beehive Inn and the court moved to the pub to examine the location.

By the end of the trial, it was apparent to the foreman that the jury would not be able to agree. The two women members were convinced of Kelly's guilt but worried that Connolly would face execution because of his position as accessory. After some discussion, ten of the jury agreed upon a compromise: a verdict of guilty but with a strong application for mercy for Connolly. However, one juror, a man who had a deep prejudice against the police, refused to join in any of the jury's discussions and to agree to the compromise. In the end the jury had to file back into the court and announce that they could not agree.

A second jury was selected and the trial repeated. This time Kelly was sentenced to hang and Connolly was given a ten-year prison sentence. The case did not end here, however, for Kelly had retained a barrister, Miss Rose Heilbron, who was on the brink of a brilliant career. Heilbron discovered that the second jury included a convicted felon and appealed the case. Her appeal, on the grounds that the jury was improperly chosen, was denied after a lengthy discussion of the Juries Act of 1825, 1870 and 1922. A final appeal to the Home Secretary was rejected. Kelly was hanged at Walton Jail on March 28, 1950, one year after his crime.

SAMMY, THE WHISPERER

An informer can prove invaluable to the police. The story of Sammy the Whisperer shows that a "grass" must be kept at arm's length.

Samuel Clifford Vosper — "Sammy the Whisperer" — was a supergrass who ended up behind bars. For sixteen years he supplied information to the police that led to a thousand convictions and the recovery of 300,000 pounds worth of goods. In the end, however, he tried to play the system at both ends.

Sammy discovered that informing could be big business with a steady income from the Scotland Yard Informer's Fund. He set himself up in London as a shady dealer in surplus articles — the sort of shop where goods "fell off a lorry" or "got knocked off at the docks," as the British say. Sammy's shop had a few additions not normally found in second-hand stores. Remote-control cameras and tape recorders (installed by Sammy) picked up every detail of his transactions which was passed straight to Scotland Yard.

Soon Sammy set his sights even higher, and donning a variety of disguises, he travelled around Britain checking criminal cases and claiming the rewards. Despite his regular income from the police, he was a greedy man and decided that he could make crime pay even more. Each time he reported a robbery, he would turn in only part of the loot and claim the full reward. The rest of the stolen goods, he sold. Not content with catching criminals and selling off their loot, Sammy decided to set up the crimes himself, claim the rewards and sell the proceeds. It was at this point that Sammy became unstuck. One of his plans went wrong and he was arrested for his part in a 21,000 pound robbery.

Sammy was convicted, but because of his "public service" his sentence was only for six years. But even six years were too much for Sammy and he was outraged. From his prison cell, he wrote letters, suggesting that the London police force was corrupt and that he, Sammy, had extensive evidence to prove police bribery. Sammy would not give up and in the end a police enquiry was formed to look into the alleged corruption, but none of his accusations was proven. For the police, it was a cautionary warning to keep a snout at arm's length.

CRIME AND PUNISHMENT

The interrogation is the final step in a murder hunt. But how does a policeman persuade a killer to condemn himself?

The writer Fyodor Dostoyevsky showed considerable insight into the relationship between the hunter and the hunted. *Crime and Punishment,* published in 1866, was written under the compulsion of an inner fever when Dostoyevsky was living in conditions of extreme poverty. The novel explores the inner thoughts and actions of a murderer, Rodion Romanovitch Raskolnikov.

Like many students, Raskolnikov was obsessed with radical ideas. In nineteenth-century Russia such ideas took the form of Slavic nihilism which viewed the majority of people as worms dominated by a few individuals of superior power. Raskolnikov recognized that to such exceptional leaders the law of the masses should not apply.

Tormented by his undisciplined intellect and the squalor in which he lived, Raskolnikov challenged himself. Was he of the same stuff that Napoleons are made of? Did he have the courage to perform an act of robbery/murder — an act that would set him free from his economic dependence on others and demonstrate his superiority? In a fever of excitement he killed an old pawnbroker and, by misadventure, her half-sister Lizaveta.

Raskolnikov soon discovered that though he was brave enough to commit murder he was unable to live with the memory of his crime. His action became an aching tooth, obsessive and ever present, so that Raskolnikov was forced to return to the scene of the murder and even discuss the crime with his friends.

As a novel of detection, *Crime and Punishment* rings true, for the investigator in charge of the case, Porfiry Petrovitch, comes to suspect Raskolnikov through a combination of logical deduction and psychological insight. After the murder, when others stepped forward to enquire about the fate of their pawned pledges, Raskolnikov had hung back. Later, during a routine visit to the police station he fainted while officers discussed the murder with each other.

Convinced of his suspicions, Petrovitch begins a masterly interrogation. Like the modern police-man, he makes no attempt to bully his suspect but explains Raskolnikov's own psychology to him and the inevitable conclusion of guilt which must be drawn from it. Petrovitch did not bother to arrest Raskolnikov but simply waited for the student's confession. Towards the end Petrovitch even attempts "plea bargaining" by suggesting to the murderer that the court will look well on the guilty man if he turned himself in of his own accord. Sure enough, after visiting his mother and a girlfriend who has shown faith in him, Raskolnikov returns to the police station, collapses in a chair and softly admits his crime.

THE MAIDS

Whereas British and American law decides upon guilt or innocence, the French judicial system attempts to arrive at a true account of the motives and circumstances of a crime. In the Le Mans murder of the Lancelin family, motive remained a mystery despite the efforts of the judge.

On the evening of February 2, 1933 René Lancelin, an attorney working in the town of Le Mans, had arranged to meet his wife and twenty-seven-year-old daughter at the house of a friend for dinner. When they did not arrive, René returned home to find the house locked and apparently deserted.

Lancelin called the police who broke down the door and entered the house. The ground floor was undisturbed but as the police walked up the stairs they realized that the second floor was awash with blood. Blood splattered the walls and floor together with fragments of torn clothing, teeth, pieces of bone and, horrifically, an eye. The bodies of Madame Lancelin and her daughter were lying in a pool of blood, battered to death and with their eyes torn out.

The police searched the rest of the house and discovered the two maids, Christine Papin, aged twenty-one, and her younger sister Lea, lying naked together in bed. Christine confessed to the murder and told the police of an apparently minor argument involving an electric iron the girls had fused. As Madame Lancelin began to complain the two maids leapt at her, ripping out her eyes with their fingers. Armed with a kitchen knife, a hammer and a heavy pewter pot, the pair proceeded to stab and batter Madame Lancelin and her daughter, stopping occasionally to change weapons. The maids then washed their hands, removed the blood soaked clothes and, locking the front door, went to bed.

The case of the Lancelin murders came to trial on September 20, 1933 and the court found itself obliged to discover some reason for such a bestial act. Yet despite the judge's patient efforts, no motive could be discovered for the double murder.

The judge first explored the possibility that the maids were victims of class oppression and bore a burning resentment towards their mistresses. Yet the two young women did not appear to have particularly strong feelings along this line. They had been treated well and had spent most of their lives in domestic service — the Lancelins seemed to have been no better and no worse than any other family. The maids did, however, make one curious statement, "I'd rather have had the skin of my mistress than that they should have had mine or my sister's."

The question of lesbian love between the sisters was then raised as a possible motive. Had Madame perhaps discovered the girls in a compromising situation and threatened to report them? Had she perhaps been killed for revenge or to keep her silent?

The facts here are confused and rumours circulated that the girls were fiercely sexual towards each other. Christine is supposed to have played the role of an insatiable lover to her passive and maleable sister in a drama tinged with perversion and depravity. But such gossip could have been sparked off by the sight of the two sisters lying naked in bed together — not an unnatural action after committing a murder and removing blood soaked clothes. In court the girls behaved as if in a hypnotic trance and medical witnesses rejected any lesbian attachment. According to the experts who addressed the court, the girls were both mentally normal.

The prosecution claimed that the case was one of brutal and inexcusable murder and worthy of the sentence of death. The court agreed and prescribed the guillotine for Christine and ten years hard labour for her sister.

Christine's sentence was later commuted to one of life imprisonment and she died in a psychiatric hospital in 1937. Lea, after serving her sentence, was released into a world in which Nazi depravity ravished her country and overshadowed her one inexplicable act of murder.

The Le Mans murder was later used as the basis of Jean Genet's play, *The Maids.* His own explanation of the case was that the murder came as the culmination of a compulsive ritual between the two sisters that involved their interchanging roles with their mistress.

THE DOMINICI CASE

Rural murder is often simple to solve — suspects are limited in number and gossip abounds. But where the only suspects all belong to the same family, the police are in for a headache.

In the summer of 1952 Sir Jack Drummond, a British biochemist, his wife Anne and their ten-year-old daughter Elizabeth went on a camping holiday to France. They crossed the channel by ferry on July 27 and made their way towards the Mediterranean coast in a leisurely fashion.

On the evening of August 4 the family decided to camp beside the road near to a farmhouse known as "La Grande Terre." After arranging their camp beds, Anne Drummond walked with her daughter to the nearby farmhouse to get water. As dusk settled the family got ready to sleep.

What happened next no one will ever know for certain for the case has been clouded by accusations and counter-accusations. From the arrangement of the bodies and the pathologist's examination, it appears that Lady Drummond was shot during the night. Her husband's body was discovered on the other side of the road where he had apparently staggered before being shot a second time. Their daughter was found some distance away battered to death. The mystery deepened when it was discovered that the girl had been murdered some time after her parents and that she had been carried from the camp-site for her bare feet were quite clean.

Who was responsible for the family's murder? The police investigation concentrated on an obvious suspect — the person who first found the bodies.

The corpse of the child, Elizabeth Drummond, was found by Gustave Dominici, owner of "La Grande Terre," who called in the police and suggested that the two other campers may have been shot. On being questioned Gustave admitted to having heard shots around 1 a.m. but did not investigate the shootings until the next morning.

Gustave's original story did not ring true. He later changed it and admitted finding the Drummond parents as well. The police then visited the Dominici farmhouse and discovered that it was dominated by Gustave's seventy-five-year-old father Gaston, a hard and cunning peasant. It did not take much detection to realize that the family had something to hide — but what?

One of the locals approached the police with a story that the Drummond girl was still alive when Gustave found her but he had left her to die. On October 16 Gustave was arrested, not for murder, but for "failing to give assistance to a person in mortal peril." The evidence against him was thin and he was sentenced to a prison term of two months.

Time passed and the Drummond murders looked as if they would never be solved. Then, well over a year later, Gaston Dominici was arrested for multiple murder. His two sons, Gustave and Clovis, claimed that the old man had killed the campers and concocted a story for the family to tell the police.

After his arrest Gaston boasted about the murders and claimed that they were crimes of passion. He said that he had crept over to the camp-site and watched Lady Drummond undressing. He became excited but was discovered by Sir Jack. He then shot the couple, chased the little girl and clubbed her to death.

Gaston Dominici on trial.
Syndication International

By the time Gaston came to trial, on November 27, 1954, the confession was forgotten and he claimed complete innocence. The trial was complicated for much of the forensic evidence had been useless; the crime scene had not been sealed off and had been trampled by sightseers who had even taken away souvenirs. When the murder weapon, a United States army carbine, was found, it was passed from hand to hand before being checked for fingerprints.

In the course of the trial Gustave withdrew his accusation against his father and began to quarrel with his brother. By the end of the proceedings the issues had become so complicated that Gaston's guilt was only decided by a majority vote.

The old man was sentenced to death but, in view of his age and the ambiguities in this case, the sentence was commuted to life imprisonment. In 1960 the eighty-three-year-old peasant was released and some years later his secret went with him to his grave.

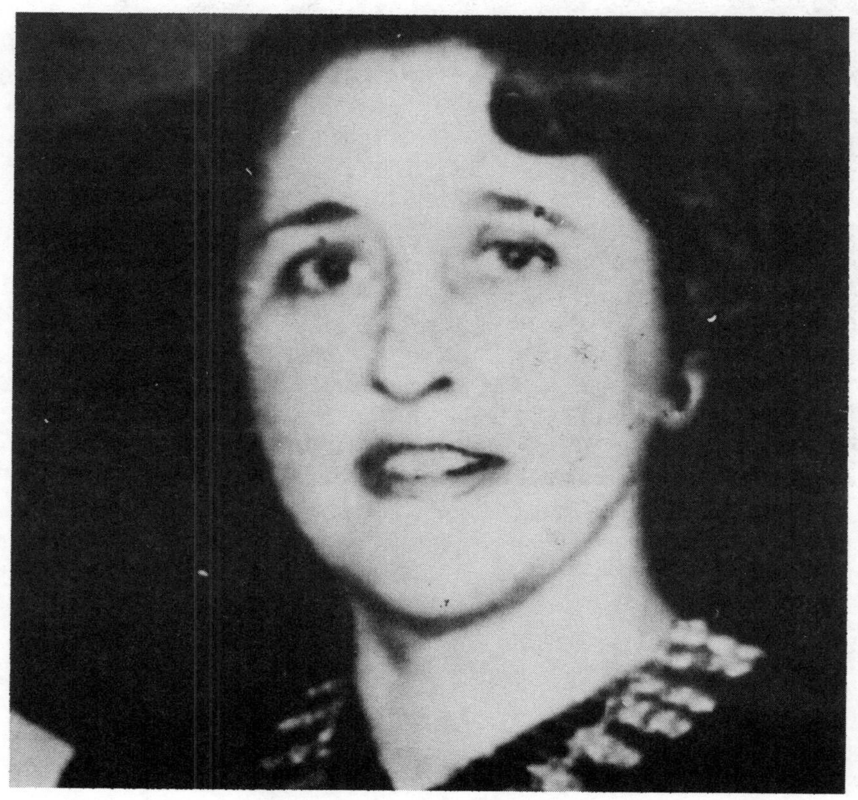

Lady Drummond — did the killer watch her undress?
Syndication International

Sir Jack Drummond who managed to stagger across the road before he was shot a second time.
Syndication International

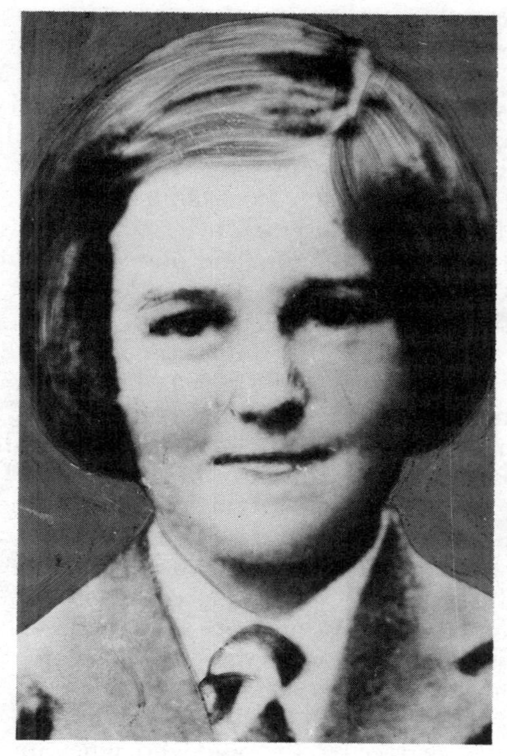

Elizabeth Drummond — was she carried from the camp site and left to die?
Syndication International

LEOPOLD AND LOEB

A killer who is brought to trial is usually judged by a jury of his peers, but in the case of Leopold and Loeb, the judge alone listened to their story.

At the height of Al Capone's Chicago career, it was not multiple murder that captured America's interest but the fate of a single kidnapping victim, Robert Franks.

The crime took place on May 21, 1924 and was the culmination of a series of robberies and petty crimes planned and executed by two wealthy students, Richard Loeb and Nathan Leopold, Jr., who imagined themselves to be supermen and master criminals. That afternoon Leopold and Loeb cruised around in a hired car looking for a victim — a situation strangely similar to that of Myra Hindley and Ian Brady, the Moors Murderers. They recognized young Robert Franks at Chicago's 49th Street and Ellis, and offered him a ride.

There remains some ambiguity as to which of the two carried out the actual killing but probably Loeb clubbed the boy, then stuffed a cloth into his mouth. The pair drove to some wasteland where Leopold had been bird-watching and placed the naked corpse in a drain pipe. The autopsy showed that Franks had not been sexually molested. The time of death was uncertain.

Following the murder the killers, using the alias "George Johnson," attempted to extract $10,000.00 in ransom money from the boy's father. But before the money could be paid, the corpse of Robert Franks was identified — not by the police but by a newspaperman working on the ransom story who had received a call after the body of a young boy was taken to the mortuary.

In the murder investigation which followed, Loeb was of considerable assistance to both the police and the press. He toured the area with them and even suggested lines of enquiry. Several suspects were arrested, questioned and later released. It was not until a pair of glasses were discovered near the drain pipe where Frank's body had been dumped that the police had their first real break in the case.

The glasses were traced to Leopold who, when interviewed, gave Loeb's name as his alibi. The two boys were questioned for long periods and Leopold showed no sign of changing his story. In the end it was Loeb who poured out a confession to the police. Faced with his partner's defection, Leopold made a statement which explained the motive behind the murder. The killing had been done "for kicks," as an intellectual exercise in crime. The identity of the victim was irrelevant and the ransom money was only an added challenge. The boys had no need of money for one of them was the son of a Sears Roebuck vice-president.

The murder had been the culmination of a perverted symbiosis of crime fantasy between the two boys. This very lack of motive was to result in a cry for "blood" from the American public and made the defence strategy that much more difficult.

Clarence Darrow, one of America's most famous defence counsels, was retained by the families. He decided that the case must never be brought to trial, for a jury would certainly condemn the boys to hang. His only chance lay in appealing to the more objective reactions of an experienced judge. In a surprise move which was kept secret, even from the accused, until hours before the opening of the proceedings, a plea of guilty was entered. In place of the trial there stood a "hearing," in which the judge listened to arguments from both sides before passing sentence. The Leopold and Loeb case was therefore never brought to a jury trial.

The hearing became a battle between Darrow and State Attorney Robert Crow. It was also a testing ground between the old and new schools of psychiatry, for Darrow pitted modern Freudian theory against Crow's old-fashioned medical experts.

The examination carried out by Drs. Harold H. Hulbert and Carl M. Bowman is probably the most extensive published investigation into the minds of psychopathic killers. It demonstrated the symbiotic relationship which had developed between the two boys. Leopold, who was a brilliant scholar, had already received his bachelor's degree and delivered papers on ornithology. Of the murder, he said: "It was an experiment. It was as easy for us to justify as an entomologist in impaling a beetle on a pin."

Fourteen-year-old murder victim Bobby Franks.
Wide World Photo

Both boys had come from privileged homes and spent more time with their governesses than with their parents. Their childhoods were not particularly healthy: Leopold's nurse encouraged him to sit naked in the bathtub with her and examine her "strawberries." She even allowed him to put his penis between her legs but stopped at actual penetration. When the two boys later met, a similar sort of sexual play developed, with Loeb as the passive partner.

The boys grew to experience considerable feelings of inadequacy and physical inferiority. Leopold learned to hide his emotions behind a scathing tongue and an adoption of the Nietzschian philosophy of supermen. When the boys met at university they realized that each complemented the other. Leopold would imagine himself as the powerful slave who would overcome stronger men. For his part, Loeb tantalized himself with thoughts of being in prison, degraded and abused. The two boys indulged in mutual masturbation and minor homosexual acts while fantasizing about becoming professional criminals. At first they carried out small robberies, including the theft of a typewriter which they later used to write the ransom note to Robert Frank's father.

Clarence Darrow in the Cook County courtroom with his clients, Loeb and Leopold.
Wide World Photo

Darrow's plea to the judge was for mercy and compassion. Although the psychiatric evidence was of great interest, it did not really explain the nature of the crime. Darrow put it simply: "Somewhere in the infinite processes that go to the making up of the boy or man, something slipped." The crime could not be excused. The two had pleaded guilty but Darrow made his petition for the future and suggested that the judge stood at the crossroads between retribution and redemption.

Darrow's argument prevailed and the young men were imprisoned for life on the charge of murder and on the charge of kidnapping for ninety-nine years.

Loeb died as a result of a prison brawl in 1936 and Leopold was released in 1958. His life outside prison was varied; he wrote a book entitled *The Birds of Puerto Rico,* did research on leprosy, worked as a social worker, and lectured in mathematics. In a sense, he was unable to devote his energy and considerable talent to any one field.

Leopold married in 1961 and died on August 30, 1971. In his last years he appears to have been tormented by feelings of bitterness and frustration that his life had been wasted and that the genius he had displayed as a teenager had never grown to fruition.

PARTNERS IN MURDER

Partners in murder are equally guilty. But what if one of them is under arrest at the time?

The early fifties was a time of rising crime in Britain with stories of cosh boys, flick knives and sudden violence in every newspaper. The public was angry and demanded a return to law and order. It was within this tense atmosphere that two young men planned their crime.

Christopher Craig, the ring leader, was only sixteen. His father had achieved the rank of captain in the First World War but Craig himself showed little promise for he suffered from dyslexia (word blindness) — a condition only poorly understood at that time and confused with a lack of intelligence. His older brother had been convicted of armed robbery, and on learning about it, Craig appears to have had a powerful need for vengeance towards the police. His partner-in-crime, Derek Bentley, was nineteen, a simple-minded youth who had earlier been to an approved school on a charge of shoplifting.

On November 2, 1952 Craig and Bentley set off to rob a confectionary warehouse in the Croydon district of London. One of them carried a gun. A neighbour saw two youths jump over the gate into "Barlow and Parker's" warehouse and called the police. Within minutes a car containing Detective Constable Fairfax and P.C. Harrison arrived and, with some difficulty, the two officers made their way onto the rooftop.

Fairfax identified himself to the two boys. From that point on events moved at lightning speed, and the interpretation of what happened next was to be crucial in the subsequent trial.

Bentley gave himself up without resistance but Craig defied the police and pulled out his gun. At this point Fairfax claimed that Bentley struggled free and shouted, "Let him have it Chris." Fairfax was shot in the shoulder while additional police officers converged on the roof. Bentley appears to have been under arrest at this point and he explained to the police that his partner had a Colt .45.

The situation had the elements of a classical stand-off until P.C. Miles, a reinforcement, arrived at the warehouse and tried to get onto the roof through a skylight. As his head came into view, Craig shot and hit him between the eyes. Using Bentley's body as a shield, the police held a hurried conference while Fairfax went to get a gun.

The siege ended when Craig's ammunition ran out. The boy stood at the end of the building and jumped. Despite the height Craig was not killed and, with his back broken, whispered, "I wish I was fucking dead. I hope I've killed the fucking lot."

The trial of Craig and Bentley, on a charge of murdering P.C. Miles, took place in London's Old Bailey before Lord Chief Justice Goddard. Christmas Humphries, for the Crown, knew that Craig, at sixteen, was too young to hang but claimed the death penalty for Bentley. He argued that both youths were partners in the crime and Bentley knew that his friend was armed. He stressed that the cry "Let him have it Chris" was a clear incitement to the violence which followed.

Bentley's counsel argued that events on the warehouse roof were confused and open to a different interpretation. He pointed out that shots had also been fired by the police and the ballistic evidence of the actual murder bullet was ambiguous. The Crown's claim, that Bentley knew his partner was armed because he told the police the make of the gun, was denied by the defence who also claimed that the damning verbal "Let him have it Chris" was never made.

Despite a spirited defence, the pair were found guilty of murder. Because of his age, Craig was "detained at Her Majesty's pleasure."

On appeal against sentence of death, Bentley's lawyers argued that the criminal partnership ended at the moment of Bentley's arrest. After all, if Bentley had been removed to the police cells and the shooting had taken place several hours later, he could hardly be held responsible. For its part the Crown made a distinction between arrest and custody. The Crown suggested that although Bentley was under arrest he could hardly be said to have been in the custody of the police for they were pinned down under fire at the time.

Bentley's appeal was denied and he was hanged on January 28, 1953. Despite its earlier call for tough measures, public opinion condemned the severity of Bentley's sentence. To many people, Bentley was the dim-witted pawn in the affair and the true killer had escaped with his life.

On the scaffold Bentley said, "I didn't tell Chris to shoot that policeman."

MURDER "UNDER MILK WOOD"

Not all murder trials go according to plan. What can the court do, for example, if the accused is unable to plead?

The township of Laugharne in South Wales was immortalized by Dylan Thomas in the radio play "Under Milk Wood." Thomas lived on the outskirts of Laugharne in a small house which overlooked Camarthen Bay. The town was a particularly clannish place (with considerable intermarriage) whose charter stretched back to Norman times. Its village head was called the Portreeve and wore a chain of cockle-shells.

On January 10, 1953 as Dylan Thomas was adding the finishing touches to his play, the daily routine of this little town was disrupted. Seventy-eight-year-old Elizabeth Thomas (no relation to the poet) was discovered beaten and stabbed to death in her cottage. Police from London were called in but found the village close-mouthed about the crime. In place of hard evidence police heard rumours that the old woman had a hoard of money hidden in her cottage, which proved to be so dusty and dirty that few fingerprints could be obtained.

What evidence could be found pointed to a handyman who was said to have been lurking around the cottage on the night of the murder. The suspect was deaf, dumb and feeble-minded. Even attempts at communication through sign language were unsuccessful. But the man enjoyed hanging around the police station and drew detailed pictures of the cottage.

After some discussion, the police charged the handyman with murder and he was brought to trial. The court was now faced with a curious legal predicament. The judge began by ruling the man "mute by visitation of God" and then faced the problem of how to proceed. He pointed out that in law the jury must decide if the accused is fit to plead *before* evidence is heard. Furthermore, a person accused of murder, but found unfit to plead, must be sent to an asylum. Yet, argued the judge, without hearing the evidence, it would not be clear if the accused had had any involvement in the crime at all, and an innocent man could hardly be sent to an asylum on the grounds that he was mute or feeble-minded.

In addition, how was evidence to be presented? How could a trial be conducted with the accused unable to enter a plea or to present evidence in examination or cross-examination. After some discussion with the Crown, the judge formally opened the trial and immediately directed the jury to return a verdict of not guilty.

INSANITY

The madman who tried to kill a Victorian prime minister forced the law to define the bounds of insanity.

It is universally agreed in law that sane persons should pay for their criminal acts. But where the insane are concerned, the law finds itself in muddy waters. Lawyers have argued that if a person's thought processes are so disturbed that he has no knowledge of what he is doing, or his actions have the random appearance of lunacy, then the question of punishment seems inappropriate. For a crime to have taken place, the *Mens Rea*, or mental intent, must be present as well as the criminal action itself.

The real problems that face the court,are those of determining the state of mind of an accused person, either during the trial or at the time of the crime, and establishing some objective test for insanity or diminished responsibility. A series of abstract deliberations were brought to a head in 1843 when the secretary to the prime minister,

Sir Robert Peel, was killed. The assassin, a man named Daniel M'Naghten, who was under the delusion that he was being persecuted by the government, shot Edward Drummond, believing him to be the prime minister.

Although M'Naghten was not examined by medical experts, he was observed by doctors in the courtroom and found "not guilty by reason of insanity." Following the trial, a committee of English judges was questioned about the defence of insanity in law. Their formal replies became known as the M'Naghten Rules and, with some variation, are now used throughout the United States and much of the Commonwealth. The M'Naghten Rules state that:

> To establish a defence of insanity, it must be clearly proved that, at the time of committing the act, the party accused was labouring under such a defect of reason, from disease of the mind, as not to know the nature and quality of the act he was doing; or if he did know it, then he did not know he was doing what was wrong.

In essence the rules state that an insane person cannot appreciate the nature and quality of the act of murder. It is insufficient to experience a minor delusion: the insane person must be in the grip of delusions so intense that they appear real and his actions are determined by this disordered perception of reality.

At the trial, a plea of insanity can be invoked both by the prosecution as well as by the defence. The former may judge that the public is best served by having the insane person placed in indefinite detention in a mental hospital. The court, however, assumes the accused to be sane until it can be demonstrated "on balance of probability" that he is mad. The judgment of insanity, therefore, differs from the judgment of guilt. It makes use of the criterion of "on the balance of probabilty" in place of "beyond reasonable doubt."

If the defence thinks that a prison sentence is preferable to indefinite confinement in an insane asylum, he may instruct his client to plead guilty to the crime. In such a case, the judge has no power to confine the prisoner to a hospital and must sentence the killer to a definite term in prison.

If, however, during the trial the judge himself suspects the sanity of the accused, he can suspend the proceeding while the subject is placed under observation by doctors. In such a case, the defence counsel can instruct the accused not to speak to the doctors or cooperate with them in any way.